Written in a personal and engaging way, General Winston Choo's memoir is an authentic voice for those of us who have had the privilege of knowing him as a leader, a colleague and a friend. It is an overdue record of an exceptional Singaporean, who has made significant contributions at all stages of a long and illustrious career in the service of Singapore. It is also important to read his life story in the context of the massive challenges that Singapore faced, and the significant role that he played in helping to ensure Singapore's survival, security, and success.

Peter Ho
Senior Adviser, Centre for Strategic Studies

I have known Lt-Gen Winston Choo since 1982, when I visited Singapore as the Commander, Regional Military Command V/Jaya.

Bilateral cooperation between Singapore and Indonesia in defence and security, within the framework of ASEAN, ran smoothly because of the spirit of friendship, both in formal matters and personal relationship, between Lt-Gen Winston Choo and me. I have lots of fond and positive memories of both our professional and personal interactions.

The experience and achievements of Lt-Gen Winston Choo in leading and building the Singapore Armed Forces should be an example and role model for Singapore's new generation.

His memoir will thus be a reference book which will benefit his family, his countrymen and the young in particular.

General (Rtd) Try Sutrisno
Commander, Republic of Indonesia Armed Forces, 1988-1993
Vice President, Republic of Indonesia, 1993-1998

General Winston Choo – my good friend and my counterpart in the military. This book, *A Soldier at Heart*, perfectly sums up the man he is – an officer and gentleman, a loving family man, efficient, disciplined, diplomatic, with a great sense of humour. The list is endless.

We shared a common language and understanding when it came to our military operations. He was always a formidable force to be reckoned with and I enjoyed working with him throughout our military journey.

It is my honour to call Winston – a man of great repute – my friend.

General Tan Sri (Dr) Hashim Mohd Ali (Rtd)
Chief of Defence Force, Malaysia, 1987-1992

General Winston Choo inspires us with his life of service to his country. I had the privilege of working with him on the Asian Tsunami Humanitarian Project when he was Chairman of the Singapore Red Cross. He was patient and decisive, completely focused on what needed to be done. He shouldered his tasks as a true servant of God and his country.

General Choo is the epitome of a soldier and gentleman, humble to a fault, always true to himself and at ease with everyone. There is much we can learn from this ordinary man who did exceptional things.

This memoir is a compulsory read for anyone interested to know how Singapore got to where it is. His revelations and lessons are relevant today.

Zulkifli Baharudin
Non-Resident Ambassador to Kazakhstan and Uzbekistan
Nominated Member of Parliament, 1997-2001
Chairman, Mercy Relief, 2003-2007

Lt-Gen Winston is a legendary figure in his country and holds the record of being the longest serving chief of the Singapore Armed Forces. He told his story in great detail, with no stone left unturned and no holds barred. His wisdom and advice on leadership are excellent pointers for future leaders to emulate. His book ends with a fine tribute to his wife Kate and his family.

Lt-Gen Winston and l go back six decades, starting with our military careers. This book rekindles a lot of nostalgic memories as l can identify many events and personalities in it. I congratulate Lt-Gen Winston for his timely presentation of this book not just to Singapore but to the world at large.

Maj-Gen (B) Pehin Mohammad Haji Daud
Commander of the Royal Brunei Armed Forces, 1986-1989

This book gives the reader an enthralling account of the beginnings of the SAF and the contributions by its pioneers.

Winston played a significant role in its development from the mid-1960s when the SAF then consisted of two infantry battalions to the late 1990s when it became a fully integrated tri-service defence force. His charisma, and his ability to make friends near and far, enabled the SAF to play an important role in defence diplomacy. As a result, trust and confidence with leaders of armed forces of neighbouring, regional and major countries were established. It took gigantic efforts to achieve this because regional suspicions in the aftermath of Separation and Confrontation had still not abated.

Tan Chin Tiong
Ambassador-at-Large, Singapore
Senior Adviser, Institute of Southeast Asian Studies (ISEAS)

This is a remarkable and inspiring memoir. It traces the experiences of a young, gifted and devoted officer from a humble beginning to the top of the Singapore Armed Forces, and follows his service as a diplomat and Chairman of the Singapore Red Cross. The story is told in a moving and compelling manner, reflecting the pursuit of excellence which is the trademark of Winston Choo's life.

I remember him as always the key person in the unique relationship with Israel, whether as military leader or as Ambassador. His contribution to the depth and richness of this relationship is invaluable and long lasting.

This is a book to be read by all.

Lt-Gen (Rtd) Ehud Barak
Chief of General Staff, Israel Defense Forces, 1991-1995
Israel Minister of Foreign Affairs, 1995-1996
Prime Minister of Israel, 1999-2001
Israel Minister of Defence, 2007-2013

WINSTON CHOO

A Soldier At Heart

A MEMOIR

*with Chua Siew San
and Judith d'Silva*

◇LANDMΔRK◇BOOKS◇

Cover photo by Patrick Lim

Published by
Landmark Books Pte Ltd

First printing June 2021
Reprinted July 2021

ISBN 978-981-18-1171-5
Printed by Oxford Graphic Printers Pte Ltd

To

my wife, Kate,
who is my forever love and tower of strength,
and the soldiers who served with me.

CONTENTS

FOREWORD

THE FIRST TIME I saw General Winston Choo, I was an Officer Cadet in SAFTI. Even at a distance, he left an impression because this was a man with presence, made more striking by his moustache. I had the opportunity to serve with him over my entire active service in the Singapore Armed Forces, and subsequently when he served our nation in other capacities. General Choo epitomised the SAF to the core. As Director General Staff, then Chief of the General Staff, and the first Chief of Defence Force of the SAF over a span of 18 years, he shaped the values and culture of the SAF and was instrumental in its development. Everyone recognised him as our country's top soldier during the SAF's key formative years, building National Service as an institution, professionalising each of the Services, and developing the Joint Staff and tri-service integrated SAF of today. He had an instinct and feel for what needed to be done and how to mould the SAF. At the same time, he was humble enough to know that he did not have all the answers and self-confident enough to listen to others and garner the best ideas. He made good use of able people in his team, guiding and leading them, to help him bring the SAF forward.

General Choo had seen action during Konfrontasi and the race riots in Singapore. He was a leader who led by example. He had clear views about what the value system of the SAF should be and he established this not only by his orders but also by the force of his own example. He parachuted and dived, jogged with his men, went down to the trenches with them, and spent long hours talking with them, listening to their problems, getting to know them and their families. I remember accompanying General Choo on many operational visits, and also spending many long nights into the wee hours with him interacting and socialising with fellow servicemen and their spouses to get to know one another beyond our daily work.

His greatest strength was his people skills. General Choo engaged people easily in his open and sincere manner, and people trusted him. He was able to bring together mobilised soldiers from the volunteer corps, police officers, those who had trained with or served in the Malaysian Armed Forces, and a new crop of home-grown, SAFTI-trained officers. He instilled in them an esprit de corps and a sense of mission to serve our new nation, believing that this was the glue that would make the SAF strong. With this, he was able to bridge the generations of officers and servicemen who formed the fledgling SAF and transitioned to the modern SAF with a professional core and National Servicemen as its strength.

General Choo could reach out and connect with anyone: soldier, sailor and airman; private and general; Sultan, President, and Minister; military spouse and the children. People could see that he was genuine, and his engaging nature and down-to-earth personality enabled him to develop relationships easily. I observed how he engaged his foreign counterparts when I sat in on his meetings with them and travelled with him to countries where we had important defence relationships, both in our region and beyond. I learnt from him how to engage foreign military and political leaders, how to win their trust and put forward our positions in a friendly but firm way. I am grateful for these opportunities. Many of the foreign leaders and officials I continue to meet I first met during General Choo's meetings with them.

General Choo built not just networks throughout our region but friendships and mutual respect that last till today. He has maintained links with them and continues to meet them. A number of them came to visit him when he was recovering from his cancer operations, including a group of about 20 retired Bruneian officers and their wives. A couple had been his juniors when they were cadets at the Federation Military College. General Choo also had warm personal relationships with many top Malaysian Armed Forces generals, some of whom were his seniors, peers and juniors from his cadet days in the Federation Military College. He had equally warm personal ties with the top Indonesian generals who played politically influential roles in the Soeharto era.

All these relationships which he nurtured carefully and skilfully were of great value not just to the SAF but also to Singapore.

And when he retired from the SAF, General Choo used his considerable networking skills and engaging personality to continue serving Singapore's interests as a diplomat and as Chairman of the Singapore Red Cross. His has been a life of service to his country and he has served Singapore most ably.

General Choo was a charismatic military leader and is one of Singapore's most important pioneers. A legend in the SAF, he has an interesting story to tell, and he tells it in his straightforward and unassuming way. I am glad that he has given us this memoir, encouraged by his ever gracious wife, Kate, who was by his side through his life's journey. It is not only a legacy to his grandchildren, but it also holds lessons for all of us.

This book tells not only the life story of an interesting and remarkable man. More than that, it also reminds us of how far we have come as a nation. It is a story that will bring back many good memories for the SAF veterans – those men and women who contributed so much to making the SAF what it is today. It is also a story that will inspire younger Singaporeans, especially those who serve in General Choo's beloved SAF, to make Singapore more secure. We all owe much to General Choo and the early generations of the SAF whom he led.

Teo Chee Hean
Senior Minister
and Coordinating Minister for National Security,
Singapore
May 2021

PREFACE

LONG BEFORE I retired from the Singapore Armed Forces, many close friends, colleagues and family members had encouraged me to publish a book on my life. I strongly and consistently resisted. I was always glad to informally share some tales of the adventures of my younger days, but I had no intention of putting pen to paper for an autobiography or memoir. I had never kept a journal or a diary, nor maintained proper records and photographs of myself. I was happy to quietly ride off into the sunset and not be writing stories about myself. I had taken to heart what I heard a publisher friend once say: that unless someone had useful life lessons to share, he had no business writing a memoir. Furthermore, given the nature of my career, I expected to find it hard to share many things without incurring the displeasure of our security officials.

It was about a year ago that Goh Eck Kheng, the same publisher who thought that someone with no useful lessons to share should not write a memoir, approached me to consider doing one. He solicited the support of my old friend and colleague, Colonel Ramachandran Menon, and they came with

Chua Siew San and Judith d'Silva, who promised me that they would help me put together a personal narrative. They assured me that given my long service in the SAF as the first Chief of Defence Force and my diplomatic roles, I would have an interesting and useful story to tell and I should share it by writing a memoir.

I thought long and hard and was engaged in an inner battle over this. Finally, I said to myself, "Don't be a coward. What are you afraid of? Never mind if people do not take favourably to what you have to share. Just be honest and truthful, don't embellish but humbly present your story." When I consulted my wife, Kate, she was most encouraging. My children, Karina and Warren, supported Kate. They argued that they had over the years heard so many memorable tales and anecdotes with life lessons from me, and I owed it to my grandchildren to record them. Let the grandchildren share in this and benefit from my stories, they said. I was persuaded to change my mind, and I conceded to recording my memoirs based on an old man's recollections and not supported by any research. I apologise in advance should there be errors or perceived omissions. My hope is that any younger person reading this may be able to draw some lessons from my story.

Seeing how far the SAF has come today gives me great joy and pride. But this is definitely not a full account of my service in and to the SAF. This is also by no means a definitive history of the major events of my life. It is a simple story of a man who is a soldier at heart – who had always wanted to join the army since he was a boy, and ended up being a general and a diplomat.

Winston Choo
May 2021

ACKNOWLEDGEMENTS

AFTER ALMOST three decades of resistance, I finally got down to producing my memoir. For this I must thank Goh Eck Kheng of Landmark Books who saw the merit in me producing my memoir and persuaded me to agree. I am also thankful to my wife, Kate, my children, Karina and Warren, and my grandchildren, whose encouragement and constant support throughout saw me through finishing this book.

Special thanks go to Chua Siew San and Judith d'Silva who consented to partner me in this endeavour. They spent considerable effort going through my oral history transcripts, speeches, essays and articles I had written, and other materials on me. They patiently and painstakingly coaxed the memories out of me to elicit anecdotes from my childhood and school days, through my entire military career up to the time I retired as CDF, over my years as a diplomat, up to today. After the initial hesitance, I found myself rather enjoying the process of reminiscing as we started putting my stories together. They spent endless hours interviewing me, aided by Irene Kan who laboured over my raspy voice to record and transcribe what I had to say. From the 20 or so sessions over 10 months they skilfully produced my story in the well-ordered and readable 30 chapters of this book. It was a mammoth task as we went over several iterations of the chapters, reviewing draft after draft. This book would not have been possible but for their doggedness and untiring effort.

Karina took it upon herself to assist me in reviewing and editing each draft. She was very thorough and took pride in her efforts, spending hours carefully going through and correcting my revisions. It meant a lot to both of us to be able to spend time discussing my memoirs and debating the merits of including, excluding or adjusting parts of the manuscript. For all this, I am thankful.

A memoir is never complete without photos. Kate had the unenviable task of trawling through decades' worth of our uncatalogued photos to help me find specific ones I wanted to include in the book. As usual, she did it with nary a complaint, and I am so grateful.

As most of the narration was based on my memory with minimal research, I had to fall back on many people to help fill in the gaps, and check on facts and dates. This meant calling on friends as well as old colleagues who had served with me, including Lieutenant-Colonel James Lim, who was my Military Assistant, and Angelina Ong, my Personal Assistant. I am grateful to all these friends for their help.

My life story would not have been worth sharing had I not been given the opportunity by our leaders, especially President Yusof Ishak, Prime Minister Lee Kuan Yew and Dr Goh Keng Swee, to take on the significant responsibilities and appointments they assigned to me. I am thankful for their faith in me and for allowing me to walk in their shadow and benefit from their wisdom, strength and greatness. And to the many who had shared my life's journey – the soldiers, sailors and airmen, the diplomats, the humanitarian workers and so many others who worked with me, and my friends – I thank you for helping me enrich this book of my memoirs.

Most of all, I am thankful to Almighty God for his healing Grace in giving me life that I may live to tell my story. Praise Him.

I

EARLY TRAINING GROUNDS

*I saw first-hand how hard it was to perform well,
how important it was to be disciplined and to persevere.*

I KNEW I had it coming. I was late. I walked through the door and stretched out my hands, palms open, ready to be caned. My father was very big on discipline and he imposed a curfew. I had been given a time to be home and I knew I should have gone home on time. But I was too engrossed playing. I was supposed to do my homework, but I had not. So I knew I would *kena* (get it). I knew that I was wrong. I was caned many times. But I never held that against my father, even as a boy; I believed that discipline was very important. That was the way I was brought up, and it had a great influence on my development.

My father was strict but reasonable, and never punished me without explaining the reason for it. He always found opportunities to share his life story with me. He was born in Singapore and was a chief clerk with Shell Company. My grandfather, whose father was an umbrella maker from Amoy in China, was also born in Singapore. He worked as an official in the Chinese Protectorate and died of smallpox when my father was five years old. My grandmother, a Straits-born Chinese, had a difficult time bringing up five boys and one girl. This difficult time growing up taught my father to be disciplined and thrifty. Some of these traits rubbed off on me. My mother was born in Bangka, Indonesia, and was adopted by her uncle, a medical doctor. She studied in a Dutch school in Indonesia. In her early teens, her adoptive father, whom we called Grandfather, brought her to Singapore.

My parents lived in my maternal grandfather's house, where I was born on 18 July 1941, just seven months before the fall of Singapore to the Japanese. I was the only son, sandwiched between two sisters. Life during the Japanese Occupation was very restrictive, and we could not go out and meet other children. Food was scarce and I was anaemic and even suffered a bout of malaria. My only playmates were the driver's children and we conversed in Malay. I grew up fairly sheltered living in that big compound house at the junction of Killiney Road and River Valley Road.

During the War, the house next door was taken over by the Japanese for the Kempeitai (military police). I do not recall much about the Japanese soldiers as I was too young to form any impressions. But I remember that one of them was kind to me and he sometimes came over and gave me toys. I never actually heard it but people in my family said they could hear the torture going on next door.

I was about five years old when we moved to our own home. My father used up most of his savings to buy the house, which was a bombed-out structure at 18 Makepeace Road in Newton. It was all he could afford. But he rebuilt it, and it became the first home of our own for my family. There, I came out of the shell of my earlier sheltered life. Those were very interesting years, full of fun. I made friends with all the neighbourhood boys. They were mostly Teochews and Eurasians, and I grew up speaking some Malay and Teochew. We spent our time catching spiders and fish from the drains, and had spider fights and fish fights. We took a bus all the way to Punggol to cut branches from mangroves because they made good catapults. We played in the open area behind my house which was overgrown with *lalang* (a tall, coarse grass). We flew kites in Makepeace Road, played football and other games on that laterite road, running barefoot over stones and pebbles. The soles of my feet became hardened like leather. If you ask me now to walk barefoot outdoors, I can't.

The things we did as kids over there developed my love for the outdoors. My life was running on the road, climbing trees, playing in drains and shooting birds with catapults. We used to shoot the birds, clean them up, build a fire, *panggang* (grill) them, and eat them with some soya sauce, pepper and salt. Our playground included the old cemetery at Kampong Java Road, which is now gone. We played hide and seek there at night. We would hide behind the tombstones and when the cars stopped at the traffic light, we popped our heads out to scare the drivers. I was mischievous by nature.

But in school I was quite a good boy. I was rather reserved and never got into trouble with the teachers. It was in 1948 that I went to Primary One in Monk's Hill Primary School, partly because it was very near my house and partly because my uncle was the Vice-Principal there. That was one reason why I was well behaved. The other reason was that I took well to discipline. The teachers were very strict. Being caned on the hand and sometimes on the buttocks was a common thing. Nobody reported to their parents. It was better not to tell them because they would say that you must have done something wrong and give you another walloping. That was how we were brought up – your teachers were your guide, your mentor, and unquestionably right. They were good and dedicated teachers, who wanted the best out of you. I had a double promotion after Primary 2, although I do not know how I got that. I was not brilliant, but I always did my schoolwork.

The schoolboys were a motley crowd from different backgrounds and races. After the War, Monk's Hill had one special class for much older Malay boys who had missed out on schooling during the war years. They were the big boys in the school. I played football with them, and of course they were better players. Recess time to me was football time. We did not have a proper field. We played barefoot with a small rubber ball in the open ground between the canteen and the toilet. Race and religion made no difference. We just played happily together.

The boys I played with were not gangsters, but there were gangsters in the area. There was a Malay gang near Kampong Java called Merah Puteh (Red and White). In Newton it was the 24 Gang. To survive, you had to know how to interact with them. I had to walk almost one kilometre from my house to Monk's Hill School. The gangsters demanded that I pay protection money or join the gang or be a runner for them. But I didn't want to give them money or to join them. So I stayed on good terms with them and didn't give them any reason to make things difficult for me. They tried to harass me, but because my response to everything was a polite "yes, yes", they eventually gave up. I didn't join them or pay them money, but I learnt all their codes, their numbers. That helped me because when the bigger boys bullied me in school, I pretended to be a gangster, throwing out numbers so that the bullies thought I was with the gang. I survived by being friendly with a few gangsters and doing small favours for them. They could not go into the school, so I helped to pass messages to boys in the school and bring protection money out to them. My father did not know this. He would have killed me if he did. This was my environment when I was growing up and I learnt to survive.

There were boyhood experiences at Makepeace Road that helped me appreciate the need for perseverance to succeed in sports and also the meaning of working hard for money. A few of the older boys in the neighbourhood were very seriously into athletics. One was a sprinter, another a hurdler and a third a long-jumper. I would follow them to their training.

I carried their running shoes, set up the hurdles, raked the long-jump pits, timed their runs and even ran circuits to warm up with them. I saw first-hand how hard it was to perform well, how important it was to be disciplined and to persevere. That had a deep impact on me in my own pursuit of sporting excellence and in my life in general.

Then there was my neighbour who had an office equipment business. Every other week he would receive a supply of knocked-down filing cabinets, cupboards, tables and chairs that needed to be assembled. He would offer a few of the neighbourhood boys an opportunity to do the assembly. I think we were paid 50 cents for each item we assembled. It required skilled and delicate work which we had to learn. At best we could complete only two pieces in one afternoon. Another of my neighbours had a provision shop. Together with his son, I used to run deliveries for him for a small payment. My father was aware of what I was doing to earn extra pocket money. He allowed me to take on the jobs as long as my schoolwork did not suffer. He thought there was merit in what I was doing, as he saw this as good exposure to work ethics and the meaning of hard work. I learnt well.

II

A FORETASTE OF THE MILITARY

*All hell broke loose on Christmas Eve when I told my parents
that I was going to military college in less than 10 days' time…
It was the start of what I always wanted – to be a soldier.*

I WENT TO Anglo-Chinese School (ACS) at Barker Road for
my secondary education. My father wanted me to go there.
My maternal grandfather had made a significant donation
to ACS many years earlier, and my father and his brothers
were from ACS. I transferred from Monk's Hill to ACS just
before the entrance exam to get into secondary school and
escaped the exam because that was a requirement only for
government schools and ACS was not one. Now my grandsons
are the fourth generation in my family to have attended ACS.

The environment in ACS was completely different from
that in Monk's Hill. The Monk's Hill boys were a mixed lot,
mostly from lower-income and middle-income families. In
ACS, many were from well-to-do families, who went to school
by car. I walked from Makepeace Road to Barker Road. The
bus fare was 5 cents each way, but by walking I could save
10 cents out of my daily allowance of 50 cents. I also did not
spend much at the tuckshop. Just a drink, a plate of noodles
or something, amounting to 15 or 20 cents. So I could save
30 cents a day to spend on things that I wanted to do or
buy, especially outdoor stuff which I found useful or gifts for

friends. I had to save for two months to buy a penknife. With a torchlight, I could go out at night, do things with it. I didn't buy books. But I did borrow comics from friends.

Most of the teachers in ACS were very dedicated. They enjoyed teaching; it was a calling. They were strict and stood for no nonsense. One of them was notorious for his slaps. He was tall and huge. We used to try to predict how many times a boy would spin when he was slapped. I somehow was one of the few who escaped his slaps. We remember most of our teachers fondly, and even invited those who were still around to our gathering in 2007 to mark 50 years after O-Levels.

One teacher I will always remember is Mr Gurdial Singh, my literature teacher in Secondary 2. He was a big man with a very gentle soul. He gave me a prize for submitting a poem that inspired me most. These lines from the poem "The Ladder of St Augustine" by Henry Wadsworth Longfellow became my guiding light: "The heights by great men reached and kept were not attained by sudden flight, but they, while their companions slept, were toiling upward in the night."

I enjoyed my classes, and even studied Latin as my father had visions of me becoming a doctor or lawyer. But I spent more time on extra-curricular activities than studying. Sports was my big love. I joined any team that wanted me. So I played football, rugby and hockey. I played football all the way until I was in Pre-University (Pre-U), the equivalent of junior college. I was the school captain. I played hockey as a goalkeeper for the ACS and Combined Schools teams. After ACS started rugby when I was in Pre-U 1, I played that until I went to military college. There were seasons for the various sports, so I could participate in every sport I enjoyed through-out the year. Every week I would train a couple of afternoons and play a couple of games. It was wonderful because I'd rather be outside on the field than being stuck indoors. I also played individual sports like badminton, and I swam and ran.

But I preferred team sports because I enjoyed the thrill and camaraderie of working together to achieve a common goal. I believe that team sports teach you to work together with people, help you to understand people, and provide opportunities to develop leadership skills. I reckon I did well later in military college because I was a sportsman. I could take the rough and tumble, I understood teamwork and could get people to work with me. That is why I feel rugby has a special place in the military. When I was Chief of Defence Force (CDF), I made rugby compulsory for Officer Cadet School (OCS). I did it because it involves sheer physical contact, unlike other games. It is a game for ruffians played by gentlemen. You need not only teamwork but also strategy and tactics. You must be able to think fast, and you need guts and character.

The other thing about sports is the importance of sportsmanship, a trait that is so consequential in life. During a football game with St Joseph's Institution, a small scuffle between two players degenerated into an ugly punch-up between the teams. I was really ashamed of what happened. I consulted my football master and we came up with the idea of inviting the opposing team over for tea. A week later we hosted the St Joseph's football team and their teachers to a small reception in our tuckshop. This gesture was our way of expressing how sorry we were. We shook hands and I really felt relieved and so much at peace after that. To me it was a small way to emphasise the importance of sportsmanship.

I had a pair of football boots which I used for playing football, rugby and hockey. It was handmade by a cobbler in Selegie Road. I brought that pair of boots with me to military college. Nowadays it is very different. People buy one pair of boots for each sport and replace them frequently. My pair of boots lasted me six years. I would have got new boots if I had asked my parents. But I didn't see the need if I could still use those boots, because I took good care of them and they worked perfectly well. I treasured my possessions.

When I went to ACS, I was still living in Makepeace Road

and the neighbourhood friends were still around. By then we were all in secondary school – the Eurasian boys in St Joseph's, the Teochew boys in Victoria School and other government schools. We did not have much time to play together anymore because we were busy with our own school activities and I had joined the 1st Company, Boys' Brigade (BB) in Prinsep Street Presbyterian Church, where my family worshipped. I went to Sunday School there and later was a member of the Youth Fellowship. To me, the good thing about attending church and participating in these activities was that I got to mix with youths from all sorts of backgrounds, different schools, different areas; they were also people with the same beliefs and upbringing.

In my early teens, sports and the BB were not the only things that occupied my time beyond schoolwork. Sunday School, Youth Fellowship, the BB and school friends also exposed me to social interaction with girls. There were lots of events and activities that included girls. Though I was by nature gregarious, I was quite shy and reserved where girls were concerned. But going to social events, parties and picnics soon made me less self-conscious. In those days most parties, for birthdays or other celebrations, were held at home and always under the close scrutiny of the elders.

There was dancing, with music from a gramophone. My mother taught me to waltz and foxtrot, while I picked up rock-and-roll from friends. Restaurants and clubs were unheard of. There was a little one-on-one dating then, but we normally went out in groups. I recall the times when we went as a group to matinee shows in the cinemas. Matinee shows were on Sundays at 11 in the morning. Tickets were 50 cents. The boys would collect the money from the girls and line up to buy the tickets. Then we would get in to *chope* (reserve) the seats using handkerchiefs. The boys would sit along the row leaving alternate seats empty so that when the girls came in they would have to sit between the boys. It was crafty, and it worked.

By the time I was in Pre-U, I was already comfortable being around girls. I was in the Arts class where the ratio of girls to boys was nearly two to one. I got along well with the girls and even had them help me out with my essays whenever I was late with submissions because of my sports and extra-curricular activities. Class outings and parties were common affairs. These wholesome activities afforded through school, church Youth Fellowship and the BB were wonderful opportunities for me to develop my social skills and stood me in good stead to being an officer and gentleman.

I joined the Junior BB when I was 9 years old, then called the Life Boys, and from 12 to 17 I was in the Senior BB. I joined because it was expected of me. Everyone in my family, my cousins, and all the young people in church were in either the BB or Girls' Brigade (GB). At that time, most companies of the BB were started in churches. Today they are in schools but affiliated to churches. But after I joined the BB, I found that I actually liked what I was doing there. The BB became a big and very important part of my life.

My deep involvement in the BB while I was in secondary school kept me occupied and off the streets. It also provided me a moral compass and spiritual ballast. The BB laid a tremendous foundation for my life, and for what I eventually did in the military. What appealed to me most were the uniform, discipline, teamwork and camaraderie – the whole way of life, which I really valued. I enjoyed drill, and I enjoyed the outdoor activities, especially camping. I attended every camp I could. Sometimes a group of us would camp out by the beach during the school holidays. These were on top of official BB camps. We even invited the GB girls to picnic with us for the day. They would come by bus and we would meet them at the bus stop and *tumpang* (give a ride) them on our bicycles to the camp site. We were a band of brothers bonded by strong friendship. I also joined the BB Band and was a bugler. In fact, my very first trips out of Singapore were to Malaya to attend BB camps and tour with the BB Band in Malacca, Kuala Lumpur, Ipoh and Penang.

The activities in the BB included classes to gain proficiency and qualify in various skills, upon which we would be awarded badges. We were given points for every badge awarded. There were badges for gymnastics, swimming, first aid, lifesaving, band, knowledge of plants, animals, birds, Bible education, and so on. The Queen's Badge was the highest award. We had to have a specified minimum number of years of membership as well as near-perfect attendance for five years and chalk up points from the badges we earned. Only after attaining all these could we apply for the Queen's Badge. It took a lot of time and hard work. Today it is called the Founder's Award. In 1958, I was conferred the Queen's Badge by the Governor of Singapore, Sir William Goode, at a parade in the Padang. It was a very proud moment for me.

I left the BB at 17 when I was in Pre-U 1. Some people in my batch left as sergeant or staff sergeant. I left as a corporal. I had the Queen's Badge and I was one of the better ones, although not the best. I left earlier than I should have, which is something I regret to this day. You see, I had applied for selection to attend the BB international camp overseas. I applied twice, and the second time I went all the way to the finals but did not make it. I was devastated. It had taken me so many years. I had done so much, but I still wasn't good enough. In those days, being selected to attend such an international event was the only way for me to get to travel overseas. The disappointment was eating me up and I reacted badly. I left prematurely. It is easy for me now to think back and see that it was the wrong thing to do. But at that time, I was upset and extremely disappointed. I felt very sorry later. I realised that it was very immature of me to think that way. And I told myself: "You must never react this way again." Later, when I was a young military officer and was not among the chosen few to go overseas for courses, I did not react impetuously. It was wrong for me to feel that it was my entitlement. I recognised that it may not be my turn to go or I was just not slated for that duty; there must have been reasons why others were chosen instead of me.

Many years later, when I contributed an article for the book published by the 1st Company BB, I related this episode and said that I had failed. Then one of my mates clarified that I was wrong. He said that in fact I had been one of the two selected but because they wanted to give it to only one person from the 1st Company, someone from another company who perhaps was not as good was selected instead of me. But at that time, I had felt that I was a failure, because I worked extremely hard for everything I wanted. I was very achievement oriented – in sports and in the BB. This lesson served me very well later in life. I learnt not to react too hastily.

So I had taken myself out of the BB prematurely, which I should not have. I even joined the Sea Cadets for a short time after that. Fortunately, I am still regarded as a distinguished member of the BB. And now I have been designated the Honorary President, a lifetime appointment. We have very good people who were in the BB, like pioneer civil servant Sim Kee Boon and President of the Singapore Industrial Arbitration Court Tan Boon Chiang, and many others who later became regulars in the Singapore Armed Forces (SAF). It is a pity that today, kids are usually limited to one co-curricular activity (CCA) in school. In most schools, you cannot join a uniformed organisation if you are doing another CCA. But I think being a member of a uniformed organisation is irreplaceable because it prepares a child, boy or girl, for life. I sit on the selection panel for the President's Award for Primers, who are BB members who have gone beyond their O-levels. I meet these young men and I can see what the BB has done for them. They stand out. Similarly, when I interviewed people in the SAF I could also see the difference – how working hard and doing well in a youth organisation can help put you a notch above the rest.

In Singapore during those days, a military career was not something anybody talked or thought about. But I was thinking about the military since the time I was in secondary school. At first I thought of joining the police because it also had the things I liked – uniform, outdoors, discipline. There were friends from the BB who had joined the Police Force. But a distant relative who was an Assistant Commissioner of Police discouraged me, saying there was no future because we were still under the British.

I wanted to join the Singapore Volunteer Corps (SVC) but was too young as I was not yet 18. Then the opportunity came when I was in Pre-U 2. They wanted to form a corps of drums, so they took in people my age – I was a bugler, Edward Yong (later a colonel in the SAF) was a drummer – even though I was not quite 18. I joined as a private and was promoted to lance-corporal within a couple of months. We did basic military training and shooting. Volunteers had to attend at least one parade every week. Then there was weekend training at the SVC camp at Tanah Merah. We were paid $2.50 for each parade and $4.50 for the weekend camp. I could make $7 a week, which was good money. I was a lance-corporal in a platoon in A Company, 1st Battalion of the SVC. That's where I got my first exposure to military life. As for the corp of drums, we once combined with the Singapore Military Forces (SMF) Brass Band to perform at a ceremonial parade. One of the marches we played was the rousing "Mechanised Infantry", composed by D McBain, which features bugles. I was so thrilled!

When there was an advertisement for people to join 1 SIR (1st Battalion Singapore Infantry Regiment), I was very in-terested. We were self-governing then but defence was still under the British. 1 SIR was part of the SMF which had its headquarters at Beach Road Camp. They called for people to apply as cadets to be trained in the Federation Military

College (FMC) in Port Dickson. The first interview was face-to-face with mostly British officers. I was short-listed to do the initiative test at the field in Tanglin, which was the British Land Forces HQ. They set up situations and observed who took the initiative and demonstrated leadership. I was short-listed again and had to do a medical test. I was taking my A-Levels history paper on the same day and I rushed through my paper so that I could go to do the medical, and then rushed back for the next paper in the afternoon. That was how determined I was to get into the military. My parents did not know anything up to this point. My father still had hopes of me becoming a doctor or lawyer.

All hell broke loose on Christmas Eve when I told my parents that I was going to military college in less than 10 days' time. They were very upset. I said, "I am so sorry, but I want to be a soldier." I had received a letter saying that I was selected to attend FMC and was given a railway warrant to travel to Port Dickson in Malaya. Four of us had been chosen – Kesavan Soon, Edward Yong, Royston Desker and me. When I had earlier gone to see my principal in ACS to ask for a testimonial, he told me that good ACS boys did not join the army. Still, I am proud and thankful to have been in ACS and can truthfully say that the school prepared me well to take on the challenges of a military career. On 2 January 1960, the four of us took a train to Seremban where we were put on a truck and driven to Port Dickson.

So I achieved what I had set out to do. It was the start of what I always wanted – to be a soldier. For this I was willing to accept two things. First, the hardship I would have to go through to become a soldier. I knew this from the stories I heard from many military people I had met and from my SVC experience. The second thing was the lack of career prospects. At the time I joined 1 SIR, there was only one battalion. The Commanding Officer (CO) was a British officer, and his company commanders and some others holding senior ranks were British. But I was determined to join the army. I thought at best I would end up a major, and have a Land Rover to drive me home. Never in my wildest dreams did I think that one day I would have three stars on my shoulders.

III

NEVER AN EASY ROAD

It was a tremendous experience.
It was a hard life. But I really enjoyed it.

I WAS FILLED with apprehension as we made our way to FMC in Port Dickson. Even though I was mentally prepared and had experience in the SVC and BB, and for a short while as a Sea Cadet, I had a sense that I was plunging into the unknown when I boarded the train at the Malayan Railway Station at Tanjong Pagar.

We got off at Seremban and there was a sergeant-major waiting to drive us to Port Dickson. When I climbed into the 3-tonner, it suddenly hit me that I was in the army now. It felt surreal. On the ride to Port Dickson, no one was looking at the scenery. I kept thinking: "What am I getting myself into?" The moment we arrived at FMC, it was pandemonium. We ran here, we ran there – to find our way around, locate our accommodation and get ourselves kitted up. Everything was done on the double. We had no time to think. And before we could settle down, the ragging started. During the first two weeks, the senior cadets could take it out on us. The four Singaporeans had a rougher time. We stood out because everyone else was Malayan. The idea of the ragging was to cut us down to size. To mould us into something more uniform because we were all from different backgrounds. Only those who came from the FMC Boys' Wing, which was for boys who attended secondary school at FMC, knew what to expect.

I told myself that I wanted to be in the army, I wanted to be a cadet. I would take whatever came my way. And I wanted to show them that a Singaporean could take it. The worst part was that the three senior cadets from Singapore gave us junior Singaporean cadets a rougher time than the Malayans did, because they wanted to demonstrate that they would not show their fellow Singaporeans any favouritism.

The things they did to us! Sometimes a senior cadet would give instructions to wake him up in the morning when it was still dark. Whoever was assigned had to go to his room, climb on top of his cupboard, squat there flapping his arms and crow like a cock. Sometimes people fell in the dark. The seniors threw things at us, belittled us and called us "stupid fellows". During the day when we were at training, we were not with them. But during the breaks, lunch time and dinner time, they would come after us. The worst time was the evening; when we were carrying out personal tasks like ironing our uniform and polishing our boots, they would pounce on us and rain insults on us. The verbal abuse was terrible; they really made us feel like dirt. Many of my fellow junior cadets broke down. My roommate, a very quiet Malay boy from Johor who was an intelligent mathematician, had a really tough time taking the ragging and I spent a lot of time assuring him and calming him down. But I decided that I would not break. I would stand tall. You can do what you want to me, I will take it.

I will never forget an incident just after the two-week period when ragging was supposed to be over. I was sitting outside my room, cleaning my rifle after shooting range, and a senior cadet, a Chinese, came up, kicked me and called me, "You bastard!" I said, "Why do you call me that?" "Because your father never married your mother." Something snapped when I heard that. I fixed the bayonet to my rifle and went at him. He ran and I chased him until some cadets stopped me. When I think back, I always wonder if I would have thrust the bayonet into him had I caught up with him. I really don't know. But I was so angry at the time. The ragging period was over; you can insult me, but don't talk about my parents. This senior cadet apologised to me later and we eventually became good friends.

A tough life at FMC was something that I expected having been in the SVC, but it was worse than I anticipated. The barracks were wooden huts and bathing facilities comprised a water trough and a ladle. What was grimmer was that the area was ridden with malaria. We got up at 5.30 in the morning, went all the way until late at night, and then started all over again the next morning. The parade square was within a laterite airstrip. Our highly polished boots were ruined after each drill lesson. The drill sergeant-major used to threaten us with his favourite scare: "If you drill like ducks, I'll move you so fast, you'll take off like a plane!" My previous exposure to the military in Singapore was nothing compared to FMC. We were cadets, and cadets get a harder time than even the recruits in basic training. We were often reminded that recruits were soldiers, but cadets were non-persons and the lowest scum of the earth. But because we were all suffering together, the junior cadets developed a very strong sense of camaraderie. I was fortunate because I could speak Malay and I am quite a friendly and gregarious person, so I got on quite well with the other junior cadets.

Six months into my junior year, cadets like me who were not from the Boys' Wing were packed off to the Outward Bound School on Pangkor Island for a two-week course. We thought it would be a walk in the park for us but it turned out to be physically and mentally demanding. There was physical training, jungle trekking, canoeing, seamanship, and confidence-building exercises. It was quite different from the military training we had so far and was an exciting experience.

The trainees included private-sector executives, teachers, civil servants, even managers of rubber estates. With such a mix, it was all the more challenging to work as a team and build team spirit, and harder to perform as a leader. But it was a refreshing change. It helped me become less dogmatic and rigid, and forced me to adopt a more balanced approach to work, duty, comrades and self. I became a better cadet too. This exposure in the Outward Bound School was not only memorable, it also benefited me to the extent that I could say it made an impact on my life.

In my senior year, the training programme included a deployment to Cameron Highlands for out-field training in a different environment. It was so cold, especially in the evenings. The last mission was to navigate in small groups from Brinchang Camp in the highlands through the jungle, eastwards and downhill to the railway line. We were to get to a railway station and find our way back to FMC. We were given survival equipment and combat rations for seven days as it was estimated that we would take at least four days.

Then it happened that a smart-aleck cadet had a contact with the leader of the Orang Asli (indigenous people) community and managed to arrange a guide for each group to bring us through the jungle to the railway line. We thought that was a clever move; no need to suffer unnecessarily. But we were not so clever after all. We got to our destination too quickly, with most of the groups taking only two days. We got caught out and the Officer Commanding (OC) blew his top. Our punishment was to repeat the jungle navigation exercise at a different location. But, by divine intervention, it was called off because a search operation was in progress after a military plane crashed in the area.

Was what we did a correct exercise of initiative? Some of us thought so. But on pondering further, I felt that we were wrong and misguided to think that we could explain this away by claiming that we had been taught to use our initiative.

We failed to accomplish the intended objective of the exercise, which was to test our map-reading, jungle navigation and survival skills. After the bravado wore off, and good sense set in, I became troubled by this episode. It taught me an important lesson on integrity.

Our training in FMC was in both the classroom and the field. In the classroom, it was a mixture of military subjects and academic subjects at Higher School Certificate (HSC) level (the equivalent of A-Levels). So I have two HSC certificates – from ACS and FMC. The CO of FMC and the OC of the Cadet Wing were British. The instructors were mostly British; they included the Regimental Sergeant-Major (RSM) from the Coldstream Guards and the Cadet Wing Sergeant-Major from the Black Watch Regiment. We had a few Malay sergeant-majors, and a Chinese one. For the HSC classes, British officers and some civilian teachers taught us. The military subjects were taught by both British and Malayan officers. One of my platoon commanders – my instructor, Yaacob Mohd Zain – later became the CDF of the Malaysian Armed Forces (MAF) just before I retired from the SAF. Till today we are good friends.

I told myself I must excel. It is in my DNA that whatever I undertake I try to do my best and do well. It was like this in school, in the BB, as a cadet, in the various military courses I attended later, and when I went to Duke University and Harvard. The same attitude. Never mind that I was not born with great intelligence. I will work hard and do my utmost.

And that was what I did. Not only in the academic and military part of my training but also in sports. Sports was an especially important thing in FMC. I played football and was captain in my second year. Boxing was compulsory. By British Army tradition, boxing was a noble sport. Spectators even had to turn up in formal dress, in mess kit. We all had a go in the ring. It was what was expected, regardless of the outcome. In my second year, I fought in the cadet competition and got knocked out in the first round. Though I took it on my chin, I was not upset as I had given my all. I am still in contact with Ariffin Rosli, the cadet who knocked me out. He is now a retired Malaysian Brigadier-General. He still feels bad, but I told him, "Come on, Ariffin, it's okay!"

I was also in the rugby team. We would go to the field at 4 o'clock in the afternoon for rugby training. Every training session began with us jogging a couple of miles in our army boots. And mind you, Port Dickson is a very hilly place. After resting for half an hour we would go on to play a match. I was the hooker, the man in the centre of the scrum. That's often a terrible place to be in. You are right in the middle when the scrum collapses and the bodies pile on you.

I was once badly injured in a game we played against the British Forces, when someone stepped on my knee and twisted it. My knee swelled so much that for one week I couldn't play rugby. The next week the swelling had gone down a bit. I strapped up my knee and went back to play. It was pride, and also the compulsion to meet expectations. Because in FMC you were finished if you showed that you were weak. So it was something I had to do; I wanted to show that the injury did not bother me. In hindsight, that was foolish. Today they will not allow you to do that. If I had gone to the medical officer, he would have excused me from playing. But I did not want others to think negatively of me. So I played. I did not see any reason not to run if I could. For a long time I suffered because I never gave my knee time to recover. Even up to my forties, I was plagued with knee problems. But if I were young today, I would still do it!

As cadets we had to undergo a battery of assessments. There were the academic and field tests, and the appraisal of your character. The character assessment was very important and your performance in sports played a very big part in this assessment. So like they say, "die-die must do". There were those who did not participate in sports. But those of us who played sports, and played well, benefited with higher grades in character assessment than those who did not. Perhaps that helped me get chosen, at the end of the first year, as one of the four Cadet Under-Officers (CUOs) in my senior term. There were four platoons, two senior and two junior, with a CUO and a Cadet-Sergeant in charge of each platoon.

I was put in charge of one of the junior first-year platoons. Being appointed a CUO was an honour. Even better, it was excellent training exposure for me. It allowed me to command at a very early stage, especially as I was given a junior platoon and not a senior one. Seniors did not need much help, but the juniors really needed guidance and looking after. They often came to me for counselling. As a CUO, I had a sort of office across from my room where the junior cadets could come to talk to me about their problems. I had to strike a balance between my studies and training and looking after the junior cadets. It taught me how to manage my time and how to manage my men.

I found that I enjoyed looking after people. In my junior platoon I had two Bruneian cadets and one Singaporean cadet. One of the Bruneians broke down during the ragging period and wanted to resign. He gave me his letter of resignation. I told him to go back and think about it. I said that this ragging period was the worst part, but once he overcame this, life would be okay. But he was adamant: "I cannot take it anymore. If the army is like this, then the army is not what I want." That night, I brought him to the Cadets' Mess and we shared several drinks. His mood improved tremendously. Then I sent him back to his room to sleep. The next afternoon, after training, I called him up and asked how he was. "Sir, can I have the letter back? I withdraw my resignation." This cadet later rose very high up in the Bruneian military and government as did the other two who were my juniors in FMC. We developed a strong bond of friendship and are still in contact.

Cadets sometimes gambled during their free time. I used

to gamble when I was a schoolboy. But as under-officers, we had to stop the cadets from gambling and we had to set an example. So I did not gamble. One of the Bruneian cadets gambled and lost his airfare to go home for the term break, so he had to stay back during the break. I have not gambled since FMC. Kate's family always played mahjong and gin rummy. When we got married my father-in-law told her: "You married a man who can't even make the fourth *kaki* (player) in mahjong." I refused to play. I told myself I'd rather spend the money on other things than lose it in gambling. There was another cadet who had frequent nose bleeds. Once his roommate ran to me at 2 in the morning, saying that the fellow was dying. But I knew he was prone to bad nose bleeds and there was no need to panic. I got to know my men and it helped me manage this kind of thing – advise people who ran out of money, counsel people to behave themselves, manage girlfriend and other personal issues.

The FMC cadets were popular with the girls from the university and the teachers' training institute, and nurses. We had many cadet events, parties where we invited them. For the mid-term ball, I had not invited a partner as I had been too busy as the CUO responsible for organising it. A junior cadet came to me and said, "Sir, you can dance with my date." I danced with her once, danced with her twice, three times. He came up to me and said, "Sir, can I have her back?" It suddenly dawned on me what I was doing. I enjoyed her company and I liked her, but I forgot that this girl was the cadet's girlfriend. It struck me that I had to draw a line: you don't *potong jalan* (cut in on) a fellow cadet. It wasn't the gentlemanly thing to do.

It was training for life. I learnt about personal, even intimate, relationships. The junior cadets who had problems, like girlfriend issues, would come to me. I was barely older than them, and I was counselling them on matters that I hardly knew myself. So I had to improvise, and I grew up quickly. If I have to live my life over, I don't mind being a cadet in FMC again. It was a tremendous experience. Over the two years, there were life lessons and a great introduction and exposure to the military and to being an officer. It was a hard life, but I loved every bit of it.

There was strong camaraderie, and I developed very deep friendships with both juniors and peers. I am from the fourth intake. We commissioned in 1961 and 60 years later we are still in contact. We used to meet at least once a year, but not so frequently now that we are getting on in age. Now we communicate by group chat. When I was CDF, I hosted one of my intake's reunions in Singapore. And when I was High Commissioner in Canberra, I could not come back for one of the gatherings, so they said we would meet halfway. They arranged the reunion in Perth and I flew from Canberra to join them. This is the kind of comradeship and affinity we have, the bonds forged in the baptism of fire we went through during training. There are lots of good memories that we retain to this day, and we still reminisce over them. When we commissioned, I think there were 32 of us. More than a third of the class made one-star general and higher. When I was CDF, the relationships developed from FMC helped me in my dealings with the Malaysian military. We had a special rapport.

FMC was run like Sandhurst, the British military college, because it was inspired and formed by the British. They wanted to make us officers and gentlemen. Cadets had their mess and we were taught mess life. We ran the mess as cadets just like we would run a mess in the unit. The training included accounting as we had to learn how to manage mess accounts. We were taught etiquette, reinforced by occasional interactions with the officers and their wives. We had to dress up. In the evening, we wore a tie and long sleeves. When we went out on the weekends or in the evenings, even to the night market a few miles from camp, we wore a tie. We all looked like idiots walking in the night market with ties. But that's the way it was. We had uniformed waiters serving us in the Cadet Dining Hall. But the food was terrible. We got either beef or fish. Only it was not really beef but *kerbau* (buffalo). We never had chicken or lamb. The food was the same, day in, day out. The smell was the same. We all sat down properly to eat. Then when we could not tolerate it, we rushed to the canteen after that. I wouldn't say I could not stand it. But once in a while I gave myself a treat. It could be expensive – $1.50 for a chicken chop, which was the big thing in the canteen.

We had moved to FMC's brand new, purpose-built college facilities in Sungei Besi, Kuala Lumpur, during our senior year and we had the privilege of being the first batch to graduate from there. The passing-out parade was an event that I will always remember. Lots of preparation, rehearsals, practices. The words of the RSM during the many rehearsals still ring in my ears many years on. He would say, "Be proud, stand tall, step out, look up and march with a swagger for soon you will be an officer." Our cadets don't march with a swagger these days! I was selected to command one of the contingents. In Sandhurst, the Queen or a member of the Royal Family would be the reviewing officer. In FMC, it was the King – the Yang di-Pertuan Agong. This was the Sovereign's Parade. It was a big thing; there were some Sultans and Ministers present. My parents drove up to Sungei Besi.

It was a wonderful parade and even today I can still hear some of the martial music in my head. This is the soldier in me. To this day, when I do my evening walks, I put on headphones and play military music, and I actually march. I like to walk to the military beat with a swagger even at my age. I walk with my dog and carry a stick, as if I'm carrying a swagger stick. Sometimes I bump into my old soldiers and they still salute me. Occasionally, I am reminded of my first salute, the one I received immediately after the commissioning parade. The Wing Sergeant-Major approached me, came to a sharp halt, gave me a smart salute and said with a strong voice: "Congratulations, Sir!" I returned the salute, shook his hand, handed him two dollars and replied, "Thank you, Mr Smith," as was customary. That was my most memorable salute; I will never forget that.

On the evening of the passing-out parade, we had the commissioning ball. We were already second-lieutenants, because we had received our commission in the morning parade. We wore the mess kit of the regiment we would be posted to. We had returned to our units one and a half months before commissioning to make our mess kit, unsure if we would graduate but fervently hoping to. I wore the Singapore Infantry Regiment mess kit. There were also the Malay Regiment mess kit, the Reconnaissance Regiment mess kit, and so on. The British officers wore the mess kit of their parent regiment. It was a very colourful evening. Both the Sovereign's Parade and the commissioning ball were grand and unforgettable events. I believe such traditions are important because they make the military; they make the difference.

It was most heartwarming that when I went to my military college Intake 4 reunion in Kuala Lumpur in 2019, my Wing OC, William Crafter, who was about 90 years old, told Kate that I was his "best cadet". I suppose it was because of how I always tried to do my best. That was why I had aimed to be a Cadet Under-Officer. I did not win the Sword of Honour, but I was one of the top cadets. This is the message that I always have for people: you do your best in whatever you decide to do. Whatever hardship there may be, take it. There is never an easy road to success.

IV

FIRST COMMAND –
LEARNING LIFE LESSONS

*When you are given a responsibility, you must consider
every minute detail from the beginning to the end.*

I KNEW EXACTLY where I would be posted to when I returned
to Singapore – 1 SIR in Ulu Pandan Camp. That was the only
battalion we had in 1961, when I was commissioned. The CO,
adjutant, company commanders, quartermaster and sergeant-
majors were British. A few Singaporean captains held Company
Second-in-Command appointments, but most were lieutenant
or second-lieutenant Platoon Commanders. I was assigned to
command 11 Platoon, Charlie Company.

This first experience of a real command was challenging.
I started from square one despite the preparations I had in
officer cadet training. I was barely 20 while my men were at
least five years older. These were professional soldiers, with
different problems and challenges in life. More than half of
them were married, and many had problems at home. They
were Chinese, Malays and Indians, all regulars as there was
no National Service (NS) at that time. Not a single one of my
men had O-Levels. A small number had gone to secondary
school but most had primary school education at best. They
spoke a mixture of English and Malay with a bit of Hokkien,
but not much because most of the Chinese could speak Malay.

It was not easy to handle them. The moment I went in, they tested me to see how far they could get with me. Military college did not prepare me for this but I soon realised that while I wanted to be approachable, I also had to hold my ground. Here I was, a 20-year-old bachelor who, apart from leading in military aspects, also had to look after my men and solve their problems, including marital problems and other difficult issues. That was where I also learnt early on to depend on my Platoon Sergeant. Treat him like a mentor for he was the de facto guardian of the platoon. This probably does not happen in our NS battalions as the platoon sergeants are equally young. I was fortunate that I had a very good Platoon Sergeant, also a bachelor – Nelson Sng Cheng Chye – who was a *laojiao* (old bird, meaning old hand). He eventually became a Senior Warrant Officer in the SAF.

I managed quite well and rarely had to go to my Company Commander for advice on how to deal with my soldiers' problems. The Company Commander and Sergeant-Major, both British, left us on our own most of the time as they had a system of monitoring our performance. My Company Second-in-Command was a Singaporean captain, Peter Stuart, who became a lifelong friend. I had to prepare the training programme for my platoon, according to an overall company training plan. We trained frequently in the open ground where Pandan Valley condominium is. It was undulating scrub land, divided into training areas A, B and C. Sometimes we trained in Mandai.

The camp in Ulu Pandan had wooden buildings with zinc roofs. All the officers lived in the mess except the married ones. We had a single room each. Air-conditioning was unheard of. As an officer, I had a batman who was a soldier from my platoon – what we now call a runner. But the batman did a lot more; he was also a valet. Every morning he would wake me up and tell me, "Sir, the training programme today is such and such. This is the uniform you must wear." He prepared my uniforms, polished my boots, made my bed, cleaned my room. Out in the field he would put up my *basha* (tent), lay out the bedding, prepare my ration meals, dig the trench, so that I could concentrate on my job as platoon commander. My batman's name was Sivalingam. He was a speed walker and a member of the battalion team. One reason he wanted to be my batman was that it gave him time to train for his speed walking. Besides receiving his pay as a private, he also got a small allowance which I gave out of my own pocket.

Pay, given twice a month, was in cash. The more senior officers in the battalion took turns going to the bank to draw the money to pay the whole battalion. Though they went with armed escorts, a British officer was once robbed of all the money he had withdrawn for the pay. He was shot dead in the Land Rover on his way back from the bank, and was buried in Ulu Pandan Military Cemetery, which is now Pine Grove Estate.

The platoon commanders took turns to pay the men in the company. We had to account for the amount we paid out, to the last cent. There were times when paying officers made up the difference from their own pockets to avoid the hassle of resolving shortfalls. The soldier would come up to you, salute and put out his hands, one over the other. He would get $80 to $100 after deductions for equipment losses and other minor expenses, say "Pay correct, Sir", salute and march off. He had to upkeep a family with that, but he was provided quarters. A second-lieutenant was paid $360 a month, a lieutenant $400, a captain $545. Married officers were paid almost twice the amount because they had what was known as marriage allowance. They could also stay in quarters. So quite a lot of young officers got married early.

Officers had to have a bank account for their salary. I had already opened a bank account as a cadet even with a pittance of $240 a month. For the $360 I got as a second-lieutenant, a little more than half went to the mess. We had to pay for everything which we bought there – food, drinks, even toothpaste. But beer was duty-free. At the end of the month, we had just enough money to go on one date with our girlfriends. We could not go out too often because, as an officer and gentleman, we had to pay the girl's share. I also gave some money to my parents, not because they needed it but because it was the right thing to do in those days. By then I had also bought a sports car – a second-hand MGA – and that cost money to maintain. So I stayed in the mess most of the time – and chalked up my mess bill. It was a vicious cycle, month after month. We learnt, early in life, the need to manage our finances.

Mess life was very active, and it helped develop camaraderie. We used to have two dining-ins a month – one for only the bachelors while the other included the married officers. For the dining-in, we dressed in mess kit and sometimes in black tie. It was very different in those days. Officers were expected to dress well and we were given a uniform allowance. Our uniforms were not from the quartermaster's store but were made to measure, by a civilian contractor called Union Merchant Tailors at Bras Basah Road. To be *sikit atas* (classier), we purchased higher-grade stuff – wool from Fox Brothers in England – for the puttees (gaiters) we wore over our ankle-boots. Our hats were ordered from the hatters Herbert Johnson in New Bond Street, London. Sam Browne leather belts could be bought in Singapore, but one of the officers gave me a British-made belt which he managed to scrounge.

We were rostered to be Duty Officer at least twice a month, from 7 am to 7 am the next day. The first duty was to dismount the previous night's guards. Then to the cookhouse to check that the fresh and dry rations delivered by the civilian contractor were accounted for. The swill was then taken away. Now and then the swill man would be in cahoots with the cooks. As the Duty Officer, I sometimes had to put my hand into the swill bin to check if canned food was being smuggled out in the swill. Nasty work! This kind of hanky-panky was prevalent from the days of the British until even after 1965. Eliminating such crooked small-time food suppliers was one reason for then-Defence Minister Dr Goh Keng Swee setting up Singapore Food Industries to supply provisions to the SAF.

In the morning, we dressed up to do all the checks and then changed into whatever training uniform was required to train our platoon. In the evening, we changed into a smart uniform with boots, puttees, Sam Browne belt and service dress cap to mount the guards for the night. We did a muster of the duty personnel at the Staff Parade at 10 pm – falling in the guards, people on duty in the cookhouse and medical centre. We also checked on the detainees to make sure they were accounted for. In addition, we had to go to the Istana to turn out the guards there. For that we wore ceremonial No. 1 dress. The time for the turnout of the guards both in camp and at the Istana was always a surprise because the Duty Officer had to go to the Adjutant in the morning to draw a lot for the time. If you drew 3 am, you would go at 3 am to the Istana. So it was *tikam tikam* (a game of chance).

One of the duties of the Duty Officer which always amused me was to close up the bar at the Sergeants' Mess after the Staff Parade at around 10.30 pm. We had to check the accounts and lock up the money. There would always be sergeants in the mess offering you drinks to hold you back so that the bar would stay open longer. In the interest of cultivating a strong bond with the senior Non-Commissioned Officers (NCOs), I would usually *cham siong* (compromise) a little and close the bar only after staying for one or two drinks.

I had a momentous experience as Duty Officer one Saturday night – a royal encounter. It was almost midnight and I was the only one left in the mess when in walked a well-dressed Malay gentleman who announced himself as the Tengku Mahkota (Crown Prince) of Johor. He was accompanied by his bodyguard. The Tengku Mahkota, who later ascended the Johor throne as Sultan Iskandar, said that he had "ordered" the guard commander at the guard room not to alert the Duty Officer as he wanted to do a surprise check. He declared that he was an honorary member of the mess as his father, the Sultan, had gifted a tiger skin to the mess. I hosted him until 3.30 am when I had to go to the Istana to turn out the guards. He quipped that he thought I was dressed in No. 1 to receive him.

He made subsequent visits and always asked for me as the other officers would take off when he was around. We developed a special relationship right up to when he was the Sultan of Johor and I was CDF. I had the honour to meet and get to know other members of the Johor Royal Family, including his son, the present Sultan. Years later, I had the pleasure of playing regular golf games with Sultan Iskandar in Johor, often followed by a gracious invitation to Kate and me to have dinner at his Istana Bukit Serene with him and his family.

An officer also had other regimental duties. I had to learn how to referee basketball games and boxing matches and, for that, was sent for a one-week course at the British Army Physical Training School at Tanglin. I was appointed the battalion basketball officer. 1 SIR then had a very good basketball team and we played with all the other British units in Singapore and the Far East. The carrot for doing well was a possible trip to Hong Kong where the finals were always held. We got to the finals but, after some wrangling, another officer senior to me went in my place. The story of my life! But I took it in my stride. I was also the messing officer, responsible for the food in the Officers' Mess. I had to work out the daily menu with the contractor and when my fellow officers thought the food was lousy, I got cursed at. You could not please everyone.

There was a lot of internal security training – riot control drills, roadblocks, cordon-and-search. In fact, 1 SIR was preoccupied with internal security. By the time I joined, they had already dealt with the Hock Lee Bus Riots and the public utilities workers strikes. The internal security duties included escorting night-soil trucks, along with dealing with all sorts of disturbances.

We held regular internal security exercises jointly with the police as, according to the law, the military operated only in support of the police. At one exercise, my platoon was based at a police station. The medical orderly attached to my platoon offered me a cigarette. I smoked it and became woozy and quite sick. He had given me a spiked cigarette. Unfortunately, the Brigade Second-in-Command decided to visit my station to be briefed on the operational situation. I could barely stand up from the stretcher I was lying on but managed to stumble through the briefing. Before he left, the colonel smiled and whispered to me to be careful with what soldiers gave me to smoke. He knew. Wise words which I remember to this day.

We put our internal security training into practice in the race riots in July 1964. I remember what happened the day the riots erupted. It was the Prophet Muhammad's birthday holiday. My two sisters and their boyfriends, and my girl-friend, Kate, and I had driven to Mersing in Johor for a day picnic in three sports cars. When we returned in the evening, we went to Ulu Pandan Camp for a drink before sending the girls home. We found the camp on standby. One of the guys had to send Kate and my sisters back as two of us were officers. We were mobilised because the riots had broken out and there was fighting between the Malays and Chinese. Our married soldiers were living in quarters in Queensway, and the drivers were also living there. Some of the officers had to drive 3-tonners to Queensway to pick up the drivers so that they could come back for more vehicles to ferry the married officers and soldiers back to camp.

I was sent out to do patrols in various parts of Singapore including Kampong Silat in Kampong Bahru, a hot spot for riots. My platoon had all races – Malays, Chinese, Indians.

What struck me most was the attitude of my soldiers. It was a serious race riot; people were being killed. But there was no racial issue or tension within my platoon. Nobody talked about the fight between the Chinese and Malays. We saw ourselves as soldiers and carried out our duties professionally, dealing with each person the same way, regardless of race.

While we were well trained in internal security drills and tactics, there were occasions when we had to think hard about how to handle particular situations and apply common sense. For example, when we had to help housewives go to market, we had the Malay soldiers escort the Chinese housewives, and vice versa. This way, we ameliorated hostile encounters with Chinese or Malay groups. And when we handled the rioters, we just regarded them as rioters and not as Malays or Chinese.

Singapore had joined the Federation of Malaysia when it was formed in 1963, together with Sarawak and Sabah. A Malaysian officer took over as CO of 1 SIR and the name of our regiment was changed to Pasokan Infantry Malaysia (PIM). That made us very upset, especially as the acronym PIM was unflattering to say the least. We continued to call ourselves SIR; we never used PIM.

President Sukarno of Indonesia opposed the union and declared Konfrontasi (Confrontation) against Malaysia. 1 SIR's training was then directed towards preparing ourselves for operations. In early 1964, I brought my platoon over to Jason Bay in Johor on my own, with a Land Rover and a 3-tonner, and spent one week training there. We were very independent.

I remember my Company Commander came to visit us. He got out of his car and asked, "Is everything all right?" We said, "Yes", and he got back into his car and returned to Singapore. That was the time when I really felt a sense of purpose. I was responsible for my men and had to prepare them for operations soon. It was serious training, conducted by me, my Platoon Sergeant and Section Commanders.

Before 1 SIR was deployed for operations in Sabah, the

CO wanted me to be the Regimental Signals Officer (RSO), and command the signals platoon. This was my regimental duty after being a platoon commander. I went to the Royal Malaysian Signals Corps' School of Signals in Kuala Lumpur for three months of training. I had also been sent to Port Dickson earlier for an infantry weapons course. I was unfortunate. Almost every platoon commander had gone to the United Kingdom (UK) for weapons and platoon commander courses, to Hythe and Warminster, but I went to Kuala Lumpur instead. I had missed out on overseas training again. I was very disappointed but, by then, had learnt to accept such letdowns.

The course at the Malaysian School of Signals turned out to be professionally conducted; it was excellent. The CO and some of the warrant officers who were instructors were seconded from the British Royal Signals. I learnt a lot and benefited from the course. Over the 12 weeks in Kuala Lumpur, I managed to sneak back to Singapore to see Kate. I left some Saturdays at 12 noon in my MGA and was home by 5 pm. Then I would return on Sunday night at around midnight and was back in class by 7.30 am on Monday. But I was serious and studied and worked hard throughout the course. I did well, had a good report with an "A" grade and returned to 1 SIR well prepared to lead the signals platoon into operations.

Before we left for Sabah, the whole battalion went to Taiping in Perak. This was when I learnt another very important life lesson. The battalion's stores and luggage were loaded on the train for Taiping and I was put in charge of them as the baggage officer. There were guards in some carriages where there were important stores. We had to account for the baggage when we got to Taiping and found a crate of rifle magazines missing. There was an inquiry and I was put on the line. I was very certain that the crate had been loaded and there were guards in the carriage. But I could not explain how it was lost. The guards were soldiers from the same battalion, although not my platoon, and I trusted them. It bothered me. I was telling the truth but at the back of my mind I questioned whether I was just trying to save my own skin by insisting that the crate had been loaded and the guards were in the carriage. Halfway through the inquiry, we received a call from the Malaysian Police to say that they had found a box of magazines by the railway track. There was an uproar at the inquiry and they asked, "Did Winston lie about securing the carriage?" They questioned the guards. Then the guards admitted that they had opened the door of the carriage and gone to sleep. The crate must have fallen out when the train went round a bend. The guards said they had not known that it had fallen out, but they admitted that they had opened the door because the carriage was so hot and poorly ventilated. They did not say all this until the police found the magazines.

That was a defining moment in my life. I could have been court-martialled. With the Communist insurgency still on, it was fortunate that it was not a crate containing weapons that fell out, only magazines. I was lucky. I got off with a severe reprimand. It was a lesson that stayed with me for the rest of my life. When you are given a responsibility, you must consider every minute detail from the beginning to the end. Did I take things for granted and was I not thorough in executing my duty? Frankly, I was not sure if I had specifically instructed the guards not to open the door, or even considered whether it was reasonable to expect them to keep the door closed with such poor ventilation. It was a black mark against me. I remember the British major who conducted the inquiry said to me, "Winston, you screwed up." And I accepted that I had.

We were in Taiping for three months and the training was good. I was RSO by then. Life in Taiping was different as we were operational. We patrolled the Thai-Malaysian border carrying out counter-insurgency operations. This was the tail end of the Malayan Emergency and there were still some Communist Party of Malaya insurgents running around in the area. The idea was to give us experience in jungle opera-tions and in possibly engaging a real enemy. It was a warm-up for the battalion's deployment to Sabah, where we would be operating in a similar environment. We took what we were doing in Taiping very seriously because we knew we would soon be facing Indonesians who would be trying to kill us. Some soldiers from other units had already been shot and killed in Sarawak and Sabah by then.

Taiping was a beautiful town. One big problem was keep-ing the soldiers out of trouble when they returned from the jungle. There was an outdoor eating place where the men used to go. There were girls who would come to sit with our soldiers for a couple of dollars. The local gangsters were not happy and they beat up one of our men. The soldiers went back to camp and, without the Duty Officer knowing, drew their bayonets and brought more soldiers with them back to town to take on the gangsters. (1 SIR had been involved in a similar incident many years earlier when the whole battalion went to fight in Holland Village after some soldiers were beaten up.) There was hell to pay. Fortunately, the Taiping magistrate was understanding and dismissed the case, accept-ing that soldiers, being soldiers, tended to do such things after being on operations for some time. We banned the soldiers from further visits to town. By this time, we were already getting ready to go to Sabah.

V

DANGEROUS STUFF

*There were times when I was lulled into complacency
but would be jolted out of it at the thought of being blown
up or shot and killed as the enemy was always nearby...
we lived and slept with loaded weapons all the time.*

WE WENT DIRECTLY from Taiping to Sabah in September 1964. I was in the advance party, together with the CO, the Intelligence Officer and some others, including members of the Tactical Headquarters. We flew from Butterworth to Tawau in a Royal Malaysian Air Force Dart Herald propeller plane, which seemed to be an endless journey because it was quite uncomfortable. We were to contact the Royal Malay Regiment battalion to take over their duties on Sebatik Island. The Battalion Tactical Headquarters was in Wallace Bay, where the sawmill and office of a British timber company were also located. The rest of the battalion arrived shortly after in batches, in Royal Australian Air Force C-130s.

The Battalion Main HQ was located in Tawau and the three rifle companies took up positions stretching across the northern half of Sebatik – at Wallace Bay, Sungei Limau and Sungei Melayu – with their platoons dispersed in various locations. The southern half of Sebatik was part of Indonesia. Our mission was to defend the Malaysian half and prevent incursions by the Indonesians. Our Sungei Melayu position also faced Pulau Nunukan, the main Indonesian troop base.

I had told Kate before I left that I hoped I would come back; I wasn't sure I would. When we arrived in Sabah, we quickly settled down and soon were in our positions. We were in operations and constantly exposed to danger. It hit me – hey, this really is dangerous stuff! But soon after, I took the danger in my stride, as part of my life. You just had to look after yourself and make sure you did the right thing.

The troops were in trenches in defensive positions facing a real enemy. They were usually alert and staunch. But there were times when they got jittery. One night, a soldier fired off a shot at some floating embers from a forest fire earlier that day, thinking that it was the enemy. That started a chain reaction and the whole company front started firing, thinking we were under attack. The firing stopped only when the Company Commander realised what had happened and gave the order to cease fire. Over time though, I could see that the men were getting more confident, alert and better able to cope with the constant danger. Our missions included mounting long-range patrols into enemy positions to gather intelligence. When the Intelligence Officer and I briefed each patrol, I could see the confidence and determination in the men, even though the missions were perilous. At the debriefs after the missions, they were upbeat. One told a story of how they were so close to the enemy position that an enemy soldier almost peed on his head, not realising he was right there.

The Indonesian soldiers facing us were marines from the Korps Kommando Operasi (KKO). Our battalion did not engage in any skirmishes but there was small arms fire and shelling, and reports of contact with the enemy by our forces. From time to time, they would also lob a couple of mortar bombs at us to make life more interesting for us, reminding us that they could kill us. We sometimes saw bodies of Indonesian soldiers being brought in.

There were times when I was lulled into complacency but would be jolted out of it at the thought of being blown up or shot and killed as the enemy was always nearby. There was a constant possibility of contact and we lived and slept with loaded weapons all the time. I remember an officer from 2 SIR told me that when he chatted with some Indonesian soldiers whom they had captured after a fire-fight, one of them told him, "I had you in my rifle sight. Why I didn't pull the trigger, I don't know." An officer from the battalion that replaced mine was shot and wounded when he was in the very same assault boat that I had used all the time in Sebatik. This happened one day after he took over from us. It sent shivers down my spine when I heard about it. That could have been me.

We patrolled the rivers in the assault boats and on foot in areas within our front. The Royal Malaysian Air Force supported by flying its Alouette helicopters for reconnaissance flights and light troop movement. Heavy-lift helicopters like the Belvedere were operated by the British Royal Air Force. We had a battery of 105-mm artillery guns manned by the British Royal Marines in our location to support us and the Royal Marines group. Some of the other activities conducted there included psychological operations where we dropped leaflets from the air using Beaver light planes flying very low. I participated in two such sorties. It was scary as you could not tell if you would be drawing small arms fire from the enemy on the ground.

My key responsibility was to provide reliable communications to the various locations in Sebatik Island as well as our Main HQ and the Brigade HQ in Tawau. I had my work cut out for me. The outgoing Signals Officer from the Royal Malay Regiment had cautioned me that radio communications in the location were bad and he had problems getting through most of the time. When my CO overheard this, he said to me in no uncertain terms that this would not be the case for 1 SIR. I saw that the British Royal Marines unit nearby was using VHF (Very High Frequency) radio equipment, so I switched to similar equipment which I had brought along in addition to the HF (High Frequency) sets that were being used. My challenge was how to get that set up, but I managed after experimenting with different types of antennae for the base station and specially designed antennae for the sub-stations, constructed from scrap material we had scrounged.

We had reliable communications with our companies and sub-units throughout our deployment in Sebatik, which was vital as our units were widely dispersed across the island. Later, I also had to devise special communications and cipher systems for our long-range patrols. Our only means of getting around was assault boats and all our logistics support came by them. It took too long to go overland. Since we could not use our trucks, our drivers became boat operators. Occasionally we could hitch a ride by helicopter.

In Sebatik, I also played tour guide to President Wee Kim Wee. He was then a journalist for *The Straits Times* and wanted to report on 1 SIR's operations. I accompanied him to various sub-units across the island by assault boat. When we were leaving our last stop, Bergosong, the tide had receded, and we had to get out and push the boat through the mud. He gamely hopped out and helped. It must have been an exciting experience for him to literally have gotten his feet wet. He exclaimed good-humouredly, "*Apa ini* (What's this), Winston? Are you trying to make things *susah* (difficult) for me?"

Prince Philip, the Duke of Edinburgh, went to Wallace Bay to visit the British forces and he visited 1 SIR as well. The English manager of the Wallace Bay Timber Company, together with his senior staff and their wives, made a special trip to meet the Prince. They were quite a sight, decked out in their Sunday best baking in the blazing heat. We were in combat gear and carrying weapons. That was when I first heard the expression "Mad dogs and Englishmen!" – and it came from Prince Philip.

While you demand that your men stay alert and focused when on duty, it is good to find opportunities to take their minds from their worries and fears and show that you care. There were some light moments on the frontline in Sebatik. We prepared *char siew* (roast meat) from wild boars that were blown up by booby traps we had laid for the enemy. We were also treated to venison from a deer that happened to run across the rifle sight of a soldier. We picked oysters from the jetty and cooked *orh luak* (oyster omelette). So, we were not stuck with eating only combat rations. We had to resolve the challenge of our Muslim soldiers wanting to fast during Ramadan. It was just not possible as they were not allowed to make a fire in the dark to prepare food for their morning meal before they started their fast. It was a sensitive issue and we had to delicately explain to the troops, after seeking the blessings of the religious teacher. I discovered quickly that soldiers can be resilient and resolute when properly led.

Maintaining the morale of the soldiers was of vital importance in an operational situation like this when they were facing constant danger. Most of the time they were in dugouts, exposed to the elements, eating combat rations. Clean water was rarely available. Drinking water had to be brought in jerry cans by assault boats. For bathing and washing we had to make do with whatever we could rustle up, usually murky and brownish water. There was a funny situation when a British company commander stripped and stood in the rain to bathe. He had soaped himself, but the rain stopped before he could rinse his body, leaving him soapy. Then there was a troubling incident when another British company commander commandeered two jerry cans of drinking water for his bath. The water had to be lugged by his soldiers some 300 metres up a hill to where his company was positioned. His soldiers were mightily upset, and I was sent by the CO to investigate. The company Quartermaster Sergeant was up in arms and had some really foul words about his OC as he had to make the ration and water runs from Tawau. It was not a healthy situation in an operational setting as it seriously affected the morale of the troops. After my report, the CO read the OC the riot act.

After we pulled out from Sebatik, the battalion was given the mission to man observation posts along the coast on the mainland and two companies were deployed to Semporna and Lahad Datu. We were at these deployments for a little over a month before we reassembled in Tawau for our flight home.

I had a harrowing experience in Tawau. I had to disarm a soldier with a cocked and fully loaded machine gun who wanted to shoot up my signallers at the Signals Centre. He had gotten drunk after he returned from duty at one of the observation posts on the coast. I approached him very carefully and managed to get close enough to kick away the weapon. I must confess that I was really frightened but I had to get the job done. Whenever I met this sergeant years after, he would never fail to say to me, "Sorry Sir, I almost killed you."

Before 1 SIR left for Sabah, we had heard Malaysian officers rubbishing us: "These city boys can't fight." Our operations in Sabah proved them wrong. When the Commander of the 5th Malaysian Infantry Brigade, our immediate higher command, visited our Tactical HQ in Wallace Bay, he commended the battalion on our good performance, especially in conducting the special patrols into enemy locations. He got on well with us and was quite fond of me. He even joked about having to get my permission to visit our position, calling me "Governor of Wallace Bay".

After seven months in Sabah, we returned to Singapore. The moment we arrived, even before we could unpack and see our families, the battalion was put on standby for operations. It quickly sank in that while our operations in Sabah may have been over, we were still in for dangerous times. Within the week, we were deployed to Jason Bay on the east coast of Johor following a report of an enemy landing. The whole battalion rapidly mounted up and crossed the Causeway to go enemy hunting. We did not encounter any, and a few days later we were told that it was a false alarm. We spent the next few months on alert and ready for action against enemy incursions in Southern Johor. Whenever there were reports of landings, we would be deployed on search-and-destroy missions.

There had already been several such landings while we were in Sabah. An attack on a platoon from 2 SIR had taken place in Kota Tinggi, southern Johor, so we were well aware of the danger. That platoon had been on a search patrol for an Indonesian incursion, and the enemy attacked them when they were harbouring for the night. A number of the soldiers were killed, some very brutally. 2 SIR conducted a search-and-destroy operation and killed or captured all the enemy in that group.

The Indonesians we encountered in Sabah were regular soldiers. The ones going into Johor were also regulars but portrayed as para-military volunteers known as Sukarelawan (volunteers). President Sukarno claimed they had volunteered to "liberate" the people of Malaysia. They did not wear uniforms. They carried Malaysian currency, with the intention of buying the support of the locals. When they were captured or killed and stripped, you would find the money in their underwear. I suspect that 2 SIR's central welfare fund was boosted that year.

Then came Separation. I was still in 1 SIR and already a captain. We were aware of the slogan "Malaysian Malaysia" and the disagreements between the People's Action Party (PAP) leaders in Singapore and the Government in Kuala Lumpur. One morning, the news broke that Singapore had separated from Malaysia. Then there was Lee Kuan Yew's press conference. Everybody was glued to the television and the image of him emotional and tearing was very vivid.

Initially we did not know what to make of it. When the significance of the Separation sank in, I was subdued, worried about what would happen next. Most of the Singaporean officers in my battalion were feeling the same way. But some of the seconded British officers were quietly celebrating, which surprised me. I suppose they did not take to being under the Malaysian Armed Forces. One silly fellow was about to remove the photograph of the Malaysian King in the Officers' Mess. We told him to leave it alone. 1 SIR was majority Singaporean, but our CO was a Malaysian and we had some Malaysian officers.

In those early days, we were more worried about our own future than the political future. I was not even sure if there would still be a battalion, still be an army. I had many concerns running through my mind: What was going to happen to us? What was going to happen to the military? What was going to happen to the battalion? Change our name back from PIM to SIR, or what? The other Singaporean officers had the same concerns. Then came the offer to all of us, officers and men. We were asked: "Do you want to stay or go?" I am a Singaporean; I said, "Of course I will stay." Most of the other Singaporeans, except for perhaps one or two, stayed. But all the Malaysians left. Soon enough, the political significance sank in – now we were on our own. Whatever we had to do, it was now for Singapore.

But I maintained the proper attitude and continued to be respectful to my CO, Lieutenant-Colonel Mohd Ghazali Seth, or Colonel Gary as he was fondly known. I believed that as military officers, we had to be professional and not act like little children. Besides, he was an excellent CO and a pukka gentleman, and we had developed a warm and close relationship, especially during our deployments to Taiping and Sabah.

When he was about to return to Malaysia, I was then Aide-de-Camp (ADC) to President Yusof Ishak and arranged for the President to host him and his wife to dinner at the Istana. When I was CDF, he was CDF of the MAF. When 1 SIR celebrated its anniversary, I invited him to join the celebrations and he was Guest-of-Honour at the Trooping of Colours. He came with some former 1 SIR officers who returned to Malaysia after Separation. We were joined at the celebrations by Major Jim Boddington, my first Company Commander in 1 SIR, who happened to be visiting Singapore. I treasured the opportunity to express our special bond of friendship. It was a small gesture but an important one. General Gary was also very touched and appreciated what I did. We are still in contact and exchange messages and greeting cards.

VI

A ONCE-IN-A-LIFETIME EXPERIENCE

The talk in the SAF and the talk of the town was that I must have done something wrong, made a mess at the Istana.

SHORTLY AFTER SEPARATION, probably in late August, four bachelors in 1 SIR were called by the Adjutant and told to report to the Istana for an interview. I was one of them. We learnt that we were candidates for the job of ADC to the President, Yusof Ishak. When we became independent in 1965, Prime Minister (PM) Lee Kuan Yew instructed that a professional military officer be given the job. Yusof Ishak had been Head of State as the Yang di-Pertuan Negara since Singapore became self-governing in 1959. Before 1963, he had police officers as his ADC. When we were part of Malaysia, a schoolteacher was seconded to do the job. He was given an honorary rank of captain and wore a military uniform. Rather demeaning for a Head of State!

We were interviewed by the President himself. He told us what he wanted of an ADC. One important requirement was that the ADC had to be a bachelor and live in the Istana. I was already engaged to be married and I told him so. He said to me, "If I choose you, then you wait. Postpone your wedding." I thought he was joking. Surely he would not select me because he knew I was going to get married. That same evening, when we were back at 1 SIR, I was instructed by the Adjutant to pack my things and go straight to the Istana. When I reported to the President, I said, "Sir, I had informed you that I'm going to get married." "Ya, and I had told you: you can wait." So I telephoned Kate and told her, "I don't know whether this is good news or bad news. I think we can forget about the wedding for a while." We had become engaged in June 1965 soon after I came back from Sabah, and I had accumulated enough money from the additional allowance from Sabah – we called it "danger money" – to afford to buy her an engagement ring. Although we had not settled on a date for our wedding, we expected that it would be within the year. But my posting to the Istana was for two years. Later, President Yusof, probably feeling sorry for me, told me I could get married after one year and bring my wife to live in the Istana, "but no children".

I was only 24 years old at the time, and had been promoted to captain a year earlier. I was given a local rank of major for the Istana posting. PM Lee wanted to know the rank of the ADC of the Malaysian King, the Yang di-Pertuan Agong. I knew the man; he was a lieutenant-colonel. When PM heard that, he told President Yusof to get the Ministry of Interior and Defence (MID, later called the Ministry of Defence or Mindef) to make me a lieutenant-colonel. I asked the President not to do that because I would be a laughing stock. I had never commanded anything more than a platoon. If he made me a lieutenant-colonel, I would only be wearing the rank.

I remember Dr Goh Keng Swee laughed when he said, "Winston, PM wants to make you a lieutenant-colonel." When I said that it did not make sense, he told me to go and convince PM. Mr Lee called me up, "Don't you want to be a lieutenant-colonel?" I said, "No. I may wear the rank, but people will not look at me as a lieutenant-colonel." He asked, "Can't you hold your ground?" I said I could, but people would know that the rank was only for show. "Okay, stay as a major."

After a century, the Istana at that time looked rather like a tired old grand dame in need of a face-lift. There were vestiges of the colonial past, like the grand ballroom on the second floor. There were many other rooms on that floor, but the main activities were held in the dining room and State Room on the first level. The President and his family lived in Sri Melati, a bungalow within the Istana grounds. There were two other bungalows. One used to be the British Attorney-General's residence, which was used as a guesthouse in the 1960s. The other was Sri Temasek, which to this day is the Prime Minister's official residence. PM Lee did not live there, and the building was used for meetings and small functions by the PM and the Ministers.

In the main Istana building, the only occupants in the night were the telephone operator, the police guard on the ground floor and me. My accommodation was a very old suite comprising one bedroom, an adjoining sitting room, a pantry and a bathroom. The sitting area was right under the hipped roof of the Istana, where the flag flies, and my bedroom was to the rear. The furniture was antiquated and there was only a big bathtub, no shower, in the bathroom. It was spartan indeed. I told myself: "It's okay, I'm a soldier; I have lived in worse conditions." I was comforted when I realised that I had a valet, Ismail Ghani. He looked after my needs, cleaned the quarters, prepared my uniform and clothes, and even cooked my breakfast. Ismail was the son of one of the butlers and later became a butler himself. He still makes sure I get my Scotch and water whenever I am a guest at the Istana.

About two or three months after I moved in, Mrs Lee Kuan Yew asked if she could see my quarters. So I brought her up in the very old rickety lift. When she saw the rooms, she exclaimed, "This is squalor!" and asked to speak to Tan Beng Kiat, the Public Works Department (PWD) man. He was quite bewildered when he came. Mrs Lee told him to put in a proper bath with shower, proper toilet, air-conditioning. "Do up his accommodation so that it's liveable," she said. There was a complete renovation. I even got a new bed. Mrs Lee kindly made that place comfortable for me.

It was quite overwhelming when I got my first brief from PM Lee. He wanted me to "turn this place around; it must be as good as the Istana Negara in Kuala Lumpur." I told him I had never been to the Istana Negara. "Never mind," he said, "You just listen, and I'll tell you what to do." The first thing he wanted was to get PWD to spruce up the place. Then he wanted me to change the uniforms of the household staff and drivers because they were too colonial. I had no idea where to begin, but I knew that the uniforms should be military-inspired, more comfortable and yet sufficiently elegant. I used some imagination and some common sense, consulted the Comptroller and even had a chat with the staff to get their views before I put the designs together – different designs for the serving staff, the butlers, and the drivers. Then I worked with a tailor to bring the designs to life. It was a relief when PM approved the new designs. Then he said, "Line them up, teach them how to stand up straight. Those who cannot, remove them." That was how much he wanted the highest standards for the Istana, to showcase Singapore's Independence.

As the ADC, I had a Comptroller working with me, and he had household staff under him, which included two butlers. There was also a horticulturist to look after the 43 hectares of the grounds, and a police inspector in charge of security. I had an assistant who was a clerical officer. I was also responsible for the motor pool – the Istana vehicles and the state cars for the PM and Ministers, which were parked in the Istana. The ADC's office was a small room near the pantry and kitchen in the main Istana building. President Yusof's office was in the Annex building. He said I was too far away from him, so they set up a room in the Annex for me.

My duties as ADC were to look after all the President's

official engagements in the Istana and outside. My urgent task was to work on the various ceremonies held in the Istana, the first and most important being the Presentation of Credentials. I worked with the Chief of Protocol from the Ministry of Foreign Affairs (MFA) to design the ceremony for foreign ambassadors to present their credentials to the Head of State. This had never been done before because, until then, Singapore was not a sovereign country. We went to find out how it was done in the UK and the Commonwealth as well as non-Commonwealth countries, including the United States. The form for the Guard of Honour and the format of the presentation itself were easy enough. But we learnt that in some countries the practice was for the Ambassador-designate to ride in a horse-drawn carriage with cavalry escort from his residence to where the ceremony was held. Where would we find a horse-drawn carriage? We decided that it would be a Mercedes-Benz, with police outriders on motorcycles. We tried to make the ceremony as grand and dignified as possible without being overly elaborate, and ended up with what I think we still practise today.

I had to learn how to organise a state banquet. So I read books and looked at how banquets were organised in the big hotels. The two butlers told me not to worry; they had laid out banquets since the days of the British Governors and had done so during the period before Independence. But I was not sure if PM wanted something different now. President Yusof was meticulous but not fussy. PM's main concern was to ensure that we gave top-class service – waiters had to stand erect, arm stretched out straight when serving, and PM would not tolerate water or anything being spilled. So I had to carry out drills for the serving staff. Fortunately, the menu was the domain of the President's wife, Puan Noor Aishah. Being an accomplished cook, she had already established menus with the chefs. Beef *rendang* and rice replaced roast beef and Yorkshire pudding. The special dessert usually served was the renowned *gula melaka* dessert, her secret recipe.

We had dress codes for the various functions in the Istana. PM was particular about this. There was once a banquet where the dress code was black tie. Some Members of Parliament (MPs) from the PAP did not know what black tie was. One came in a brown suit with a black necktie. I kept a box of black bow ties in my office for such eventualities but could not help him when he showed up in a brown suit. When PM saw him, I was instructed to tell him to go home. I had to remove his chair and adjust the seating plan on the fly. That was the sort of thing that happened in the early days. After that, I had to send a note to the MPs to explain what to wear when we say black tie, lounge suit, informal or casual, with a picture and a write-up for each. Fortunately, the officer cadet training I had was very British, so I knew these things.

The Istana was a hive of activity during the early days after Independence. We had to cater for morning coffee or tea with foreign dignitaries, lunch and dinner functions hosted not only by the President and PM but also by some Ministers. Garden parties, held for the Singaporean community, were always a challenge because of rain. Fortunately, the military prepared me to work out contingency plans. Timely transfer of the party indoors was honed to a fine art. Canvas covers had to be laid over the carpets in the State and Dining Rooms to protect them from being soiled.

These responsibilities together with my other duties to serve the President were putting a great strain on me, so a second full-time ADC, Assistant Superintendent of Police (ASP) Robert Woodworth, was appointed to assist me. He was married and did not need to live in. He, together with an array of honorary ADCs from the SAF and Police who came for big functions, were of great help.

Then PM wanted to change the President's car, which was the British Governor's old black Rolls Royce, and told me to go and buy a new one. Can you imagine a 24-year-old going to Malayan Motors to choose a Rolls Royce? I chose a top-of-the-line silver Rolls. Not black, because President Yusof did not want it black. I selected woollen floormats and lambskin seat covers. I remember I issued a cheque on behalf of the Government for $75,000 and took delivery in time for the first National Day Parade. President Yusof wanted to put white cloth covers over the seats, like the state cars and taxis. I dissuaded him, reasoning that we had paid good money for the lambskin seats, so please do not cover them. He agreed. But on the way to the National Day Parade, the very first time we used that car, I had to hurry into the car after him and the hook on my sword belt made quite a deep scratch on the seat. President Yusof looked at me and said in exasperation, "I told you to put on the white covers!" I had to go to Malayan Motors to ask them to restore the upholstery. Sometimes I joked with my friends, "What car did you buy? I bought a Rolls Royce."

I found it easy to work for President Yusof. He was open and frank. He would tell me whenever I was wrong, and I would accept it. That was the way I operated and got things done. Sometimes I had to remind him of the dos and don'ts. I even drilled him to march in uniform wearing a sword, at the Istana tennis court, to prepare him for the National Day Parade. He took it in his stride and never complained. He was a keen grower of orchids and even taught me how to grow them, giving me a few plants to start me off. He was also a very keen photographer and got his materials from Tithes, a shop on Middle Road well known for photographic supplies and services. Once in a while he wanted to go to the shop himself, without any security officer or staff driver. I would drive the Istana car which I used for my duties and he sat in front with me. I always carried a pistol in a holster under my bush jacket when I went out with the President.

Once, after finishing our business at Tithes, he wanted to go and eat satay. I said I would buy the satay and bring it to the Istana for him. But he insisted on eating there, at the old Satay Club in the lane next to Alhambra Theatre down at Beach Road. I parked the car and we sat on stools. Someone spotted us and reported back. I got such a scolding from PM. After that, every time President Yusof wanted to eat satay, I told him I would buy and bring it to him. But he would reply, "Don't want. The taste is not the same." He was stubborn like that. I had to tell him that I would get into trouble if I brought him to the Satay Club again. I empathised with his desire for some freedom, but I had to explain that he could not try to go out incognito; it was just not possible.

I learnt a lot about life and grew up very quickly at the Istana. My exposure was a once-in-a-lifetime experience. The things I had to do, the people I met. There were diplomats, Ministers, important civil servants – people like Howe Yoon Chong and Sim Kee Boon – and Singaporeans from the different communities. Whenever I organised the President's small dinners, I had to make sure that there was a good mix of Malays, Chinese, Indians, Eurasians, plus one politician and one civil servant. Always that mix.

I had to make sure that everything was organised down to the smallest detail of the timing and protocol. I always prepared a brief for President Yusof before each function, detailing the order of proceedings and timings, and listing the people he would meet with a short write-up on each of them. He occasionally visited Eusoff College and Raffles Hall at the University of Singapore because he was Chancellor of the University. Once at Eusoff College, he said to the female undergraduates who lived there, "This is my ADC. Good-looking, not married yet. Young ladies, you should spend some time talking to him and get to know him."

There were seven guest bedrooms in the Istana then and sometimes foreign guests stayed there. They were fascinating people. I will always remember two of them in particular. One was a Russian Minister who came with a weapon. I had to tell him diplomatically, "Sir, may I put this away for you? I will return it to you when you leave." I do not know how he got into Singapore with that. When I returned the pistol to him, he gave me a jar of caviar – the best Russian caviar according to him. I declared it to Treasury, and they let me keep it because it was perishable. Another interesting person was Emperor Haile Selassie of Ethiopia. I always imagined that he would be a big man. But he was a very small fellow; his two daughters who accompanied him were bigger than him. We put him in the guest bedroom, and he brought his two little poodles to sleep in the room. President Yusof went ballistic. "How dare you put a dog in the room?" I said, "Not dog. Dogs. Two." When Emperor Selassie left, he gave me a gold Rolex watch stamped "King Solomon's Mine" on the back. He asked me if I was married. When I said I was engaged and about to marry, he gave me a very heavy gold necklace, also stamped "King Solomon's Mine". Treasury valued them at a price I could not afford on a major's pay. Till today, I regret that I did not beg, borrow or steal to buy the watch and necklace.

PM was at Sri Temasek most evenings. He would play golf for exercise and inspect the grounds. Unless I had to go out with the President, I did not leave the Istana until PM left as there could be a phone call at any time. He would sometimes tell me to deal with issues he had spotted, such as an ailing tree or a dead stray dog which needed to be disposed of.

One day, PM called me up and said there were a lot of weeds in the grounds. I jogged around the Istana every morning and if I spotted something, I would call the horticulturist to follow up. But I did not know about the weeds. PM said they were Elephantopus, so called because they spread out like the footprint of an elephant and they grew deep. They were rampant in the Istana grounds and would require more manpower than the groundsmen we had on our staff to dig them out. PM told me to deploy the Workers Brigade. We had formed these brigades after Independence to give jobs to unemployed people and take them off the streets. I brought in two companies of them to weed out the Elephantopus. One day, PM called me up and said he had observed that the work was not done properly. He told me to line up all the men from the Workers Brigade. He scolded them, "You are lazing around. You have been told what to do, but you don't do it. Where are you from? From Malaysia? You go back. We try to give you a job, but you don't want to work properly." Then he told me to get two good RSMs to manage the workers. "All they need is proper supervision." The weeds were removed without delay.

The Istana had a five-hole golf course. PM instructed me to put in two more holes and told me where to locate them. I did not play golf then and did not know much about the game. He said he would tell me what to do. He put stakes into the ground where he wanted the new greens and asked me to get help from the Singapore Island Country Club to get them done. I put that experience and knowledge to good use years later when I was CDF and was instructed by Dr Goh Keng Swee to take over the Sembawang golf course from the New Zealanders and redesign it. We rebuilt it from nine to 18 holes for $72,000. Today it probably costs $1 million to construct just one hole.

The other thing about working at the Istana was that I learnt to put a name to a face, because I had to greet people and meet diplomats. Fortunately, I am blessed with a good memory for names. But sometimes I had to use little memory tricks, like associating a name with a person's appearance; for instance, Hensley ... hen ... chicken-like. You have to if you want to be efficient, to do what you are supposed to do. After some time, I got rather good at it. Even now, I am pretty good at putting a name to a face. Most times I can still call the old soldiers by name when I bump into them. It is harder for me to remember new names now, but I try.

I was supposed to be at the Istana for two years. But after just under a year, Dr Goh wanted me back in the SAF because they wanted me to help build up the Signals corps. Although I was an Infantry Officer, I had been trained as a Regimental Signals Officer while in 1 SIR. So somebody must have said to somebody, "Hey, Winston Choo has some signals training."

When President Yusof heard this, he blew his top. "What are they trying to do? Why the change? I'll stop it!" He put his foot down and refused to release me. Dr Goh spoke to PM and convinced him to speak to the President. PM called me up and told me Dr Goh wanted me back to start some organisation or other. He said I was better off doing that than "pushing chairs in Istana". It was so disparaging. I had worked so hard and he said I was pushing chairs. Those were his exact words. I replied that I was a soldier and would follow orders. I told him the President was very angry, very upset. PM said he would speak to him. Then President Yusof called me up and said he would let me go and "now you can get married."

The worst part of it was that when I left, I had to remove my local major rank and go back to my substantive rank of captain. I was supposed to be in the Istana for two years, but I was leaving after less than one full year. The talk in the SAF and the talk of the town was that I must have done something wrong, made a mess at the Istana. I got tired of trying to explain, so I just said, "Too bad. They want me to leave, I leave. Go back to the SAF, so I go back." Fortunately, three things happened to erase the speculation that I had screwed up. First, I was soon given command of a new signals unit. Second, when I got married, President Yusof gave me a reception at his home in the Istana. He even gave approval for his Honorary ADCs from the SAF and the Police to mount the honour guard as sword bearers at my church wedding. Third, I was retained as the senior Honorary ADC. I would have loved to serve the full term at the Istana. I enjoyed the job, seeing things happening there, and I benefited from the exposure to so many different things. At that age I could never have dreamt of such an enriching experience.

VII

A NEW VOCATION

I had to make sure that I was well equipped to
do the job I was supposed to do when I returned.
The only way was to put in very hard work.

I RETURNED to my true calling, soldiering, in September 1966. Having been away from the SAF for almost a year in a completely different environment in the Istana, I was looking forward to getting back into action in the Army. My first job was to bring together a diverse group of signals people from different organisations and set up a signals unit. I was appointed the OC of 1 SAF Signals. It was quite daunting for a 25-year-old infantryman with only Regimental Signals Officer training. Some men had returned from the Malaysian Signals after Separation while others were Singaporeans who had served with the British Royal Signals based in Singapore. Fortunately, there were very good signals officers among them. My second-in-command, Leslie Terh, who helped me manage the squadron, had returned from the Malaysian Signals. He was among a large batch of Singapore cadets who went to FMC when we were part of Malaysia. We had a few Chinese and Indian senior NCOs but the majority were Malays, and they were very good radio operators and signallers.

The squadron was undermanned and so we had to start recruiting. NS was not in force yet. We were able to recruit a better racial mix reflecting Singapore's racial make-up. The recruits we brought in were better educated, although nothing like the soldiers we have today. Maybe one or two had O-Levels but most had not completed secondary school. Altogether, I trained two batches. They were the first corps of regular signallers in the SAF. Many later became instructors at the School of Signals while the others became the backbone of the Signals corps in the different units. Over the years, up to the time I was CDF, I used to run into many of them serving in key appointments in various units in the SAF.

The unit was based in Beach Road Camp which was ill designed to house a signals squadron. It was a headquarters facility and there were no living quarters. Everyone lived out, which was not at all conducive for building esprit de corps. We turned vehicle garages into makeshift living quarters for the recruits and brought in standing fans for ventilation. A cookhouse was constructed near the vehicle washing bay and the dining hall was under an archway. Classrooms were created from storage sheds. My office below the Drill Hall was partitioned, with three of us sharing one fan. The quartermaster and signals equipment stores were adjacent to my office. It was good that we were hardly in the office but running around making sure the soldiers were trained properly. We learnt to make do with what we had and got the job done.

The unit conducted basic training for the recruits. Being infantry trained, I had no problem designing the syllabus and overseeing the recruit training. The basic Signals vocation courses were conducted by the senior NCOs with the help of our Israeli advisers. It was a proud day when we held the passing-out parade for the first batch of signallers. I felt a great sense of achievement. We had managed to turn out well-trained signallers from scratch, despite the odds. My boss, the Chief of Communications and Electronics (C&E), took the salute.

One of our early missions was to send a signals detachment to Bangladesh to provide communications for the SAF humanitarian team doing flood relief operations. The detachment did a good job in maintaining communications between Singapore and Bangladesh under difficult conditions with antiquated radio equipment. It was an early test for the unit.

A big challenge for 1 SAF Signals was that we were the only signals unit in the whole SAF at that time. We also had to provide the communications and Signals Dispatch Service (mail) for MID and the SAF, and communications support for the major training exercises of the SAF Training Institute (SAFTI). Not many may remember that Singapore had Grand Prix races at Old Thomson Road every year from 1961 until 1973. And many would not know that it was 1 SAF Signals, from the time the unit was operational, that laid out all the telephone lines backed up by a radio network to enable the officials to manage the races. The public address system for major SAF events and the National Day Parade was always contracted out to us. We did all these events with old equipment that was left behind by the British and Malaysians. Most of the radio sets were civilian equipment for internal security operations such as civil unrest and riot control. We had to adapt and make use of them until we could get proper military-grade equipment.

The Chief of C&E, as the Chief Signals Officer was known then, was a Police Superintendent who was transferred to the SAF as a lieutenant-colonel. He had headed the Police Radio Unit responsible for police communications and for providing and maintaining police radio equipment. He was an electronics engineer who, understandably, did not know much about the requirements for military communications. He was also very PGO (Police General Orders). PGO was an expression I had learnt from some police friends that referred to someone who was a stick-in-the-mud, inflexibly adhering strictly to the book. Fortunately, one of the staff officers in

ABOVE *First family photograph – taken with father Keng Ho, mother Njoen Swee and sisters Sally (seated) and Jeanette, February 1946.*

RIGHT *With Kate, starting young – I was 14 and Kate was 13, 1955.*

ABOVE *Standing in the centre of the front row among my ACS Form II schoolmates, 1954.*

TOP *Captain of ACS Football Team, seated right, 1957.*

BOTTOM *In action, 1957.*

LEFT *Being presented the Boys' Brigade Queen's Badge by Sir William Goode, Governor of Singapore, 1958.*

LEFT *Lance-Corporal,
'A' Company, SVC, 1959.*

RIGHT *Officer Cadet, 1960.*

BELOW *Cadet training in
Port Dickson, FMC, 1960.*

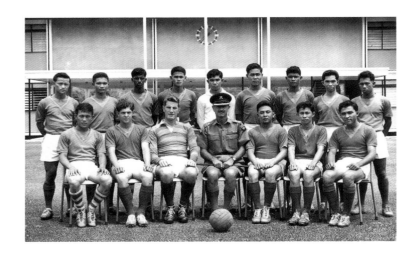

TOP LEFT *Captain of FMC Cadet Wing Football Team, 1961.*

LEFT *As a Cadet Under-Officer inspecting junior cadets, FMC, 1961.*

ABOVE *My Commissioning Ball with my parents in attendance, FMC, 9 December 1961.*

RIGHT *With my batman Pte Sivalingam, 1962.*

BELOW *C Company 1 SIR with OC, CSM, CQMS and platoon commanders, 1962.*

FAR RIGHT *1 SIR Tactical HQ Sebatik, Sabah. Konfrontasi, 1964.*

ABOVE *Prince Philip visiting
1 SIR in Sebatik, Sabah.
Konfrontasi, 1964.*

TOP RIGHT *With signallers
travelling to Sebatik in an
assault boat. Konfrontasi, 1964.*

RIGHT *With Tactical HQ
radio detachment at Tanjung
Sedeli, Johor, during a
search-and-destroy operation.
Konfrontasi, 1964.*

ABOVE *With Kate, and my sisters and their boyfriends, Jason Bay, 21 July 1964.*

RIGHT *With Kate at 1 SIR Dinner and Dance, 1963.*

FAR RIGHT *Our engagement, 5 June 1965.*

ABOVE *ADC to President
Yusof Ishak at the 1st Session of
Parliament, 22 December 1965.*

RIGHT *ADC to President
Yusof Ishak at the Inspection of
Guard-of-Honour during the
ceremonial opening of the 1st
Parliament, 22 December 1965.*

LEFT *Our wedding at St. Andrew's Cathedral, 3 December 1966.*

BELOW *With Kate during our "second honeymoon", Trafalgar Square, London, 1969.*

his HQ was a signals officer who had joined us from the British Royal Signals, and that made things a little easier. It was frustrating to manage my unit of professional military signallers with a very PGO ex-policeman as my boss. I did not think he liked me much, but I had a job to do and I did it.

It was fortunate that we had the assistance of two Israeli advisers, Lieutenant-Colonel Moshe Paran and Major Levi Barak. Paran was in charge of advising the SAF on communications and electronics matters, while Barak was involved in starting up the School of Signals in SAFTI to train some from the first batches of officer cadets as well as the early batches of regular NCOs to become signals officers. The school later trained National Servicemen (NSmen) who were enlisted from August 1967 onwards. We had to do a lot of planning, adapting and improvising, and we depended heavily on Paran. He was an electronics engineer, an experienced signals officer, very professional and a brilliant man. He was the de facto deputy in the Israeli advisory delegation, which was headed by Colonel Ya'akov "Jak" Elazari. Paran was among the few Israeli advisers proficient in English and his knowledge extended beyond signals. Unsurprisingly, he was the one who wrote the first SAF staff manual, adapting from British and American staff systems.

Even though it disrupted my work in the unit, I was happy to be given the opportunity to attend the Preparatory Course for Instructors together with some 30 other officers at SAFTI. The chief instructor was an Israeli paratrooper. I had missed out on an earlier course, which was conducted soon after the SAF was formed in 1966, as I was ADC to the President then. This course was designed to induct SAF officers from disparate backgrounds into a common training system, based on the training system of the Israel Defense Forces (IDF), so that they could be deployed as instructors to the various SAF units and schools. It was back to basic military training for us when most of us were by then already majors and some were lieutenant-colonels. We lived in at SAFTI and were bashed around for four weeks. Our training days started at 5.30 in the morning with 5BX (physical training), included 5-km runs in battle order, and finished late into the night. The course covered familiarisation with weapon systems, navigation and small unit tactics, and ended with a live-firing exercise. It was physically tough and mentally trying but I felt that it was time well spent. After completing the course, I knew that I was better prepared and ready to contribute to the development of the SAF.

After a year, in March 1967, 1 SAF Signals was upgraded to a signals battalion. It was named the MID Signals Battalion (later renamed 1st Signals Battalion), and given more manpower, new equipment, and an expanded role. I was appointed the CO and promoted to major shortly after that. One interesting additional duty I had, together with a couple of the senior NCOs of the unit, was to run signals and radio procedures training courses for officer cadets of the People's Defence Force (PDF). They were all volunteers, and were senior civil servants, private sector executives and Members of Parliament, including some Cabinet Ministers. The better known among the volunteers were Othman Wok, Jek Yuen Tong, Lee Khoon Choy, Chan Chee Seng and Fong Sip Chee. As they were among the VIPs I had looked after when I was ADC to the President at the Istana, it was somewhat awkward and quite something to have them filing up, coming to attention, saluting and addressing me as "Sir". To me they were trainees and I treated them like I did any trainee, with care and respect. But I must say that they were very serious about their training and played their part to a T. I salute them for their commitment.

After a year, it was decided that I be sent on a signals course to receive formal training as a signals officer. The Chief ordered that I hand over my duties as CO, MID Signals Battalion to a non-signals-trained officer and move to HQ

C&E as a staff officer, before going for my course at the Royal School of Signals in Blandford, UK. He made me Assistant Head of the Operations, Organisation and Training Branch under a captain who was the Head. The Chief had put me, a major, under a captain. Obviously, I was not happy. This is done only in exceptional cases in the military. Though it felt somewhat demeaning, I tried to rationalise that this was not to put me down but more to park me temporarily in the branch, as I was to leave shortly for the UK. I made the best of my time in HQ, learning more about the roles of the branch and preparing for my course.

I left for Blandford in June 1968. I was delighted because it was the first time I was sent overseas for a course. Up to that point, almost all my peers had gone overseas for training. The farthest I had gone for a course was to Kuala Lumpur. I was also grateful because I would be getting comprehensive training for my job in Signals. Thus far, I had been trained only up to RSO level. Everything else that I knew was improvised and learnt on the job. The Officers' Telecomunications and Electronics course in the Royal School of Signals was designed to prepare mid-level signals officers for squadron commander and senior staff appointments at brigade and division levels. The theory part of the course would arm me with sufficient technical knowledge to employ signals equipment effectively and be able to discuss technical issues and problems with the electronics and telecommunications experts. The practical and operational parts would include field deployment exercises for battalion, brigade and division-level signals operations.

The course was very technical, so I had to prepare myself before I left for Blandford. The last time I did any mathematics or physics was for O-Levels as I had switched to the Arts stream for A-Levels. I had to go back to the books because I did not want to make a fool of myself in Blandford. I sat with Chew Bak Khoon every evening after working hours and had him tutor me. He was an engineer who joined the SAF from

Singapore Telecoms, and eventually became Chief Signals Officer. I even got him to teach me how to use a slide rule, and revise mathematics formulae and physics with me so that when I started the course at least I would not be going in blind.

Going to Blandford was my introduction to the UK. From Heathrow I took a train to Victoria Station, then another to Waterloo Station, and a third train to Salisbury on which I travelled first class. When I got into the first-class carriage and greeted the elderly lady seated there, she gave me a very hard stare and said, "This is not the place for you." I said, "I beg your pardon? I have a first-class ticket." And she replied, "But you are not English." I said I was indeed not English, but I could buy a first-class ticket. I thought to myself: "So, this is England." A military vehicle had been sent to pick me up at Salisbury and take me to the school. Happily, during my time in Blandford I discovered that the British were all right and I got on very well with them.

In the course, I found the field exercises particularly interesting. We went out to do radio and long-range deployment exercises in Salisbury Plain and areas further north. The English countryside was just as charming and pretty as I had imagined and seen in the books I had read in school. But winter was punishingly cold. It was particularly difficult to lay telephone lines or join two cables together, with gloves on. The British students did it with bare hands. I learnt to cope with the weather, and l learnt to keep in my pack a flask of hot coffee laced with a tot of rum.

For the theory lessons, I had to work very hard. As I said, my science and mathematics were out of date and the signals course was very technical, so it was tough for me. I spent many evenings in the library studying and trying to brush up to make sure I could follow the lessons. I told myself that I had to do well. I always felt compelled to try my best in whatever I did. And now I could not let Singapore down as well. Moreover, I had to make sure that I was well equipped to do the job I was supposed to do when I returned. The only way was to put in very hard work. Fortunately, some of the instructors knew my handicap, sympathised with me, and helped me out. As it turned out, I was among the few students who graduated with an "A" grade. I was also given an excellent course report.

I tried to make the best use of my time in England even as I kept my nose to the grindstone as this was my first time in the UK and, in fact, the first time that I had gone abroad. I was used to the British military mess life in 1 SIR, but in my first exposure to an actual British mess at Blandford, I found them steeped in tradition and rigid in the way they did things and the way they expected you to behave. The only arrangement that was unusual to me was that we had female officers living in the mess. There were separate baths, showers and toilets which both the men and women could use. These were along the same corridor as our rooms, so we had to wear our bathrobes to get to them. This was tiresome, and I never got used to it. But generally, I had no problems and enjoyed the mess life.

One of the things I found rather amusing was that I had an old British ex-serviceman as my batman. Every morning he woke me up with a cup of tea. This was something I could not get used to. First, I did not like tea. Second, I could not consume anything before I went to the bathroom and brushed my teeth. One day he said, "Sir, I think you don't like tea." He had noticed the untouched cups of tea next to my bed. I said, "No, it's not that I dislike tea. I don't like to drink tea first thing in the morning." He offered to bring me something else, but I asked him to just wake me up and not bring me anything, which he did. I was used to having batmen; they had been my soldiers when I was in 1 SIR. But to have an elderly person serving me made me uncomfortable. I decided to treat him like an uncle, engaging him whenever he came and chatting about his family and his service life in the military. This was more to put myself at ease than to put him at ease because he was quite used to serving young officers. After some time, we got on very well. He even confided in me that he was a Tory supporter and had strong views about how Britain should be governed.

Living in the mess was fine but there was one inconvenience. During Christmas week, the mess would shut down. The British officers went home to their families but we overseas officers were literally thrown out into the street. I had to go to London and book into a bed and breakfast. I knew no one in London and Christmas in England is a family thing. On Christmas Eve, I cut a forlorn figure hanging out cold, alone, and rather lost in Trafalgar Square admiring the huge Christmas tree. I missed the warmth of my family. It was the loneliest Christmas of my life.

There were many international students and I wanted to make use of the opportunity to learn more about the world. They came from Uganda, Ghana, Nigeria, Sudan, Jordan, Sri Lanka, Malaysia and even Ireland. We all stayed in the Officers' Mess. That was a learning experience for me, to live and go to school with such a colourful assortment of people. One of the Ugandans later took part in a coup and rose quite high up the ranks. There were two Ghanaians, very polished officers. After they returned home, one took part in a coup, the other did not. The one who did, became a Minister; the other lost his life. Then there was a Jordanian who spoke little English and asked for my help to buy a car and get a driving licence. He was very grateful after I got him what he wanted and offered to drive me to Blandford town any time I wanted to go. Unfortunately, he got into an accident and I helped him again, to deal with the police and to settle the insurance issues. The Kuwaiti major was one foreign student whom the British were very attentive to. They treated him like a king when we visited the companies manufacturing communications equipment. Later, I found out that Kuwait had placed a big order for the equipment, enough for four brigades. He told me that his army had only one brigade, and if any equipment broke down, they would just replace it with a new one from the three lots of spares. The generosity of their defence budget astounded me.

The Nigerian was something else. He went to Blandford town every Saturday dressed in a three-piece pin-striped suit with a bowler hat and an umbrella and walked up and down the High Street. I asked him why he dressed that way, and his answer was that the British dressed like that. But the British did not dress like that to go to Blandford town to eat fish and chips! The officer from Sudan became quite a good friend. I remember that during a break in the course we went to London and visited a casino. I did not gamble but enjoyed the free flow of drinks and titbits. At one point, he was winning quite a lot at blackjack and refused to leave the table when I urged him to. Inevitably, he lost it all. But, without him knowing, I had earlier pocketed a handful of his gambling chips. So he was pleasantly surprised when I took him to the cashier to cash in the chips I had squirrelled from him. He bought me dinner as the chips amounted to 300 pounds. I built some good relationships with my course mates, such as the Malaysian student "Syd" Idris who later became Chief Signals Officer.

I enjoyed going to Blandford even though it was a very small town. My normal Saturday routine was to go there and have fish and chips for lunch. Syd and I made friends with the owner of the fish and chips shop. He and his wife took a liking to us and invited us a few times to their home above the shop for a roast beef or chicken dinner. I would also get a bigger serving of fish and chips for my Saturday lunch, for which I felt very grateful. I found the British people, especially the ones in the small towns, very friendly. There was nothing much to do in Blandford and sometimes we took a bus to other towns such as Poole and Bournemouth. Occasionally we made a trip to Salisbury, which was a bigger town, and went to the movies. I wanted to immerse myself in the British way of life and understand the British people.

Kate joined me in the UK just after I finished my course at Blandford. That was quite an adventure and experience for both of us, more so as it was winter. I went to London to receive her at the airport. She took a long time to appear and I was getting quite anxious, wondering what had happened to her. When she finally came through the arrival gate, she said she was delayed waiting for her luggage which had not arrived with her. Fortunately, I had the foresight to buy a few blouses, a pair of slacks and a sweater before she came. So she managed to get by during the two days before her luggage arrived. The first thing we did together in London was to go to a Singapore restaurant in a basement in Kensington High Street. Kate complained that she had just come from Singapore and I was asking her to eat *char kuay teow*. I told her it was not for her. Eating familiar food to remind me of home meant a great deal to me.

It was a good thing that I had a short break after the course, so Kate and I travelled to Europe. We were on a US$5-a-day holiday package which provided bed and breakfast and two tours in each city. We went to Copenhagen, Amsterdam, Vienna, Hamburg, Paris, Venice and Rome, staying two or three days in each place. It was our very first such experience and we tried to do too many things in too short a time. After the guided tours, we would walk to see many places not covered by the tour. It was tiring, but we were young then. And we had little adventures in each city. We wanted to see how people lived, find out more about them, and engage them. I would not say we were country bumpkins, but we were pretty close to that, always excited and sometimes bewildered by all the new sights and sounds.

There was an unpleasant experience in Paris where we were given the run-around by a man in a tourism booth and rudely told that "if you don't speak French, don't come here." That was my first impression of France. The Italians were very friendly but also very volatile. When the cab driver got angry with the car in front, he put half of his body out the window, raised both hands and screamed at the other driver. I told Kate to close her eyes and not fret. The Germans would answer exactly the question you asked, and not say one word more. The Austrians and Dutch were friendly. We loved the exposure to so many cultures and languages. We were discovering that people in other parts of the world could be so different. Besides the short cruise we had taken to Hong Kong for our honeymoon, this was the first time we were really seeing the world. Our second honeymoon – and a great learning experience.

VIII

AN EYE-OPENER

*The deeper understanding I had gained of the
IDF's military capability convinced me that we had
made the right decision in getting the Israelis
to advise us on the development of the SAF.*

OUR HOLIDAY ENDED in Rome and we flew to Israel, as
I was instructed to go there after my course in Blandford. Dr
Goh Keng Swee wanted officers returning from courses overseas to stop over in Israel to get a better appreciation of the
operations and workings of the IDF. I was to spend two weeks
there. I was very excited as it was my first time in Israel.
Moreover, I was expecting the visit to be interesting as it was
just after the Six-Day War in June 1967. I had read some articles
and accounts of the war and was looking forward to seeing
some of the battlegrounds. Some Israeli advisers had quipped
before I left for Blandford that I was lucky to be visiting Israel
after the War as they had acquired much more real estate
and there was more for me to see. As for Israel itself, I had
only a vague idea of the country gained from the Bible and
tourist brochures. So while I did not know what to expect, I
knew that I had a specific mission to learn as much as I could
professionally.

Our hosts had laid out a very comprehensive programme for
me, throwing in some sightseeing. Kate was included for the
sightseeing but was on her own when I was doing the official

visits and calls. After the hectic tour of Europe, she was grateful for some free time to recuperate. My escort was a captain named Yael, a petite young lady who toted an Uzi sub-machine gun wherever we went. Despite all we had heard about the dangerous situation in Israel, we never felt any threat at all.

The first item in my programme was a call on the Israeli Chief of Signals, Colonel Moshe Gidron, who preferred to be called by his nickname, Musik. He had obviously been briefed by our adviser Lieutenant-Colonel Moshe Paran and was familiar with the situation in Singapore and the state of the build-up of our Signals formation. He gave me a very useful briefing, and what was particularly beneficial was his sharing of the problems and the lessons they had learnt from the Six-Day War. We got on well although I was much junior to him. We remained friends and maintained contact even after he retired. When I became Ambassador to Israel years later, I arranged to meet some of the former Israeli advisers. I specially asked to meet Muzik and he came even though he was not very well and was already 88 years old.

I was highly impressed when I visited the IDF's Signals school and units. The camps were spartan but functional. The school was professionally run and well equipped, and the instructors were experienced and impressive. It was the same at the units where efficiency and a strong no-nonsense attitude prevailed. It was evident that the SAF Signals was still in nursery school and had plenty to learn and much catching up to do.

They also arranged for me to visit several companies in their electronics industry. Of special interest to me was Tadiran which was producing, under American licence, the VRC series of tactical radio equipment we were ordering for our units. Having done similar visits to British electronics companies like Plessey and Racal, I got the impression that the Israeli companies, while lacking the frills, were trim and efficient, and very inventive. I was told that their defence industries included companies manufacturing artillery weapons, ammunition, and other army, air force and naval equipment. I sensed the urgency and importance the Israelis attached to being self-reliant, and their sharp focus on developing their own military industrial capability. Singapore, under Dr Goh, was on the same page and had begun setting up our own defence industries right from the early stages of the SAF's development.

The battlefield-cum-sightseeing tour was a special treat, professionally. First was a helicopter ride into the Sinai. I had read some accounts of the major battles of the Six-Day War. Of particular interest to me was the Battle of Abu Ageila, a strategically located road junction and the key gateway into the Sinai for the IDF. General Ariel "Arik" Sharon, in command of the 38th Division, was given the mission to capture this strategic position held by an Egyptian division in well-prepared and strongly held defensive positions. He conducted a brilliant operation and scored a decisive victory. The Israeli operation in Abu Ageila became a textbook operation, studied in military schools all over the world. Flying over the desert was exhilarating. I could not really relate the terrain to the battle but I managed to appreciate the factors involved in battle in the open desert. It was rugged tank country, much like the tank battles fought in North Africa in the Second World War between Rommel and Montgomery.

They took me on a side trip to Mount Sinai, where Moses receiving the Ten Commandments and the burning bush of the Old Testament came to life for me. I visited St Catherine's Monastery and was shown the cellar where a rather gruesome sight greeted us. There were piles of skeletons and bones of the monks who had died there. It was a tradition for the bones to be piled in the cellar after the remains of the monks were exhumed.

On the road trip from Tel Aviv to Jerusalem, the burnt-out military vehicles strewn on both sides of the narrow two-lane road made an unforgettable sight. That road was the only link to Jerusalem and fierce battles had been fought there during both the War of Independence and the recent Six-Day War. In Jerusalem, I was shown how the paratroopers had conducted urban warfare, fighting house-to-house to take the whole city. The bullet holes, the damage from the shelling and fighting were still very evident. I could visualise a hard-fought and bloody battle. All these left a deep impression on me.

While this was primarily a work trip, I was grateful that Kate and I also had the opportunity to visit some holy sites in Jerusalem. We toured the Old City, accompanied by the trusty Uzi-armed Yael and a squad of soldiers to protect us as the alleyways were crowded with a mix of pilgrims and Palestinians. We walked the Stations of the Cross. It made the Bible come alive for us, but sadly it was also a terrible first impression. The place did not look the least bit religious and did not feel holy at all. It was a bazaar, crowded, filthy and narrow. There were frequent interruptions by merchants peddling trinkets. As Christians we were distressed to see all that commercialisation. We had to draw on our Christian faith and values to feel spiritual and to have a sense of pilgrimage, which we prayerfully did. Foremost in our thoughts was that this was where our Lord Jesus Christ walked on the way to His crucifixion.

We went to the Church of the Holy Sepulchre, which is built over Golgotha, the site of the crucifixion. I wanted to light a candle. The priest held out a plate and I put in 10 Israeli pounds. The plate did not move. I put in another five Israeli pounds; the plate did not budge. I put in yet another five Israeli pounds, and the plate was still there. The priest was obviously not satisfied. Yael told me not to give any more money. I finally got to light a candle because she grabbed a candle and gave it to me. I was very, very upset, and so was Kate. Nowadays this does not happen. The Church of the Holy Sepulchre is run by several Christian denominations. Because they were fighting over the ownership, it is an Arab family living down the road that holds the key to the door of the church to this day. At the time that I was there, they had ceremonies by the different denominations throughout the day. Just imagine – the Catholics, the Greek Orthodox, the Armenians, the Coptics and others all praying and singing at the same time! They led processions to all the holy parts of the church, and they quarreled and fought. What a cacophony! It was a dreadful display of irreverent behaviour. But not anymore; now they have a schedule.

Another notable trip was to Masada, the ruins of a mountain-top stone fortress overlooking the Dead Sea. It gave me an insight into how the IDF made good use of the history of the Jews to motivate their men. People walked up to Masada, but I was lucky to be brought up by helicopter. I learnt that IDF recruits trekked up to Masada as part of their passing-out ritual. There, in the midst of the ruins, a swearing-in ceremony was held at last light for them to take an oath of allegiance to the nation, ending with the words "Masada shall not fall again". Masada stands as a powerful symbol of heroism and determination for the Israelis. In AD 74, a group of Jewish rebels had made their last stand at Masada against the Romans. After a long siege, every one of them died, committing suicide rather than surrender. I still recall the wonder I felt on that visit to Masada. It was 5 o'clock in the evening and the sun was setting; bathed in that light, Masada was an awe-inspiring sight. I understood why the IDF had chosen to make it a tradition to swear in their recruits there. Today, the recruits are still made to walk up even though there is now a cable car. We cannot draw on such a historically inspiring location in Singapore to conduct the passing-out ceremony for our recruits, but I hope that the NS Square at Marina Bay will have the same effect of stirring the patriotism of our young NSmen.

Visiting the Golan Heights was another very fascinating excursion. Israel had recently seized this from Syria in the

Six-Day War. To appreciate the strategic significance of the Golan and the tremendous military feat of attacking and taking this strategic highland, I was first brought to Tiberias on the shores of the Sea of Galilee. Galilee was also of biblical significance as it was there that Jesus first met his disciples and preached. We visited Capernaum and the site of the Sermon on the Mount and teaching of The Beatitudes. We stopped at a kibbutz, a collective community, situated on the shores of Galilee. There we were told of the constant threat kibbutz members faced from the Syrians up on the Golan overlooking the valley. They were fired upon daily and shelled at night. The farm tractors had to be armour-plated and the people slept in bunkers. I was awed by the tenacity of these people.

And as I looked up the steep slopes of the Golan that loomed over the valley, I could truly appreciate the challenges that the assaulting Israeli force faced. It must have been literally an uphill battle to fight all the way up the mountain with the Syrians entrenched in well-prepared defensive positions. They had dug in their tanks, turning them into pillboxes to shoot at the Israelis coming up from the Galilee valley. The Israelis suffered heavy casualties and it took great ingenuity for them to win that battle. Later, when we went to the top and looked down into the valley to get the Syrian perspective, I better understood why the Syrian forces had been so sanguine.

During that visit to the Golan, I was treated to a good lesson in military operations under impossible circumstances, gained insight into the brilliance of the commanders and heard accounts of the indomitable fighting spirit of the Israeli soldiers, all while seeing first-hand the aftermath of an intense battle. We visited the battleground where fierce tank battles had been fought. The IDF was only starting to clear some of the battle wreckage. We drove through captured Syrian territory right up to Quneitra, a Syrian town 60 km southwest of Damascus, and had lunch there. Imagine sitting there on a stool having lunch in a blown-out building, looking around at all the bullet holes while listening to an officer from the Golani Brigade explain the various aspects of the battle. It was surreal. Many years later I had the same feeling when I was having a meal in Umm Qasr, a captured Iraqi town, with our officers in the United Nations Peacekeeping Force after the First Gulf War.

Then I had to go to Beersheba in the south, on the way to the Negev desert. We had bought second-hand French-made AMX-13 tanks from the Israelis. The IDF had used these light tanks in the Six-Day War to great effect, as in General Sharon's battle for Abu Ageila. Though they were not employed as main battle tanks, they were exploited for their swiftness and agility and skilfully used in special missions such as tank hunting. The British had thought that our terrain was not suitable for using tanks, but the Israelis thought otherwise and had proposed that we use the AMX-13 as it was a light tank. Those AMX-13s served very well as an introduction to armoured warfare for the SAF. When I became CDF, we had a major upgrading programme for the AMX-13 as a suitable replacement was not readily available then.

Our Armour officers, later nicknamed the 36 Camels as they had acquired a set of 36 wooden camels to represent each one of them, were going through a tough and thorough training programme on the AMX-13. The Israeli trainers were very hard on them, with no holds barred. While it was a love-hate relationship, our officers took to the training and learnt the lessons well. That was the genesis of our Armour corps, one we can be proud of today.

I had hardly been in a tank before this and I found it novel and thrilling riding in a tank in the desert. After being with the tanks the whole day, one could not tell that I was a Singaporean. My face and the exposed parts of my body were all covered with fine dust and I had "blond" hair. The temperature range in the desert was extreme. The day was so hot that you could not touch the tank. One of the tankees promised that I could fry an egg on the hull. Regrettably, I didn't have an egg with me to try this. At night it was freezing cold, and if you touched the tank, your hand could get stuck to the metal. I had a most interesting time out in the desert with my fellow SAF officers.

After the incredible experiences visiting the many battle and historical sites, I spent a fruitful afternoon with the operations people at the IDF HQ. They briefed me on their organisational set-up and gave an overview of the Six-Day War. Though I had hoped to meet one or two of the generals who featured prominently in the War, such as Yitzhak Rabin and Arik Sharon, it did not happen. Rabin had gone to Washington as Israel's ambassador. I did get to meet him some years later when I was CDF during one of my visits to Israel. He was then the Prime Minister. I remember that he was very intense, but patiently took time to put his points across. He smoked non-stop during our meeting. He would light the next cigarette with the one in his hand – literally a chain smoker. It was no wonder that his voice was so raspy.

I was sent to Israel to learn more about their signals organisation. By the end of my visit, I felt that I had learnt a great deal, going way beyond signals. I had gained a good grasp of the Israeli military capabilities and how they operated. I had been given the opportunity to visit some of the battlefields of the Six-Day War and came to appreciate the odds the Israelis faced. I had better insight into their war-fighting mentality. They had persevered and were victorious. And they did it all in six days. It was mind-boggling.

What struck me as well was their different military culture. I found it strange to see privates calling officers by their first name. We would consider that *kurang ajar* (ill-mannered) in Singapore. They were more relaxed and informal and not bound by hierarchy. There was open fraternisation between male and female soldiers. There were many female soldiers because women were conscripted. In the evenings along Dizengoff Street, Tel Aviv's shopping belt, it was not uncommon to see a lieutenant-colonel walking arm-in-arm with a female corporal, most probably a conscript, both in uniform. This was also foreign to me. During a visit to a field exercise, I was in a latrine with my zip down when in walked a female soldier. I came out and spoke to a major who happened to be there. Unperturbed, he told me: "If you are worried, whistle or sing so that the female soldiers can hear you and won't go in."

When the Israeli advisers in Singapore initially tried to impose a culture of informality on the SAF, I didn't understand why. The Asian culture ran contrary to theirs and their culture did not sit well with us. So we resisted. But they were doing it in good faith as they thought we could be comfortable with their ways. After spending more time talking to their officers and watching their exercises, I realised that this informality did not affect them in operations. They had been very successful in war because they were firm and strict on operational discipline and did not compromise the command structure in the battlefield. It is their culture and their strength. But to adopt their ways wholesale would not work for us. We had to create our own culture that fitted us. This was something I had to grapple with even as CDF.

My two weeks in Israel was a big eye-opener. The deeper understanding I had gained of the IDF's military capability convinced me that we had made the right decision in getting the Israelis to advise us on the development of the SAF.

IX

BACK TO SIGNALS

As a professional, you must stand your professional ground.

WHEN I RETURNED to Singapore, I couldn't wait to see my daughter, Karina, for the first time. She was born when I was in Blandford. While I was there, Kate and I used to write to each other at least three times a week. After Karina was born, Kate would fill her letters with details about our daughter's progress. I also received lots of photos, but all that didn't make up for seeing her in person. When I first set eyes on Karina, she was already seven months old. The joy was tinged with trauma though, because whenever I tried to hold her she would howl. I had to go into stealth mode each time I wanted to carry her, by approaching her from behind. I couldn't help but feel rejected. But Kate consoled me, saying that was natural and I should give my daughter time to grow accustomed to my face. And soon enough, she did.

I went back to Signals. And, for the second time, I found myself regressing. That sort of thing could happen in the early days of the SAF. I had been CO of MID Signals Battalion before I left for the UK to upgrade my professional qualifications as a signals officer. While I was away, command of the battalion was taken over by a non-signals-trained officer who had joined the SAF from the SVC and had become a regular. To my chagrin, Chief C&E posted me to be second-in-command of that same battalion. I did not know his true intentions. If it was to place me somewhere until my substantive posting became available, the least he could have done was to not put me in a position that seemed to belittle me. Or perhaps it was to add insult to injury because he had earlier put me, then a major, under a captain. Regardless, I sucked it up and did my job; there was no point in thinking the worst of my situation.

Though decidedly challenging and bruising to my ego, I saw these setbacks as life lessons and made the best of them. My view was: I am a soldier, I am put in a job, I do my utmost in the job, whatever that job may be. At the same time, I was determined to prove that I could do a good job, especially now that I had been properly trained at Blandford. Not long after, I was posted to HQ C&E and appointed Head Operations, Organisation and Training Branch – the job I was temporarily assistant to just before I left for the UK. This time I felt that I was qualified for the job and could really contribute. I was aware of some of the shortcomings and the areas that required attention. So I sat myself down to getting the job done, working with the help of the Israeli adviser Lieutenant-Colonel Moshe Paran. By then we also had more signals officers posted to the HQ, who could be brought in to help in the work.

Before I could settle down in my job, I had to join a mixed batch of officers in the School of Advanced Training for Officers (SATO) at SAFTI to attend a course that prepared company and battalion commanders for combat units. These were still the early days of the SAF and there was a need to get as many as possible of the pioneer batches of officers, who had come from different backgrounds, through this programme. So the first few courses at SATO had participants ranging from young lieutenants and captains to majors and lieutenant-colonels, which included the first batch of officer cadets trained in SAFTI. Their ages ranged from mid-twenties to over forty years. Even the SAF Paymaster, who was in his late forties, was a student.

The CO of SATO, a Singaporean named Michael Seth, was assisted by two Israeli advisers. The course was both physically and mentally tough and demanding. Most training days extended well into the night and there were many field exercises. Live-firing exercises were conducted with the participation of infantry troops supported by artillery and armour. I take my hat off to the older ones. Even as a 28-year-old, I faced tremendous strain during the course. But when it was over, I felt a great sense of satisfaction and achievement. More importantly, on completing the course I could consider myself no less than any other mainstream combat officer.

During one of my visits back to HQ C&E I ran into the MID Permanent Secretary, George Bogaars, in the corridor of Pearl's Hill Lower Barracks. He asked me how I was faring and before I could reply, he said that I should not be too worried. He hinted that I would be taking over as the Chief C&E soon, and that I would be promoted. I did not know what to make of that conversation and decided to keep it to myself and not think too much of it. Shortly after that, I was promoted to lieutenant-colonel. That was the biggest batch of promotions to lieutenant-colonel. There were 10 or 12 of us, with me being the youngest. Those promoted included officers from the first, second and third FMC intakes, and others who had joined as regulars from the SVC and some Malayan military ancillary units. It dawned on me that with this promotion I was now on par in rank with some who were senior to me in service. I had even overtaken some senior to me who had not been promoted. I told myself that I should not let it get to my head. At the same time, I could not help but feel some trepidation.

I was summoned to the office of the Chief C&E who, after

handing me the letter of promotion, pointedly told me "I have nothing to do with your promotion", making it very clear that he did not think I deserved to be promoted. My response was, "I am sorry you think that way." I took the letter, saluted and walked out of his office. Despite what he had done to me, I can put my hand on my heart and say that I didn't take offence or bear any grudge against him; I just swept it aside and moved on. I was only 28 and over the decade from the time I joined as an 18-year-old – a short duration in an army career – I had already gone through a lot. Exactly a month after my promotion the Chief C&E returned to the Police, and I took over as Chief C&E, or Chief Signals Officer.

Mr Lim Kim San had taken over as Defence Minister from Dr Goh Keng Swee by that time. It was a difficult period because we were fully occupied taking over British assets. The MID Signals Battalion had moved into Fort Canning, a British facility. Our Air Force and Navy were in a nascent state with no signals set-up in their organisations, and HQ C&E had to provide communications and electronics support to them. The Navy was not taking over British assets. They had a couple of old ships, one inherited from the Singapore Naval Volunteer Reserve and a second-hand riverine iron-hull boat, and we supplemented the naval communications equipment with army radio sets.

The Air Force requirements were more demanding. We had taken over the air bases from the British, which meant having to operate and manage all the communications equipment. A tougher requirement was to take over and man the static radio relay stations around the island connecting the air bases, the Bloodhound air defence missile units and the air defence radar station on Bukit Gombak. The British had a special signals regiment just to do that. We needed not just signallers but also technicians as they had to operate and maintain specialised communications equipment. We were not ready and did not have sufficient people with the expertise to replicate the British regiment. So we formed a very much smaller unit called the Static Radio Relay Unit to take over those facilities from the British. We were very stretched and had to quickly recruit and send technicians to the UK to be trained. I was fortunate to have Chew Bak Khoon as Head Technical Branch in the HQ. As an experienced electrical and electronics engineer who was familiar with the equipment and the technical intricacies, he was of tremendous help.

It was during this period that something happened that almost cost me my career. We had a retired British Air Chief Marshal, Sir Rochford Hughes, as Special Adviser to the Prime Minister and Defence Minister on air matters. He had been the British Commander-in-Chief Far East Air Force based in Singapore. I got on the wrong side of Sir Rochford for a few reasons. The first problem arose when he wanted Singapore to take over the British troposcatter equipment which provided the communications link between Bukit Gombak in Singapore and Western Hill in Butterworth, Malaysia. This was for air force communications in the Five Power Defence Arrangements or FPDA.

I discussed this with Bak Khoon. We concluded that this equipment had immense technical problems and was highly unreliable as it would frequently break down, sometimes for long periods at a time. We also needed the Malaysians to agree to take over the Western Hill end if we wanted to operate it. I asked the Malaysian Chief Signals Officer for his views and he said he was not interested in taking over the Western Hill station. He must also have assessed that the equipment was unreliable. Sir Rochford insisted that the SAF should take over the troposcatter station on Bukit Gombak. Fortunately, Bak Khoon shared with me an article in a British electronics journal written by a British engineer who called the tropo-scatter system the two white elephants of Singapore, because of the two gigantic white antenna dishes sitting on the side of the hill. He had written a comprehensive article on all the things that were wrong with the system. I cut out the article and sent it to Minister Lim Kim San to support my recommendation not to take it over. He sent it to Sir Rochford and told him that our Signals people felt that it was not worth taking over and he tended to agree with them.

Sir Rochford called me up and his exact words to me were that I was "recalcitrant and obstructionist". I told him that as Chief C&E, I could only give my professional recommendation, and this was my professional recommendation. I pointed out that he had read what the article said, and that was from an independent British journal. And I reminded him that the Malaysians did not want to take over their end, so taking the Singapore station would serve no purpose. Eventually, we did not take it over. We opted instead, with Malaysian agreement, to use the civilian trunk system which ran all the way up the Peninsula. It was cheaper and more reliable, though not solely dedicated to our operations. That did not endear me to Sir Rochford.

I had another run-in with Sir Rochford later which further strained our relationship. The Singapore Government had given him quarters in Keppel Harbour, overlooking Labrador Park. He lived in a beautiful bungalow and he had a yacht. He had four telephone extensions in his house and asked for one more for his servants' quarters so that the servants could hear the telephone ring. The request came to HQ Signals because we were responsible for all telephone equipment in MID and the SAF. I decided to tell him that we could not give him the fifth telephone for technical reasons. So he complained to the Minister, and the Permanent Secretary asked me why we would not give Sir Rochford a telephone. I said he already had four and didn't need a fifth. The Permanent Secretary agreed, and Sir Rochford did not get his additional telephone extension. However, I did fix a bell in the servants' quarters and connected it to the telephone system. At that point, Sir Rochford was ready to recommend that I be removed.

Fortunately, I survived because Minister Lim Kim San said that there was nothing wrong with me.

This is the lesson I learnt: as a professional, you must stand your professional ground. Even if you should be sacked or removed, you can sincerely say that you had been professional. It was a professional decision that we made not to take over the troposcatter equipment from the British. And we were proven right.

Then we started receiving the American tactical radio equipment (the VRC series) manufactured under licence by Tadiran of Israel. This was the same equipment the IDF was using. For brigade-level and longer-range communications, more powerful vehicular-mounted high-frequency equipment and radio relay trunk communications equipment were acquired. We even introduced new teleprinter equipment, and field telephones and telephone exchanges.

One thing I learnt from my predecessor was to be very prudent in spending. We sometimes adopted unorthodox solutions to overcome budgetary constraints. For instance, military specification batteries for signals equipment mounted on vehicles were very expensive, so he taught us to use normal car batteries and carefully encase them in wooden boxes with the necessary protection. They were not to military specification, but they served their purpose and cost much less. We designed our own mounting for antennae on our vehicles and got them made in Singapore. They were not elegant, but they worked well. That was the way things were done in those days – making do with what we had. We continued to use second-hand equipment. We learnt very quickly how to improvise, how to make do and get things done. The Israelis were very good at it. And they were surprised to see that Singaporeans could also do it.

My aim at that time was to develop a signals corps. Any self-respecting army must have its own signals corps. It was a challenge to train enough people in the School of Signals to man the signals units we needed. We trained the first batch of signals officers from the first batch of SAFTI-trained regular officers. Later, the school also trained SAFTI-trained regular NCOs as signallers. Together with some of the NCOs whom I had trained in the garages in Beach Road camp, we built up the Signals corps. By then we had also sent officers to the US, UK and Israel for training courses.

As the Army expanded with the establishment of NS battalions, we raised signals platoons in the new infantry units. Signals units were also raised for the Armour, Artillery and Engineer formations. Signals companies were formed to provide signals support to the infantry and armour brigades. To ensure the supply and maintenance of our new electronics and communications equipment, the Electronics Supply and Maintenance Base was set up. Slowly but surely, by the time I handed over, we had the semblance of a respectable signals corps.

Not long enough in the job, I had to take a break and have Bak Khoon stand in for me as Chief. I was to be a student again, this time at the Singapore Command and Staff College (SCSC). Though I had a relatively short tenure as Chief C&E, it was nonetheless a most interesting and challenging time, and a tremendous experience. I had the privilege to play a major role growing the organisation from its infancy. Starting from a ragtag group of signallers from the Malaysian Signals, British Royal Signals and SMF volunteers, with me coming from the infantry, we managed to build the nucleus of a signals corps. Being involved with signals right from the time I returned to the SAF from the Istana in August 1966, Signals has a special place in my heart. I am proud and honoured to be accepted as a valued member of the corps.

X

A LIGHTNING BOLT

"Eh Winston, Old Man wants to see you."

I WAS ONE of the pioneer students in SCSC at Fort Canning, which was officially opened by PM Lee Kuan Yew in February 1970. Although one of the main reasons I joined the military was to stay away from studies, as I much preferred the outdoors, I found myself frequently in school attending one course after another over a period of 10 years. I had started with cadet training in military college in 1960, closely followed by the Weapons and Signals Officers courses both in Kuala Lumpur, then the Telecommunications and Electronics course in the UK, and the Preparatory course and SATO course in SAFTI. I realised that to be a true military professional I should not stop learning. I had to keep improving my knowledge, skills and competencies. I continued to study and could not escape from books and the classroom right up to the day I retired from the SAF.

The SAF's first Command and Staff College course was attended by most of the senior officers in the SAF then. It was a high-powered group of students. The top SAF officer – the Director General Staff (DGS) who was concurrently the Director of SCSC – was himself a student. The others included formation chiefs of Infantry, Armour, Artillery, Engineers and Logistics, and Heads of Departments in the Ministry. Most were lieutenant-colonels and a few were majors. As in staff college courses overseas, the participants included a few senior officers from the public sector and the Police to provide a good mix of people with different working experiences and responsibilities. My roommate was a senior officer from the Internal Security Department.

The curriculum was designed by the Israeli advisers, adapted from the syllabus of their own staff college and other overseas colleges. The bulk of the course focused on maritime, air and land operations at tactical, operational and strategic levels. Lectures were followed by a series of map-planning exercises involving combined arms and joint operations. We also did work on military thinkers, military technology, and leadership. The students were given broad exposure to government policies on defence and security as well as finance and budget issues. The course requirements included a term paper on assigned subjects.

The teaching staff was a group of very experienced Israeli instructors brought in specifically for the SCSC. They were supported by the other Israelis who were already in Singapore as advisers to the various formations. For one of the major exercises, we were fortunate to have a visiting IDF general, a war veteran, to take us through various stages of the exercise. This was especially helpful and enlightening. The college also organised the "Director's Evening", when distinguished personalities were invited to talk to the students. PM Lee was the keynote speaker at one of those evenings.

We were given accommodation in the college as the programme usually extended beyond the eight-hour workday. Most of us lived in, especially during the exercises, which ran for a few days at a stretch. But there was time for mess nights and informal gatherings when we could let our hair down, have a couple of drinks and break into song. Those events gave me the opportunity to get to know the officers whom I would have to work with in the future.

The course was high-pressure and exacting, taking us away from our families. My son, Warren, was born during the course and I could not take my wife to the hospital. I was told I had a son only on the morning after he was born. This was a repeat for me as my daughter had been born when I was at the Royal School of Signals in the UK. These were some of the sacrifices I had to accept.

It was in the midst of the SCSC course that I was summoned by Dr Goh Keng Swee, who had returned as Minister for Interior and Defence. Director Manpower Chia Cheong Fook told me, "Eh Winston, Old Man wants to see you." Those were his exact words. I wondered what I had done. They sent me to the Minister's office in Pearl's Hill.

Dr Goh looked me in the eye and said, "I've got a job for you." I could not figure out what job it could be; I was already Chief C&E. He said, "I'm going to make you DGS." I answered, automatically, "Yes, Sir." It took a little while to sink in; I could not believe what I had heard. He repeated, "Yes, I'm going to make you DGS." He asked in his gruff way if I was surprised, and I said yes. I told him, "Sir, Minister, I am just 29 years old, just promoted to lieutenant-colonel. You make me DGS, you have effectively shortened my career in the SAF. How long can I remain as DGS? Five years at best, and then I will be about 35, 36 years old. I had joined the military as a life-long career. What happens after that?" His reply: "Ah, that's later. Don't think too much about it."

Dr Goh told me that he had received feedback that among the professional officers, those who had gone to military colleges, I was seen as the one who had the potential. To put this in perspective, there were no university graduates among those who had joined the military before Independence. A few of us had A-level qualifications then, so I guess I was one of the "geniuses" with A-Levels.

Dr Goh had obviously thought it through, and he laid out his plan for me. "Do your SCSC, complete the staff course. After that do what I tell you to do." I was to hand over my position as Chief C&E to Chew Bak Khoon and return to the Infantry to command 4 SIR (4th Battalion Singapore Infantry Regiment). Then I would attend the US Command and General Staff College at Fort Leavenworth in Kansas where a place had been secured for me. I told him that I was already in SCSC, and he replied that I should go to the American staff college as that would deepen my professional qualifications and enhance my résumé. He told me that I would command a brigade when I returned from Leavenworth, after which I would go to the General Staff and do stints as Head Training and Head Organisation. After all that, I would take over from Brigadier Kirpa "Kip" Ram Vij as DGS. Other than saying that I would be commanding 4 SIR after SCSC and going to the US later that year, Dr Goh did not tell me what the rest of the timeline was.

Dr Goh's revelation of his plan for me came like a lightning bolt. I walked out of his office in a daze. It was unreal and I did not know what to make of it. I did not even dare tell my wife about this until at least a week later. I was not sure whether I was dreaming, whether Dr Goh was going to call me up the next day and say he had changed his mind. I could not believe it because it did not make much sense to me – I was much too young!

Later, I figured out that this move must have been in the works for quite some time. Edward Yong, who was in my intake in FMC and had since become my brother-in-law, said to me sometime after my meeting with Dr Goh that he knew of this intended appointment but could not tell me. Edward was then the Deputy Director Manpower. When I ran into the Permanent Secretary, Pang Tee Pow, he had this to say to me: "Winston, so you know already, huh?" Then there were also the knowing looks from the Israeli Chief Adviser when he met me later in SCSC.

But why the need for a change of DGS? Kip was then in his second tour as DGS. He was the second and the fourth DGS, with Tommy Campbell sandwiched between Kip's two stints. Campbell was a volunteer officer who was a school headmaster before he came into the SAF, and had been my OC when I was in the SVC. He had taken over as DGS when Kip left after his first stint to establish SAFTI and was appointed its Director. His first time round, Kip had come in from the civil service to succeed Tan Teck Khim, who came from the Police but left after a short while. Kip had been deeply involved, playing an important and defining role in the early development of the SAF.

I was not in a hurry. Up to that point of my career, the thought of being the DGS had never crossed my mind. At 29 years old, it would have been insane to have such thoughts. I had always wanted to be a soldier. When I joined the armed forces, I did not see myself rising higher in rank than major and had no ambition to do so. That was what was available at the time that I joined, and my sole reason for joining was that I liked the military life. Then I was happy being part of the development of the Signals corps and of the SAF in general. I was satisfied with the progress in my military career and was enjoying myself.

For me to assume the post of DGS was an unusual route of military advancement. Besides, below Kip there were dozens of officers senior to me. There were those who had joined the SAF from the Malayan Forces, the SMF and the Police. There were three batches, totalling nine officers, who had gone to FMC before me, while a couple of others had gone to Portsea in Australia for an officer cadets' course. The Chief of Armour, Chief of Artillery, Chief of Engineers were all senior to me, as were the brigade commanders. A leak of the news of my coming appointment would be explosive. There would be internal discord because the military has a deep-seated belief in hierarchy and established protocols. I was very uneasy about how I would face my seniors.

When I went back to the SCSC course, my concentration was affected. I had to keep the information to myself and could not share it with anyone. It was most daunting. My feelings were not of elation but more of confusion and worry. I could not stand on a hill and say "I have arrived". There was no sense of achievement or success. Then I reminded myself that I already had some unusual experiences in my time in the military. I had wanted to get married but was told to postpone it and go to the Istana instead. When I returned to Signals, I became second in command of the battalion I had previously commanded. As a major, I had worked under a captain. Then I had a chief who told me in the face that he had not supported my promotion.

I had to get my act together and focus on my course work. There was still some way to go with important exercises to complete and my paper to submit. I had to consciously work at behaving as normally and naturally as possible. Now the challenge was to ensure that I didn't break Dr Goh's faith in me and let him down. I had to learn to compartmentalise – put my turbulent thoughts aside and focus on staying the course and continuing to perform well. It was difficult but I managed to stay positive and eventually pulled through.

XI

A SPECIAL UNIT

"You know Sir, you were a bastard. You were so tough on us.
But you cared for us. I will go to war with you."

IN LINE WITH Dr Goh Keng Swee's plan, I handed over my duties as Chief C&E to Chew Bak Khoon the moment I completed staff college, and went to take over 4 SIR. I felt excited and gratified because I was now back to commanding a combat unit. 4 SIR was a standard NS battalion. Unlike the mono-intake combat battalions of today, the rifle companies of the battalion were inducted at different times and were therefore at different stages of their training. The system then was different from what we have today as the battalion did not go into the reserves as a unit.

I remember very well the day I arrived at the battalion on 18 January 1971. Armed with experience gained at the SATO course and the recent SCSC course, I was raring to take command. The General Staff Officer or GSO – nowadays known as the S3 – received me and introduced me to the battalion staff and company commanders. Most of the company commanders and staff officers were regulars; only the platoon commanders were NSmen. They looked at me apprehensively. I was just as apprehensive. They must have had doubts about my ability to command an infantry battalion, thinking of me as a signals officer who had not been with a combat unit. To establish our relationship on the right footing, I did not tell them that I had come from the Infantry and that I had been an officer in 1 SIR in combat operations during Konfrontasi. Nor did I tell them about the extensive leadership training I had been through. Instead, I chose to tell them that I had much to learn and I hoped that they would work with me to make 4 SIR the best infantry battalion in the SAF.

As it turned out, they indeed worked very hard with me and made my time in 4 SIR fulfilling and memorable. We went through the various stages of the training regime that every infantry unit had to go through. I was fortunate to have an extremely efficient GSO, Sardul Singh, who was from the second SAFTI officer cadet intake. We worked well together, and he helped me prepare the training plans and tie up all the training areas and logistics for the battalion. The work-plan required various exercises to be conducted both day and night at platoon and company levels, leading up to battalion exercises.

I spent as much time as I could in the field with the companies when they were doing the exercises. I was interested to see how the soldiers in the various companies, at different stages of their NS, reacted to the training. As CO, I had to know the standard of their performance. Sometimes, I demanded that they repeat the exercise if it was not done satisfactorily. It is important that the officers, NCOs and soldiers see that you are interested and take time to be out in the field with them, and that you are concerned about their well-being. Every opportunity I got, I would stay and share a meal with them. That was when I could observe the standard of the rations, and also see if the officers took the trouble to ensure that the men were properly fed and that they got their food before the officers. I often stayed on for the night exercises and got on the ground to find out how the men were doing.

I usually had my Medical Officer (MO), Dr Siva, accompany

me during the visits. The MO's presence in the field helped to assure the troops that they would be taken care of should they be injured. A slightly-built man, Siva was initially reluctant to go out into the field with me, wondering why he needed to get out there. But after some gentle persuasion he was game to go. I even made him jump off a hovering helicopter. He became bold enough to do river crossings with the soldiers. Then he revelled in telling stories of his feats in the field to the other officers in the mess.

The rifle companies had joined at different times and were at various levels of training. We had to put in hard work to bring them up to scratch as quickly as possible to ensure that they were ready for the battalion-level exercises. The support company – comprising the mortar, demolition and anti-tank platoons – was manned by NSmen from various intakes and had to be put through its paces. I was fortunate to have well-trained and committed company commanders and senior NCOs who were up to the task. I was pleased that all of them answered my call to work together with me and turned out good fighting soldiers. This was evident when they performed very well during the most demanding battalion day and night live-firing exercises, which required precise coordination and well-executed plans. I was concerned because of the potential danger of live-firing exercises, and they did not let me down.

My brigade commander as well as the brigade staff came to supervise and observe the battalion exercises. By then, word had somehow got out that I was DGS-designate. I was aware that the brigade commander, who was senior to me, may not be happy with the prospect of my leapfrogging him. It may have been my imagination, but I sensed a hostile attitude pervading the Brigade HQ. One evening, during the battalion confirmation exercise, I walked into the exercise brigade headquarters tent and overheard one of the brigade staff officers saying, "Let's fix this signals officer who thinks he can run an infantry unit." Mind you, I was a lieutenant-colonel by then. I walked in and they saw me and were taken aback. Needless to say, it was an awkward moment. But I acted as though I had not heard him. Although I don't think they actually did anything to sabotage me, that was the kind of environment and sentiment I had to deal with at that time.

Then there was a brigade exercise in Pulau Tekong, which my battalion was involved in. 4 SIR was in 2nd Singapore Infantry Brigade (2 SIB) and the exercise controllers came from 3rd Singapore Infantry Brigade (3 SIB), the other SAF infantry brigade at that time. Lieutenant-Colonel Peter Lim, the 3 SIB commander, was one of the senior officers who had been vying for the top job. He gave me a tough time throughout the exercise. For instance, my battalion was made to do the river crossing repeatedly as each time the crossing was declared unsatisfactory.

CO of 5th Battalion Singapore Infantry Regiment (5 SIR) Major Robert Wee, who was the controller for my battalion, privately apologised to me one evening. He said he knew he was making me do ridiculous things, "But what to do? I am ordered." I told him it was fine, I understood. What troubled me though was that because of me, my battalion suffered. But I was relieved that my officers and NCOs stood by me all the way and just executed the missions as required. Somehow, Dr Goh Keng Swee knew what was going on. Sometime later, he called me up and told me that he had heard that I had been given a rough time and he was glad I had taken it in my stride.

My time in 4 SIR was special to me. I was happy and proud that I had fostered the camaraderie and esprit de corps in the battalion. Right from the start, I realised that I had to build a solid bond of cohesion among my officers and senior NCOs if I wanted to run a strong and successful unit. I decided that the mess was a good place for developing the bond. To encourage the officers to patronise the mess, I urged them to spruce up the place. The officers got together to redecorate the mess on a self-help basis, contributing funds to buy the materials. They were proud of the result of their efforts and were happy to invite guests to their mess. Most evenings, I had my dinner in the cookhouse and then stayed on in the mess to interact with the officers. The mess organised get-togethers and parties where the officers could bring their wives and girlfriends.

During one of these events, one of the girlfriends, Lilian Ong, asked me: "Why does George (her boyfriend) tell me I must call you Sir? And why is it that whenever you are in camp in the evening, nobody can go home?" I told her, "You don't have to call me Sir. If you want, you can call me Winston." She replied, "Cannot, *paiseh* (embarrassed) to call you Winston." "Then call me Colonel Choo. As for staying late in the unit, it is something I expect of my officers. When I am in the unit, you stay in the unit. When I go home, you go home." They have married since and whenever I meet them, I do not hesitate to tease Lilian that she had once scolded me. George Ong is now one of my golfing *kakis* (partners). I am happy that even after we all retired, we still get together for meals and golf. I cherish the relationships that I have not only with officers from 4 SIR but also with others who had served in the SAF with me.

Similarly, I encouraged the senior NCOs to have more opportunities to get together. From time to time, I asked the RSM, Ali Pawiro, to invite me to the Sergeants' Mess so that I could spend some time talking to my senior NCOs informally. I was glad that the senior NCOs welcomed me in their mess and appreciated the opportunity to talk to me in an informal environment.

I went to the field with my men, got into the trenches with them. I sat and talked to them. I made sure they knew that I was with them. I wanted them to feel confident and know that they had access to me. That was why I stayed in the unit until late at night. I was with them as much as possible. Seemingly small things mattered. Food, for instance. In those days, our food was cooked by army cooks; we did not have catered food like we do now. At the weekly muster parade, I would line up the cooks in front of the parade and ask the battalion if the food was good. If it was good, they should clap for the cooks. If the food was no good, they could boo them. This had a salutary effect on the cooks to try to produce better food. I always ate in the cookhouse and required my officers and senior NCOs to do so as well. I wanted the men to know that we were there with them and would know if the food was good or not. Also, it was important to motivate the cooks. Sometimes, they were treated with disdain because only those who were not combat fit became cooks. I knew that if they were appreciated, they would be motivated and put effort into their cooking. And when you make sure the soldiers eat well, then they know that you care for them.

Ali Pawiro was a wonderful RSM. He never shouted unnecessarily. In his seemingly quiet way, he exhibited strength and firmness and when he stood in the parade square, all the soldiers "took cover". I appreciated his excellent hold on discipline and supported him. I still meet Ali these days. While I was firm about discipline and stood no nonsense in camp and especially in field exercises, I also made myself available and approachable to the soldiers. A particular incident has stuck in my mind. Many years after I retired, a man came up to me in Ghim Moh hawker centre and said, "Sir, I was a soldier in 4 SIR. You know Sir, you were a bastard. You were so tough on us. But you cared for us. I will go to war with you." I do not know his name, just that he was a rifleman. That is why 4 SIR is so special to me.

When I went to 4 SIR, my aim was to raise a strong and combat-ready battalion. And the best way to achieve this was for the battalion to work towards winning the best combat unit award. I knew that I had my staff, my company commanders, and my senior NCOs all behind me in this quest. But I had to leave the battalion for the Command and General

Staff College in Leavenworth before the end of the assessment period for the best combat unit. Jimmy Yap, who took over from me as CO, benefitted from our hard work and brought 4 SIR to win the award that year. I was most pleased to hear of their achievement but a little disappointed to not have been able to claim the victory with my men.

It is always a challenging adventure to be given charge of a battalion of soldiers, and I had the great fortune to have this opportunity three times. But 4 SIR is special to me as it was one of the most memorable, gratifying and fulfilling times of my SAF career being the CO of a combat unit of fighting men, spending many days and nights nurturing and moulding them into a combat-ready fighting force. The officers and men were the best and 4 SIR was exceptional. To this day, I still meet many of my company commanders, staff officers and other officers who were with me in 4 SIR. We still reminisce about the old days in the battalion and they sometimes request what they say was my favourite song at the time – "Yellow River" sung by Jeff Christie.

XII

BACK TO SCHOOL – FORT LEAVENWORTH

"I am here to be a serious student!"
The whole class went silent before someone piped up,
"Hey, he speaks English!"

FOR SOMEONE WHO had never been to the US, Fort Leavenworth in Kansas was a brave new world for me. I was to be the first officer from Singapore to attend the US Army Command and General Staff College there. That was in August 1971. Up to that point, only a few SAF personnel had attended courses in the US and when I went to the quartermaster stores for warm clothing, all they gave me were a few long johns and sweaters. The SAF had not come up with appropriate uniforms for temperate countries. That was also the case when I went to the UK in 1968. I soon learnt that I had to improvise to survive the bitterly cold winter in the American Midwest.

The Mindef department that took charge of those going for overseas courses did not know what overseas allowance to give me. They asked the US Army Attaché, Colonel Rudy Kogan, and he told them that all foreign officers going on the military aid programmes were given US$8 a day by the US Government. Using this as a reference, Mindef decided that I would just get that US$8 a day, no more, no less. After I arrived in the US, I realised why my classmates on US assistance programmes could live so comfortably. In addition to getting US$8 a day from the US, they also received an overseas allowance from their respective countries. I had to survive like a church mouse. I asked whether my wife could join me. Mindef said that she could, provided the course was longer than 12 months. But the course was just about eleven and a half months. Colonel Kogan, who became a good friend, came up with a bright idea. He recommended that I be sent for an attachment at Fort Benning and Fort Riley, for exposure after staff college. That would take more than 12 months in all and then my wife could join me – and that's just what I did.

I flew to Hawaii and then to Los Angeles for a six-hour transit before flying to Kansas City. The instruction was to change into uniform when I arrived in Los Angeles, which I did. An elderly gentleman came up to me, "Soldier, which country are you from?" I replied that I was from Singapore, which he had probably never heard of. He asked where I was going, and when I said "Leavenworth" his eyes bulged out. Then he said, "I never knew they sent foreign soldiers to Leavenworth." I told him I would be one from 72 foreign countries, and he continued to stare at me. I did not understand his reaction until much later, when I found out that Leavenworth was famous for four things: the federal, state men's, state women's, and US military penitentiaries. There were many Americans who did not know about the college.

I was met on arrival in Kansas City by an American officer, Lieutenant-Colonel Paul Raetz, who would be my course-mate. He was a "snowbird", having reported early to the college, and was asked to stand in for my military sponsor to receive me. He picked me up in a Porsche. I was carrying one large suitcase. He looked at me and said, "If that's your suitcase, how am I going to get you in?" Then he put me in the car, put my suitcase on my lap, and drove like a maniac. What an introduction after a marathon flight! He drove me to the

Bachelor Officers' Quarters (BOQ) where l was to live, and told me to leave my bag in my room and go with him to the officers' club for a drink. I had eaten only a little on the plane and was hungry. But he dismissed it: "You don't need food, let's go get a drink." At the bar, I asked for a whisky and water. The barman looked at me strangely and said, "Sir, only sergeants drink whisky. Officers don't." My sponsor told me to ask for a Scotch, whereupon the barman said, "Scotch! Ah, yes, officers drink Scotch." To them, whisky was bourbon produced in the US.

There were almost a thousand students in the course because there was a backlog of US officers who had served in the Vietnam War and missed out on staff college. This was normally a course for majors but there were more colonels and lieutenant-colonels than majors. Though the college was an Army institution, there were also students from the Air Force, Navy and Marines. We were divided into divisions and sections, each section being a classroom of 30 students. In my section, there were four allied (meaning foreign) officers and the rest were Americans, mostly from the Army. I was among the younger lieuteant-colonels.

As I was the first Singaporean in Leavenworth, they did not know what to make of me. In the first week I did not say much. Sometime during the second week, there was a lesson on the US foreign military assistance programme. Broadly there were two programmes – Foreign Military Sales (FMS) and Military Assistance Program (MAP). FMS sold American services and equipment to foreign nations, while MAP provided foreign countries with full military aid for in-country services and equipment, and access to fully funded courses in the US.

An American student stood up and declared that MAP was a waste of American taxpayers' money. Foreign students were there at Uncle Sam's expense and interested only in enjoying themselves, having girlfriends, and not doing anything serious.

He looked around the class and dismissively waved his hand at "all these foreign students here". I got so angry that I stood up and said, "I am what you term an allied officer. I am from Singapore. I am not on MAP. Uncle Sam is not paying for me to be here. I am a living, breathing example of your FMS – my government paid fully for a place for me here. So don't generalise – I am here to be a serious student!" The whole class fell silent before someone piped up, "Hey, he speaks English!" Up to that point I had kept a low profile because the US Army Attaché had advised me to lie low in the early stages, not to draw attention to myself so that I would not get a "blue goose", meaning an additional assignment. After my outburst, my cover was blown and the "blue goose" started flying my way. After that slightly dramatic start, I got on well with those in my section and other classmates I knew in the college.

Before the course started, we had to collect books and manuals which must have weighed some 15 to 20 kilograms in total. That was intimidating. The course design was somewhat like those in other staff colleges and our SCSC course which I had attended. There was a good mix of military and non-military subjects. We learnt about the US system of government and administration, and there were discussions on foreign policy. There was emphasis on leadership and management subjects, using case studies. The military subjects covered tactics, intelligence, logistics, personnel and civil affairs. The topic of civil affairs was given special attention because of their experience in Vietnam. The eye-opener for me was the scale at which the US Army worked. There was nothing small for the US Army. The map-planning exercises involved various aspects of operations and were conducted at division level and higher. The exercises encompassed the use of large armour formations, army aviation, heliborne insertions, helicopter gunships, high-calibre artillery, rocket artillery, and even the use of tactical nuclear weapons.

I had to make a conscious effort not to be overawed. Coming from a much smaller army, and accustomed to operating only at company, battalion and brigade levels, the magnitude of their operations was rather overwhelming. Going through the exercises in the course, I endeavoured to think big like the Americans, even learning to use some of their gung-ho buzzwords, such as "nuke 'em", meaning to blast the enemy with heavy artillery fire. I knew that I had to make the best of my experience and understand the considerations that went into their thinking and planning. Then, importantly, I would have to learn to apply the principles and to appreciate how to adjust and scale down for our purposes. I made every effort to learn as much as I could, participated actively in class discussions and contributed sound solutions. Once, I surprised my section mates when I challenged the school solution for a logistics exercise. I pointed out that the calculation for the load factor for stores and ammunition was wrong as there was an error in the formula. I did a recalculation with my corrected formula. My table mate, Don VanEynde, said that I was a genius; this mistake had been there for some time and no one had picked it up until I spotted it.

I also tried to experience as much of life outside the classroom as I could. Besides having the military sponsor who assisted with issues in the college, allied officers were also assigned civilian sponsors from Leavenworth and Kansas City so that they could experience social life in the community. I did not go to Kansas City much and did not have much interaction with my sponsor there. But I had a very close relationship with my sponsor in Leavenworth. Don Maahs, a retired army sergeant, and his wife, Mimi, played a very big role in my experience of American society. Mimi was a nurse from France, whom Don had met in Korea. They looked after me like I was their son. It made a difference, as the BOQ could be a lonely place.

Whenever I needed something, I would drive to their house,

and the door was always open. Even if they were not home, I could go in and sit in the basement lounge, play pool, read, or watch television. I could go over in the evenings and join them for dinner. Typical American style – go to the freezer, take out a steak, throw it on the fire. No marinade, just take it off the grill and add sauce before you eat. I remained close to the Maahs.

When Lee Hsien Loong went to Leavenworth some years later, Don and Mimi were also his sponsor. I fondly remember that many years on, when I was CDF and was invited back to Fort Leavenworth, how happy and proud they were to have me in their house. Mimi made a special trip to the hairdresser's and dressed up for a photograph with me with the Singapore flag they had put up. I was so touched!

Don helped me to buy a car. Even though I lived in the BOQ and could walk to class, a car was necessary for moving around because of the distance between places. On US$8 a day, I had to use my own savings to buy a used car. I wanted a Ford Mustang, but with the money I had set aside for a car I had to settle for a Chevrolet Corvair. Don told me the Corvair was good and economical, but potentially dangerous because it was very light with the engine in the rear. He taught me to put two sandbags in the trunk in front, one over each wheel, to stabilise the vehicle. From this, I learnt how a simple trick can provide a practical solution. So, my old canary-yellow Corvair bought for US$450 gave me good and faithful service throughout my time in the US. When I left Leavenworth, the SAF officer who came after me bought over the car for US$300. And he made a profit from it, selling it for US$400 at Fort Sill, Oklahoma, where he did an attachment after Leavenworth before returning home.

To get a US driving licence I had to produce my Singapore licence and pass an eyesight test. Jean Fernandez, a Cambodian officer who spoke more French than English, asked for my help with getting a driving licence. We went together to the

Department of Transport. He could not produce his national driving licence as he had left it behind in Cambodia. With a stroke of ingenuity, I asked him if he had any form of photo ID and he pulled out a Cambodian Army ration card which had his photograph. I gave that to the Department of Transport and Jean got a Kansas driving licence.

Every allied officer was given an opportunity to deliver a presentation on his country to the school and the community, in a programme called "Know Your World". After I saw the good presentations by the British, German and Thai officers, I told myself that I would have to put in special effort for my presentation. I asked our Embassy in Washington DC if they could help me with things like brochures. They sent those, plus two cartons of Tiger beer. The beer was a big hit. Kate was still in Singapore and I asked her to photograph some of the outstanding landmarks and sights and send me the slides. I was determined to make an impact. I wanted them to know more about Singapore, where it was and what the country was about. At that time, very few Americans knew anything about Singapore. People in the Midwest, where Kansas is, were quite parochial unlike people in New York or the West Coast.

I felt a burning need to tell them more about Singapore after an incident in the dining hall. An American reserve officer from the Intelligence corps had asked me where I was from and when I said "Singapore", he expressed surprise that the US Army allowed me in when I was a communist – thinking Singapore to be part of China. To disabuse him of this, I sketched a simple map of the region on a serviette, starting with Vietnam because they were familiar with the country. I drew part of mainland Southeast Asia, pointed out Thailand, moved south to Malaysia and then Singapore. But he still insisted that Singapore was part of China and was communist.

That was why I worked hard to present a good and strong

impression of Singapore. I even cooked fried rice and served it with Tiger beer. I got the help of Singapore Airlines (SIA) to send orchids which I distributed to the ladies present. It was a lot of effort as I had to do it all by myself, being the only Singaporean student, unlike other foreign countries which had two or three students each. The presentation was well received and most of those who attended went away with a better idea of Singapore.

There were other memorable experiences which reminded me of my foreignness. Kate joined me towards the later part of the course. We were invited by an American classmate to his parents' home for dinner on the very night of her arrival, and we drove 80 miles there and another 80 miles back. It was amusing to see the wives initially trying to communicate with Kate using sign language, until she spoke to them in English. I also remember the time when my friends made use of the fact that I was foreign. We were driving in a convoy of six cars to Leavenworth town dressed in mess kit after an event at the college. We went the wrong way and were stopped by the police. One of my American friends told the police officer, "Sorry Officer, we are escorting a prince." Out the side of his mouth he told me to keep up the show. I got out of the car and he introduced me to the police officer, "This is the prince." The officer let us off. Kate asked me how I pulled that off and I told her I just had to stay silent. It was all in good fun.

Then there was the tornado. We had been warned to go down to the basement if there was a tornado. I had moved out of the BOQ when Kate joined me and rented a small, old, wooden house outside the base. One night, when I was studying for my final exam, we heard a sound which may have been a siren, but we figured that it was probably only the wind howling through the cracks of our old house. The next day, my instructor and classmates asked where I had spent the previous night and whether I had taken shelter as there had been a tornado. So the sound we heard had actually been the warning siren. The gravity of it hit me only on my drive home when I saw that houses just a few blocks from ours had been flattened by the tornado. How foolish we had been to have not taken tornados seriously and not been more alert.

Throughout that year in Leavenworth, I tried to learn as much as I could from the course to broaden my knowledge and understanding of the military and how other armies operated. I wanted to excel and project a good impression of SAF officers. I worked hard and was pleased that I made it to the Commandant's List, graduating in the top 10 per cent of the cohort. Attending the US Army staff course and doing well boosted my confidence to undertake the responsibilities that would soon come my way. It wasn't so much about filling up my résumé as it was about being able to stand tall when dealing with my SAF colleagues and foreign counterparts.

Besides benefitting professionally from the course in Leavenworth, I had the opportunity to immerse myself in American life and society. When I first arrived at Leavenworth, I was told that it would be "the best year of (my) life". As it turned out, it was not the best but surely one of the best. I had challenges, but I also had a fruitful time growing professionally, experiencing a new culture, and making many friends with Americans in the community and students of different nationalities. We became very good friends with a group of Army aviators and their wives. Paul Raetz introduced us and we were "adopted" and spent a lot of good social time together. I treasured the camaraderie and strong friendships, and to this day I am still in contact with many of them.

After the staff course ended, I went for an attachment in Fort Riley, Kansas, with the 1st Infantry Division, where I gained some insights into life in a US combat division. I had a useful learning experience when I joined the division in a field exercise operating with the M-113 armoured personnel carriers. Then I went to Fort Benning, Georgia for a short visit and spent some time with my military sponsor who had been assigned there after staff college. One disappointment was that I could not get Mindef's clearance to do parachuting in Fort Benning. Still, the attachments to the two US Army bases were a wonderful round-up to an enriching and exciting stint in the US.

XIII

A CRASH PROGRAMME

I was only 32 years old, still wet behind
the ears. But I knew that this was very serious,
so I had better grow up quickly.

IT WAS Dr Goh Keng Swee's plan to give me command and staff experience before I took over as DGS. It was a crash programme to get me ready. I was given four appointments in less than two years – the command of a battalion and a brigade, and stints as Head of Training and Organisation in the General Staff. But before all that, immediately on my return from Leavenworth, Dr Goh ordered a write-up on me in the media. It was about my return and how well I had done in Leavenworth. That made me feel rather embarrassed. And it rapidly dawned on me that the clock was ticking.

I was supposed to go to 2 SIB, but the brigade commander was not due to move yet. So I was parked in 1 SIR and took over as CO. I felt a great sense of satisfaction that I was given the opportunity to command the battalion that had been my first unit after I commissioned as an officer. 1 SIR had moved from its original camp in Ulu Pandan to Guillemard Camp, one of the first three camps built after Independence. Unlike the other two which were by the sea in Bedok, Guillemard was in the middle of a housing estate – not exactly conducive for a military camp.

This temporary posting bothered me as I did not know how long I was going to be in 1 SIR. But I decided to run the battalion on the assumption that I would be there for some time. I was happy to learn that the unit was manned by efficient principal staff officers, with very good company commanders and senior NCOs. The battalion was already in the advanced stages of its training cycle and was running very well. My predecessor had done a great job and I was fortunate that I could look forward to a smooth and trouble-free command.

My only disappointment was when I discovered, to my horror, that most of the silver collection in the Officers' Mess was missing. I was told that just after Singapore separated from Malaysia, one of the Acting COs had auctioned it all away. I could only guess that he got rid of the silver because he thought that the messes would be closed, as the Israeli advisers had not favoured separate messes for officers and NCOs. It saddened me greatly. It was the tradition for an officer joining 1 SIR to present a piece of silver to the mess, and I had given a silver table lamp. Eventually, I managed to locate one piece of silver, a very important piece. It was the Wiltshire Cup, presented to 1 SIR by its first CO, Lieutenant-Colonel R W Stephenson. He was from the Wiltshire Regiment and that cup dated back to the 1800s. I made sure that the cup would remain in 1 SIR, especially as there was little else left. That was when I urged the unit to record the history of 1 SIR. I had observed that because we were preoccupied with more important issues like quickly building up the SAF, we did not make an effort to preserve our history and traditions as we did not think that it was important at the time. I am glad that more is being done these days.

Unfortunately, I was not given enough time to soak in the satisfaction of commanding the battalion I consider to be the cradle of my journey in the Army. I was in 1 SIR for barely eight weeks before I was given the warning order for my next posting and informed of my impending promotion to colonel.

I remember my Quartermaster in 1 SIR, Ting Kiong Poh, scrambling to get the accoutrements for my new rank. He still reminds me of the headache I caused him whenever we play golf these days.

I was promoted and went to 2 SIB as the Brigade Commander on 1 October 1972. HQ 2 SIB was in Tanah Merah Camp situated near Changi Prison, on a hill by the sea. Sadly, it does not exist today, as its location is now part of Changi Airport. It used to be the training camp for the SVC, with just tin sheds like Ulu Pandan Camp. We had to make ourselves comfortable. The Signals and Recce companies were located with the brigade HQ. This time I was not as apprehensive about taking over a combat unit, as I already had my baptism in 4 SIR and 1 SIR. Still, it was a big challenge for me, and I knew I did not have much time to make an impact.

Being a brigade commander meant that I now had three battalions to look after, and three battalion COs with different styles and characters to manage. It was even more challenging because two of them were my contemporaries and not my juniors. But they were professional, and I worked well with them. It was common in those days to spend time in the mess and go out together for drinks, which we did. There were nice hangouts in the East Coast area. A favourite watering hole for the brigade was a bar in Country Club Hotel on a small hill in Upper East Coast Road. I was aware of the importance of striking a balance between being comfortable with them and becoming too familiar. Fortunately, I had no problem doing that because it was my nature to be friendly and I enjoyed a good beer anyway.

I was living in Bukit Timah and the journey to Tanah Merah took a long time in those days – the expressways were not built yet. I would leave home just after 6 am to arrive at the brigade HQ by 7.30 am at the latest, and I did not leave for home until very late. The hours were long and strenuous, but we were preparing for a brigade exercise and I put great effort into the preparations. By then, I knew that I was not going to be in the brigade for long. The plan was for me to command the brigade for the exercise before moving on. I had to make sure that I did a good job – not so much because I was going to be DGS but because I had to be able to say to myself that not only did I have the experience of commanding a brigade, I had commanded it well as demonstrated by its performance in the exercise. Fortunately, the brigade exercise had good results with the support and cooperation of my brigade staff and COs of the battalions. I was proud and pleased that I had successfully led my brigade through an exercise, even though I had only four months with them.

Then I went to Mindef to be Head Training in the General Staff. I had some concern because the last time I did any form of staff work was when I was at HQ C&E. Mindef was by then located at Tanglin in the former headquarters of the British Forces. I was told that my office used to be occupied by the British Chief Signals Officer. He had left behind a very unusual writing desk. It was about 2.5 by 2 metres with a semi-circular indentation where the officer would sit. I loved that desk and brought it with me when I became CDF.

I did not have the benefit of a proper handover in Training. So, I got hold of my staff officers there and asked them to tell me what was going on, what the priorities were and which areas I should look at. I did not want to pretend that I knew it all. I thought a good approach was to let my staff know that I wanted to do the job, but I could be effective only if they supported and cooperated with me. The best thing was to be frank with them and show them that I was willing to hear them out. I found that this approach worked well.

I reported to DGS Brigadier Kirpa "Kip" Ram Vij. I asked him to tell me what his emphasis for training was. Kip knew by then that I was going to take over from him. I had no problems with him. He was a true gentleman, quite unlike some of my seniors who were not happy that I would be leapfrogging them and even some of my peers.

I went to see Dr Goh to report that I had taken over as Head Training. He told me: "I want you to expand training opportunities." And so began my training in international diplomacy. One of my first achievements, an important one, was to arrange for commando training in the Royal Thai Army's special forces training centre in Lopburi. This would be our first access to training in Thailand. That was quite an experience. I went to Lopburi with one of our commando officers. The commander, Special Colonel (equivalent to a brigadier-general) Anek Boonyathi, agreed to everything we asked for. We wanted parachute training, special warfare training and so on, and to train with them. When we discussed payment, he said we just had to pay for fuel, food, ammunition and other logistical support they provided us. I cannot remember the exact amount. It was substantial but very reasonable for 40 commandos to undergo the training. Payment was cash on the barrel, but I had no money. I went to see our Ambassador, Chi Owyang. He advanced me the money, and I paid the Thais.

Then came the problem when I returned to Singapore. I told the higher executive officer at Mindef's Finance Division that we had to refund our Embassy in Bangkok and he jumped and exclaimed, "How can you do that? Do you have receipts?" I went to see Dr Goh and explained the situation to him. He laughed heartily and said that I was correct to pay the Thais, "and if they want you to pay in cash, you pay." I said I had paid but faced a problem with our Finance people. He ordered the Finance Division to pay our Embassy. Dr Goh knew that we could not insist on doing things our usual way in that situation. He asked if I had gone through item by item with the Thais, and when I replied that I had not, he said that I had done the right thing. That bought us tremendous goodwill from the Thai Special Forces. They appreciated that we were not bean-counting and we trusted them. That strong relationship carried on for many years and gained us good training with the Thai Special Forces. That was my first big mission as Head Training.

I quickly realised that with our army formations expanding, there was greater need for training areas. We had so many limitations in Singapore for our military training. Expanding training opportunities outside Singapore for the SAF became my highest priority. After Thailand, we went to Brunei for jungle training. Then came the relentless efforts to seek more training areas overseas.

I had learnt that the different formations of the Army had their own training requirements and peculiarities. I also had to handle the Israeli advisers at the formations because they were more demanding than the SAF formation chiefs. I understood why the Israelis were demanding. To them, training was crucial, and everything was possible. Because of their insistence, we often pushed to make the impossible happen. We had to maximise the use of SAFTI live-firing areas, fine-tuning the firing templates without compromising safety. What was most useful from my tenure as Head Training was the deep understanding I got of the constraints that our Army faced in meeting our training requirements. Hence it was imperative that we made friends with the militaries of other nations so that more overseas training opportunities would open up for us.

One day, Dr Goh called me and, to my surprise, gave me a mission that had nothing to do with my responsibility for training. He said he understood that there was a morale problem in the Engineers formation; it was not running well. He wanted me to look into it. I had to be very careful as this was not in the charter of my job. So I went to see DGS and told him that the Minister had asked me to look into this. Kip smiled at me and said that if that was what Dr Goh wanted, I should do it.

It was delicate; I knew I could not go barging in. I met

some of the officers I knew personally and had drinks with them in the mess. I also visited some training sessions and took the opportunity to casually speak to some of the officers. Slowly, I figured out what the problem was. Unlike the Infantry and, to some extent, Armour and Artillery formations which had some history, the Engineers was a relatively younger formation. Earlier on, they had a Chief Engineer Officer who was an infantry officer and not engineer-trained. The commanders were young officers who came from the first batch of SAFTI cadets. They lacked strong and confident leadership at the unit level. As a formation, they felt rather neglected, thinking that hardly any emphasis was given to them. Then there was an unfortunate incident when topless go-go dancers were brought in to perform at a mess party and someone reported them. The officers were severely punished and the organiser was kicked out of the Army. They resented it as they felt that the punishment was unduly harsh.

I thought the solution was for them to be given some attention, especially assurance from the top. What better than from the Minister himself. I asked them to organise a formation dining-in and invite Dr Goh. I told Dr Goh that it would help if he went and gave a short speech, to encourage them and show that he regarded them as important, which he did with his usual aplomb. He talked about how important the Engineers were and did not say a word about the topless dancers. That helped to lift their spirits and improve morale. Later, I realised why Dr Goh had given me, Head Training, this task to sort out a morale problem. In his usual wily way, he was still testing me.

After six months in the Training Department, I left to be Head Organisation in the General Staff. That was the equivalent of G5 Plans but at that time it was just known as the Organisation Department. I was a colonel, but I took over from a major, G Arumugam, who had been in the post for a while. He was from the SVC and not a combat officer.

He was, however, a very meticulous person who knew his job well and guarded his empire jealously. He stayed on in the department and so I had to win him over. I did not have the detailed knowledge of the job of Head Organisation and needed his help, which he readily obliged.

I understood why it was imperative that I had a stint there. That was where we planned the order of battle, or orbat, of the SAF. We looked closely at what we needed for manpower, weaponry and military equipment, and what changes had to be made. The Organisation Department was where the Israeli blueprint and the masterplan for the formation of the SAF resided. That was the first time I had the opportunity to go through them. From the formation of the SAF in 1966 to the time I got to the Organisation Department in 1973, a great many changes had already taken place. It was important for me to understand why certain things were done, what motivated the changes.

Then I was put through another test. I was given a task which again had nothing to do with my formal role as Head Organisation. In early 1974, a group of Japanese Red Army terrorists attacked the Shell refinery complex in Pulau Bukom to blow up the oil tanks. Fortunately, they failed to cause serious damage, but during their escape they hijacked the ferry *Laju* and held its crew hostage. This incident exposed the vulnerability of our oil refineries, and I was tasked to study the weaknesses of the physical security at all the five refineries in Singapore, recommend measures to secure them, and then implement the measures. This was actually the responsibility of Military Intelligence and Head Operations Department. I again consulted DGS who said that I was to carry it out as ordered.

It turned out to be a complex mission. After conducting a survey of the installations, I had to negotiate with the management of the refineries to carry out the physical improvements to their security and to accept the reinforcement of their installations with SAF troops and armoured vehicles. This required hard persuasion with some CEOs as it meant expenditure on their part. I had to talk them into agreeing without invoking the Minister's name. I completed securing the refineries within a week with the help of the Chief Armour Officer and Chief Commando Officer, as well as the Navy to ferry the troops and armoured vehicles to the refineries on the islands.

In my eight months as Head Organisation I did not have the opportunity to work on any big organisational changes. Besides having to undertake special operational tasks, I was also busy doing other things in preparation for taking over as DGS. One was to receive a series of intelligence briefings from our external intelligence agency. Dr Goh asked the Director of the Security and Intelligence Division (SID) to get his officers to brief me. I was given reading material and at 7 o'clock in the evenings, when most people had gone home, I sat through briefings by an SID officer. These gave me a deeper understanding of the dynamics in our region and what it would mean for the SAF's mission.

I was only 32 years old, still wet behind the ears. But I knew that this was very serious, so I had better grow up fast. That was a very trying time as I had to pick up so many things, take on so many different responsibilities – in a very short time. On top of that, I did not even know the timetable for when I would be taking over as DGS. Kate did not know the strain I felt at the prospect of becoming the head of the SAF. I did not share this with her at that point because I did not want her to worry.

XIV

"THIS IS IT!"

Dr Goh Keng Swee looked me in the eye
and said, "This is it! You have been prepared.
Now do your job." That shook me.

ON 1 MAY 1974, I took over as Director General Staff. I had reached the pinnacle of the SAF. I was excited, but also anxious and apprehensive. And I could not help feeling bad about taking over from Brigadier Kirpa Ram Vij. In my view, Kip had done a great job as DGS, laying much of the groundwork for the formation of the SAF. And here I was, a young punk several years his junior, taking over from him. There was no change-of-command parade or ceremony of any sort in those days. Just a handshake, "Good luck and all the best!" Kip was, like I said, a fine gentleman.

I took my time to move into Kip's room. His office was only one flight down and almost directly below my Head Organisation office. I told his Personal Assistant, Angelina Ong, to take her time to clear up his things for him before I moved in. I retained both Angelina and Kip's Staff Officer, Lim Theam Poh, because it is not my nature to turn people out when I move in. Mind you, over the previous three years, I had made several moves! Anyway, I was also rather overwhelmed by the change. One of the first things I did was to see the Permanent Secretary, Pang Tee Pow. He asked if I had taken over, and I replied that I had but for now I was just occupying the seat as I had not done anything yet. Then I went to see the Minister. Dr Goh Keng Swee looked me in the eye and said, "This is it! You have been prepared. Now do your job." That shook me.

My first thought was how I was going to get the people who were senior to me – and there were quite a number of them – to accept me taking over as DGS. It was important that they not only accepted me but, more so, that they would cooperate with me and we could work together. Although they did not outrank me, they were senior to me in service and had held senior positions, such as brigade and formation commanders, before me. Seniority is very important in a military organisation, and I had jumped three, four, five steps. There was also the matter of my age; most of my seniors were at least three or four years older than me. I thought about it for a long time. Then I decided that I should bite the bullet and meet them face-to-face. I arranged to meet them in my office. Not all of them turned up. I said to them words to this effect: "I didn't ask for this job. The powers that be made the decision. So here I am, and I want to make a good job of it. I know I am junior to all of you, but I hope you will work with me. After all, we are all professionals, and we are here because we want to serve the SAF. Those of you who feel strongly that you should be the one sitting in this chair, do see the Minister and tell him you want the job. If he gives you the job, I will willingly step aside. But if that doesn't happen, please work with me for the sake of the SAF." I hoped that would set the tone and ease the tension.

I knew there were still some who were not happy, as was to be expected. My Personal Assistant and Staff Officer assured me that I should not worry, just do my job and the SAF officers would be with me. I also knew that it was not only my seniors who were important. The younger officers from the first few batches in SAFTI mattered greatly and I had to work with them too. They were already in the General Staff, holding key jobs in the various departments. I decided that minimum movement was best for the organisation as I didn't want to destabilise anybody or anything. I spent the next couple of months meeting with the different Heads in the General Staff, getting to understand their priorities and problems. Although I had already spent some time in the General Staff before I became DGS, I wanted to learn more, especially from the Operations and Intelligence departments.

Then I had to get to know the workings of Mindef, especially the weekly Mindef HQ Meeting, which was the highest decision-making forum for Mindef and the SAF. Important matters regarding the development of the SAF, such as the formation of new units, personnel matters, logistics issues, and the acquisition of weapon systems and equipment, were discussed and decided on at those meetings. Those who attended included the Permanent Secretaries, and Directors of Manpower, Security and Intelligence, Logistics, and Finance. The Minister chaired the meeting and the Minister of State and Parliamentary Secretary were there. The DGS was the only uniformed member.

As the newest and most junior member, I had to quickly figure out the flow and dynamics of the meetings. It was important to know when to speak and when to keep quiet, and who besides the Chairman were the main movers. Things like the curry puffs served at the meeting were not as trivial as they seemed. The meeting did not start until the Polar Café curry puffs were brought in. There was enough for everyone at the meeting with one to spare. But no one touched the spare as it was reserved for the Chairman. Smoking was allowed and Director Logistics and I were the only smokers. But sometimes the Chairman would reach out for a cigarette from my pack. The meeting was held in a very small room. Today, I can't imagine how we survived with all that smoke.

Once I had settled in, I began my visits to the formations

and units. One of my top priorities was to get a sense of the morale of the troops and the officer corps. The first unit I visited was the Engineers because I knew that they had a problem earlier, the one that Dr Goh had asked me to deal with. When I met them, I did not refer to the earlier problem and neither did the Chief Engineer Officer. I then went on to visit Armour and other formations and units. Another of my priorities was to find out how the various arms were working with their respective Israeli advisers. Armour was doing very well. The Engineers were now turning around. I already knew that Signals had no problem. I left SAFTI to the last. The Director of SAFTI, Colonel Peter Lim, was one of my seniors who had been most unhappy about my appointment as DGS. The training institute was running well and there was not much I needed to do there as DGS. Still, I felt that I should make it a point to visit SAFTI to show that the training institute deserved my full attention.

Then there were the Air Force and Navy. The DGS was not directly responsible for their development and training but, through the Operations Department, coordinated the operations of the three services. Also, common SAF issues, such as standards of regimentation and discipline, and military culture, were the DGS's responsibility. The Air Force and Navy each had their own Mindef HQ meetings chaired by the Minister and I attended them.

The Air Force was run mostly by seconded British officers. Head Air Operations, the squadron commanders and the CO of the Flying Training School were all British. The person in charge of the air staff was Air Commodore John Langer. Early in my tenure as DGS, I ran into an issue with him. He made it a point to tell me that as his rank was equivalent to a brigadier, he outranked me because I was only a colonel. My reply to that was: "I may be a colonel, but as the DGS I am in charge of the SAF. You are in charge only of the Air Force." I said that it was not a matter of rank or position, but I expected him to work with me. This was British haughtiness, treating the Singaporean officers like boys, and I refused to let him walk all over me. Eventually, we reached a kind of accommodation in our working relationship. That was the sort of thing I had to deal with. In a military organisation, rank matters. Our civilians did not fathom this. Even Dr Goh, who I think very well knew this problem, told me, "You do it. Never mind about your rank. Don't worry."

The Navy was being helped by the New Zealanders. They were not in positions of command but the Royal New Zealand Navy provided instructors for the first batches of our seamen and technicians. The first batches of regular midshipmen were trained overseas. The Navy was in the early stages of its development and had recently received a squadron of six patrol craft built in Singapore. They went through a series of leadership changes. At one stage, they even had a schoolteacher, J S Gill from the Singapore Naval Volunteer Reserve, as chief. Eventually, James Aeria, who had more extensive naval training, was selected for the job. He was also from the Naval Volunteer Reserve and mobilised into the Royal Malaysian Navy, and had operational experience during Konfrontasi. I recall that he had commanded a patrol boat in Sabah.

Those were interesting times for me as DGS. I had to learn to deal with foreigners because Mindef and the SAF had advisers and consultants from various countries. Fortunately, by that time the special consultant who wanted to get me sacked, Air Chief Marshal Sir Rochford Hughes, had gone. We had a mini United Nations – the Israelis with the Army, the British with the Air Force, the New Zealanders with the Navy, and some Americans helping us in logistics. The FPDA, comprising Australia, New Zealand and the United Kingdom (collectively known as the ANZUK forces), Singapore and Malaysia, had been set up a few years earlier and there were ANZUK forces stationed in Singapore. They were then headed by a New Zealand brigadier overseeing a

New Zealand battalion, an Australian battalion and a British battalion. I chaired regular meetings with them as DGS; and all the ANZUK commanders were more senior in rank and older than me. FPDA policy matters though were handled at a higher level, at meetings attended by the Ministers and Permanent Secretaries from the member countries.

That was my first foray into diplomacy. I was only 32, whereas my counterparts in other armed forces were in their 50s. It is one thing to be appointed a leader, being accepted as one is quite something else. And in a military organisation, you must be accepted as the leader in order to lead. In my dealings with these military chiefs, I had to defer to their seniority and yet stand my ground as Singapore's representative. There was an encounter I will not forget. The Australian CDF, a four-star general, came to Singapore. When he met me, he exclaimed, "But you are a boy!" I said, "General, I may be a boy to you, but I am doing a man's job."

The culture of the SAF was a matter of great concern to me then. Our roots and the diversity of advisers meant that we were exposed to British, Israeli as well as Australian, Kiwi and American military cultures. This was something that had to be addressed. The origins of the military in Singapore had been British. Before Independence, 1 SIR and 2 SIR were run by British officers and were steeped in British Army culture and traditions. But that would not sit well with our National Service army. This was complicated by influences of our different advisers. I took the approach that the SAF's culture must be uniquely Singaporean – something we could identify with and be comfortable with. And we had to bear in mind that we were a National Service armed forces, and conscripts could not be handled like regular soldiers.

By that time, the Israelis had reduced the number of their advisers here following the 1973 Arab-Israeli War. For me, it was a constant concern to make sure that they did not try to change our culture and traditions. They had tried that earlier. For instance, they removed the Officers' Mess and replaced it with a common room for the officers, warrant officers and sergeants. It did not work; the officers did not want to go there because they could not let their guard down, and the sergeants did not want to go because the officers were there. We managed to get our messes back. Also, on the encouragement of the Israeli advisers we had lost our supply of beer, which was a standard feature of British military camps. One day, PM Lee Kuan Yew visited a camp and asked for a beer. When he was told that there was no beer, he exclaimed, "What kind of army are you!" So, the beer came back. Having been to Israel and having visited their units and their field exercises, I could understand why the Israeli advisers were trying to influence us to embrace their military culture. But military culture is a subset of national culture. We are Asians with a more hierarchical social structure, whereas the Israelis are more egalitarian. Adopting their system wholesale would not work. Over time, the Israelis accepted these differences, and we were unhindered in creating and evolving a uniquely Singaporean military culture.

The SAF, particularly the Army, was already equipped, organised and trained for conventional operations. I began to look at the suitability of the General Staff structure to command and operate a conventional army. The SAF was maturing and more professionally trained officers and NCOs were filling up its ranks. We had started with the British Army command structure. Then the Israelis introduced their modified arrangement. So I studied different models operated by different armies. I considered it paricularly important to have a similar command and staff structure at all levels – from battalion to brigade to division and the General Staff. All the major staff functions of personnel, intelligence, operations and logistics had to be included to support a command and control structure.

The General Staff Division did not have the full quota

of staff functions. We had Intelligence, Operations, Training and Organisation. Manpower and Logistics were handled by civilian divisions. But these two functions were necessary to make a fully functional staff structure. I was in favour of a comprehensive General Staff system and was attracted to the American model, which was simple and met my requirement for a common structure throughout the various levels of the Army. The problem was selling the idea to a civilian hierarchy still uncertain of the military and its capability to manage the SAF. It was crucial that this could be justified on the grounds of operational efficiency, and not be perceived as empire-building.

Our help came in the person of a German consultant. Dr Goh had always favoured opening ourselves to advice from people who had relevant experience and could show us what to do. Through special arrangements, Dr Goh brought in Lieutenant-General Siegfried Schulz in the mid-1970s. He was a godsend to the SAF. Schulz was a young lieutenant in the German Army towards the end of the Second World War and had risen up in the West German Army. He was to advise us on the Army and his views were increasingly sought by Dr Goh, who wanted a different perspective from the Israelis. Schulz remained with us for about 12 years. He was very knowledgeable and professional. He was also shrewd and understood the dynamics of the internal considerations in a young SAF and our Defence Ministry.

Schulz was a tremendous help to us because, being very young professionally, SAF officers were sometimes not taken seriously by the civilian hierarchy. So, my staff and I worked closely with him, letting him know our concerns. As a professional he could see that we needed a proper command and staff system. He was our ally. When eventually he put up a recommendation, it was exactly what we wanted because we had told him what we needed during our extensive discussions. And what he said was more readily accepted because it came from a consultant. Sometimes you find that the words of someone in your own house do not carry as much weight as the words of a visitor. That was the case with the SAF and General Schulz. Often, when we wanted to get things done, we would write the words and give the pen to Schulz to sign. When we introduced the General Staff structure, that was our work, endorsed by Schulz and accepted by Dr Goh and Mindef. If Schulz had not endorsed it, we would not have succeeded in making this change.

The change took effect on 1 September 1976, two years after I became DGS and two months after I was promoted to brigadier-general. With the reorganisation, the DGS became Chief of the General Staff (CGS). The various departments – Manpower, Intelligence, Operations, Logistics, Organisation and Plans, and Training – became G1 to G6 respectively, and the Heads were now called Assistant Chief of General Staff (ACGS) (Personnel) or G1, ACGS (Intelligence) or G2, ACGS (Operations) or G3, ACGS (Logistics) or G4, ACGS (Plans) or G5 and ACGS (Training) or G6. We used the American 1, 2, 3, 4, 5 terms because the British terms were rather wordy. We thought the SAF was too young an organisation to be mired in awkward terminology which people could not relate to. This numbering system was adopted for the staff branches at battalion and brigade levels as S1, S2, S3 and S4, and at division level as G1, G2, G3 and G4. Training normally came under operations, but we added 6 for training in the General Staff because training was a major preoccupation for the SAF and we thought there was a need for training to be a separate department. With the establishment of the General Staff, the Army now had a proper command and staff structure and the SAF had taken an important step further in its development.

XV

HOLDING OUR OWN WITH THE CIVILIANS

I always accepted the primacy of civilian authority over the military... But the lack of confidence in the military bothered me greatly; I was determined to fix it.

AS DGS, one of my priorities was to gain recognition for the professionalism and ability of SAF officers. Not just from Singaporeans at large but, more immediately, from the civilians in Mindef. From the time I became DGS, I sensed the lack of regard for the military officers and felt uneasy about our standing vis-à-vis our civilian counterparts in the bureaucracy. I think I would not be wrong to say that many of my fellow regulars, especially those working in Mindef, were not happy with the way the civilians regarded them. From the start, I always accepted the primacy of civilian authority over the military. That was never the issue and I had always lived by this. But the lack of confidence in the military bothered me greatly; I was determined to fix it.

The root of this problem was that at the beginning, when there was the urgent need to form our own armed forces after Independence, we had few military professionals to plan and lead the development of the SAF. The officers from the two SIR battalions and mobilised volunteers were deployed on the ground to be instructors in the schools and to man the units. Those working in Mindef were mostly junior officers, mobilised volunteers and even some police officers brought in to hold staff positions. Consequently, civilians dominated the HQ.

Dr Goh Keng Swee was tasked to expeditiously form an armed forces. The Israelis had recommended an integrated organisation instead of a separate Defence ministry and an armed forces headquarters, and this was accepted. A group of civilian bureaucrats who the Minister could rely on to get the job done was cobbled together. In the top planning and decision-making forum, the Mindef HQ Meeting, the only military member was the DGS, who was equal in status to the Directors for Manpower, Logistics, Finance and Intelligence. All the DGSs who preceded me had not been trained and schooled as military professionals, and the civilians knew this. The first had been a police officer, followed by two mobilised volunteers, one a civil servant and the other a schoolteacher.

In the formative days of the SAF, I would say that all the professional military input that went into our planning was provided by the Israeli advisers, and this was understandably so. The Israeli advisers called all the shots when it came to professional military matters. They had direct access to the Permanent Secretary and the Minister. One of those advisers, Yehuda Golan, published a book many years later in which he criticised Singapore soldiers for not wanting to do the things he wanted them to, and he had to complain to the civilian leadership, meaning the Permanent Secretary and the Minister. Complete disregard for the military chain of command! Such behaviour helped reinforce the civilians' negative attitude towards our military professionals.

With the emphasis and focus in the early days being to raise a military force swiftly, there was no time for niceties and no consideration for military protocols and sensitivities. When I became DGS, this culture still prevailed. I vividly recall the words of Permanent Secretary Pang Tee Pow. He pointed out to me that my predecessor was only a one-star and so was the British brigadier overseeing the Air Force; "But I am four stars! Remember that!"

I could accept some of the shenanigans of the civilians. It was the prevailing culture, and I would just have to work at putting it right. But some things truly upset me. This included ridiculous efforts by the civilians to interfere in military regimentation matters. For example, someone questioned why they had to stand for the colours at parades. In most armies, the colours – which are the standards of the units that in battle act as a rallying point for troops – are at the front of their respective units when they go on parade. This meant that during a march-past, the spectators had to stand each time a colour passed in front of them. Some Mindef civilians considered it troublesome having to stand almost throughout the march-past. So, much to the chagrin of the RSMs in the SAF, the drill was modified to group the colours of all the units on parade into one contingent at the front so that the spectators needed to stand only once and not throughout the march-past. This really irked me but, being practical, I accepted the change as it did not lessen the importance and significance of the parade or the colours. I had a difficult time placating the RSMs though.

Then there were silly questions from a senior civilian like: "Why does the Parade Commander say, 'May I have your permission to march off the parade?' What if the Inspecting Officer says 'No'?" Can you imagine! My retort to that was: "You find me one Inspecting Officer besides you who will say no." This is a military tradition, but those civilians did not bother to appreciate that. These were less weighty issues, but the ludicrous comments have stuck in my mind. Every so often, on matters of both high and low importance, a civilian would challenge our decisions and professional considerations. I always told my staff that they had to be professional. What they put on paper, they had better be able to defend it to me, because I had to defend them at Mindef HQ. In the earlier years, with powerful and assertive civilians around and me being new, I had to reluctantly accommodate. In later years, as the military staff became better trained and more familiar with their duties, we would push back when we did not agree. But this was still a long trudge.

The civilians' rather dismissive attitude towards the military in those days gave us no say in decisions on the acquisition of weaponry and equipment. The civilians in the Logistics Division decided what the SAF should have. I accepted that sometimes there may have been political or other non-military considerations when deciding whether to buy certain equipment. I also accepted that, as is the practice in most armed forces, the actual procurement process is undertaken by the civilian logistics department. What annoyed me was that the system did not cater for input from the military users. It was like: "you just worry about training the troops and leave us to decide what weapon systems to give you." I saw very early on that we needed to beef up the professional capabilities of our officers so that they could assess and define our operational requirements and arrive at specifying the types of weapons and equipment which we should consider for acquisition.

Another big issue I faced during those early days was that some of the civilian department heads would ignore and circumvent the military chain of command. Sometimes they went straight to the units, down to the company commander, bypassing the division, brigade, and battalion commanders. For the military, this is a no-no. I myself made it a practice that if I needed to speak to somebody junior to find out something, I would always let his bosses know. And I would tell the officer that I would inform his bosses. For military operations to be conducted smoothly, it is imperative that the chain of command be respected without exception. The commander must know that he is in charge, and if anything goes wrong, it is his head on the block.

I could accept criticisms but did not like the military being treated with disdain, which was blatantly obvious sometimes. That was why I felt compelled to raise the level of professionalism in our military. Great emphasis had to be placed on training officers properly, developing a professional outlook, and enhancing their military knowledge. We were fortunate that Dr Goh Keng Swee recognised the need to develop the SAF's professional competence and supported this exercise. No effort was spared to secure advanced courses overseas to expand the military knowledge of our officers and to expose them to other armed forces. They could learn from others and come back and adapt what they had learnt for the SAF so that our doctrines would be dynamic. The other unique thing Dr Goh instituted was to make it compulsory for the officers to read military journals. All SAF officers had to submit a list of the journals they subscribed to. There was a scheme to help them pay for their subscriptions. Dr Goh himself was a voracious reader and his knowledge of the military was par excellence. He could stump visiting American generals with his deep knowledge of military technology.

Our efforts to win recognition from the civilians for our professionalism and the capability of our military were given a boost by a cue from Dr Goh to take deliberate steps to raise the prestige and standing of the military. For a start, we took over the British Britannia Club in Beach Road for our NCOs. It was important that our NCOs could be seen to have a club of their own. In a practical way, Dr Goh also reasoned that it was better for our soldiers to have a proper place to drink and let their hair down than to be seen roughing it out along Orchard Road. I was asked to look out for a suitable location for an officers' club. We settled for the old Sanders Home in Portsdown Road, previously used by the British Army for recreational facilities for their families. This facility had been allocated to the Civil Service for a recreation club, but we managed to get the Ministry of Finance to hand it over to us. We named this club for officers the Temasek Club, reflecting its pedigree. In a similar vein, Dr Goh established what was regarded as prestigious quarters for the top officers. These were the black and white colonial bungalows at Alexandra Park that had been used to house senior British officers. Those staying in these quarters also received an allowance to employ domestic helpers because it was difficult to maintain the big house on your own. The house I lived in since I was a colonel is still there. It is No. 2, the first house on the left as you enter Alexandra Park. When I became DGS in 1974, Dr Goh asked me to move into my predecessor's house, a big one at the top of the hill. When I declined, he looked at me and asked, "What's wrong with you?" He was quite insistent, but I told him that I was happy where I was, and it did not make a difference which house I lived in. He relented. I saw no purpose in moving because a house is a house. I lived in that house right up to the day I retired from the SAF.

Dr Goh went one step further by developing Normanton Park Estate for SAF officers. He wanted them to have affordable homes. The architect was instructed to build point-block flats just like the HDB ones, so there was no need to draw up new plans. The larger walk-up apartments were for lieutenant-colonels and above. When the reception was luke-warm at the beginning, Dr Goh told me to go and book one to set the example. I replied that I thought it a good buy and would love to do it, but it would be awkward for the officers if the CGS lived in the same estate. "Never mind, book," he said. I booked and paid the booking fee. When the response became very good, I withdrew my booking and forfeited the booking fee. I suppose my sacrifice had been for a good cause.

With all these efforts to boost the skills, standing and morale of the SAF personnel, and the injection of more and more well-trained and professional officers, the military began to be seen in a better light and we were able to hold our own with the civilians. But it was not all plain sailing. We had a particularly difficult time with the civilian leadership after

Dr Goh left Mindef in 1979. The General Staff did not agree with many of the views expressed and would make counter-proposals. For instance, we were asked why the SAF could not teach its soldiers to fight on bicycles. After all, the Japanese had come down the Malayan Peninsula on bicycles during the Second World War. We were also asked why we had to acquire bridges; why could we not cut bamboo to make bridges as the Japanese had done? I pointed out that that was 1942, and the Japanese Army just used whatever was available – bicycles, bamboos, planks – to push down the Peninsula as rapidly as possible. My deputy Tan Chin Tiong and I went through elaborate explanations of how battles were fought differently in the past, how much more equipment soldiers now had to carry, and so on.

Worse still was the idea to set up a parallel General Staff and put the young scholars there. Chin Tiong and I decided that we would not be fazed by this but would just do our best professionally and wait and see what would actually be decided. In the meantime, we carried on with what we had to do. Shortly after that, Dr Goh, who was then Minister for Education, called me up and asked me how the General Staff was. I said it was all right. Then he asked, "What's this about the parallel General Staff?" I told him there was some unhappiness that the General Staff did not agree with some of the ideas coming out and was regarded as being unsupportive. Perhaps a younger General Staff was desired. "Rubbish!" declared Dr Goh. Not long after, Mindef had a change of leadership at the top.

This love-hate relationship between the military and the civilians in Mindef started to ease off with changes in the main players. Less powerful and pushy bureaucrats now held senior positions. More experienced, knowledgeable and professional military officers were assigned to the General Staff. Most importantly, there was a better understanding and definition of the respective roles and responsibilities. The ability of the military to contribute was expected and well received. In later years, Administrative Service officers who had the benefit of serving NS were assigned positions in Mindef, which helped greatly in developing a more amicable working relationship between the military and civilians. Things were also changing within the civil service as more and more senior officers had military experience and SAF training through their NS. This obviously raised their appreciation of military professionals. Eventually, we came into our own when the CGS was placed on the same level as the Permanent Secretaries in the national Table of Precedence. The lesson I took away from all this was that the only way to earn respect and recognition was to work hard at raising the level of our military professionalism.

XVI

TO FIGHT AS ONE

The SAF could win only if we could fight effectively as an integrated tri-service force… the SAF – as a whole – would pack a bigger punch than the sum of its parts.

IT HAD ALWAYS BEEN a pressing priority for me to develop the command and staff structure of the SAF. In the early days, we were focused on building up the various arms of the Army, the units of the Navy and the Air Force, and did not address the question of how to pull all these together with a command structure if we had to go to war. The General Staff Division headed by a Director was adequate for the early stages of the SAF when the emphasis was on building up and overseeing training. But it was not designed for operations. This was painfully evident in our response to the *Laju* incident in January 1974, when Japanese Red Army terrorists seized the *Laju* ferry after planting explosives on Pulau Bukom, and in Operation Thunderstorm when we had to deal with the influx of boat people, refugees fleeing by sea after the Vietnam War ended in April 1975. Our response was disorderly and lacked a clear line of direction for the operations. What happened was that direction for the operations came from the Minister via the Permanent Secretary and several civilian directors who gave orders separately to units of the Army and the Navy.

It became obvious that a proper command structure was necessary if we wanted to carry out operations effectively. We had to go beyond just amassing and training an armed forces. To this end, we had successfully made the case for a General Staff, and we had formed one with the help of our consultant General Siegfried Schulz. That was adequate to command a combined arms operation for the Army and to have loose control of a limited operation involving the two other Services. Then Schulz agreed with me that we had now arrived at a point where we could look beyond that.

We started to think about having proper Service organisations. The Services had developed sufficiently for them to have their distinctive identities. On 1 April 1975, the Singapore Air Defence Command was renamed the Republic of Singapore Air Force (RSAF) and the Singapore Maritime Command was renamed the Republic of Singapore Navy (RSN). Their rank structures and uniforms had to be sorted out. When the SAF was formed after Independence, we all wore Temasek green and had a common rank nomenclature and insignia. Then changes were made in small steps to the uniforms and rank insignia. The RSN changed their uniforms to beige while the RSAF still wore green but had stripes like the British Royal Air Force as rank insignia. Eventually we settled on all three Services having a common rank structure and insignia, the only exception being the Navy where flag officers adopted the conventional naval title of admiral. I used to jokingly say that I could not imagine having a general on board a ship commanding a naval fleet.

A few years later, we took the step to appoint Air Force and Navy chiefs and set up proper structures for the Air Staff and Naval Staff. At that point there was still no Chief of Army, because as CGS I was not only chief of the SAF but also chief of the Army. That set us thinking that we should do something about this inconsistency. As an interim measure, the then Deputy Chief of General Staff (DCGS), Boey Tak

Hap, became the de facto Chief of Army. That was a good first step; now all three Services had their respective chiefs and the CGS could concentrate solely on his duties as chief of the SAF.

After that was settled, I began to think about the development of the SAF as a joint force, and I discussed this with Schulz. Unlike the Israeli advisers, Schulz did not look at tactics and how to fight but was focused on the big picture and development issues. This was most useful for us at that point of the SAF's growth.

We had developed the Army to be capable of fighting effectively as a combined arms force. Our Air Force had grown in strength and capability to effectively undertake air defence and close air support for land operations. The Navy, though still comparatively small in size, had outgrown the "coast guard" image and packed the potency to carry out its defined maritime tasks. Given the limitations of our size and the likely theatre of operations, the SAF could win only if we could fight effectively as an integrated tri-service force. To achieve that, we needed a lean and effective joint command and staff structure to ensure that our tri-service force could operate in synergy, so that the SAF – as a whole – would pack a bigger punch than the sum of its parts.

We went around looking at how other armed forces did it. The American structure was not suitable because they were so big. They had theatre commands and the person at the apex of the American armed forces was the Chairman of the Joint Chiefs of Staff. We looked at the British and Commonwealth systems. The British had a joint staff with a Chief of Defence Staff who was the head of the armed forces. The Malaysians had a Chief of Defence Force, as did the Australians. The Israelis had a similar system; although they used the title Ramatkal or Chief of General Staff, he had a joint function and responsibility.

We recognised that we had to adapt and customise a system

which we could be comfortable with, that would be fit for what we needed and wanted to achieve. And we had to have the right people trained to man the positions. We knew this was the direction we should move in. We started in 1983 and it took some years, but we managed to move from a loose structure managed by the General Staff for combined arms operations, to a robust system that would be effective in joint operations of the three Services.

The command and staff structure for joint operations required the same supporting functions as the General Staff – personnel, intelligence, operations, and logistics. These functions dealt with issues related to military operations, separate from the policy matters handled by the civilian directors in Mindef. Our first foray into Joint Staff work was with committees, one dealing with joint operations and plans and another addressing joint intelligence. The next stage was to appoint someone with a staff to take charge of the function, which led to the establishment of the office of the Director, Joint Operations and Plans Directorate (DJOPD). The first DJOPD was Lee Hsien Loong, who had all the relevant training and command exposure and carried sufficient weight for the position. Subsequent DJOPDs were also well recognised for their ability to carry the job – George Yeo from the Air Force and Teo Chee Hean from the Navy. We also set up the post of Director, Joint Intelligence Directorate (DJID) and Chin Siat Yoon was appointed. That was the start of the Joint Staff. It worked well and we later took it a step further to bring in logistics and personnel, slowly evolving. I had to tread carefully so as not to give the impression that we were building an empire.

I was not made Chief of Defence Force or CDF until 1990. At the apex of the SAF, I was first Director General Staff or DGS and then Chief of the General Staff or CGS. Even after the Joint Staff was established in 1983, I retained the title of CGS. I was promoted to Lieutenant-General in 1988 as CGS.

My titles did not matter as my responsibilities remained the same and my aim was to get the Joint Staff established and accepted. At the back of my mind, I was always aware that the civilians had to be comfortable with me and the military, so I never pushed. It was Defence Minister Goh Chok Tong who thought that it was time to make the changes. First, he promoted me to Lieutenant-General, the first three-star in the SAF, in July 1988. Then he thought that it was appropriate that we should be like other armed forces and have a CDF heading the SAF. The post was created in April 1990.

One important factor that made the Joint Staff gel and carry more weight was that we now had a bigger say in the use of the budget and the acquisition of equipment. We had moved on from the early days of being responsible only for training the forces while the civilians dictated what equipment we should get. We now had more military expertise and professionalism within the SAF. The number of officers with knowledge of military technology had steadily grown over the years. By the time we had the Joint Staff, we had Weapons Staff Officers who could do weapons assessments. Besides going to the Royal Military College of Science in Shrivenham, Oxfordshire, in the UK, our officers also went to the Naval Postgraduate School (NPS) in Monterey, California, in the US. Among the first SAF officers who went to NPS was Lui Pao Chuen, who later became Director Logistics as a military officer and Mindef's first Chief Defence Scientist.

Slowly over the years, the SAF had developed the capability to define our operational requirements and our military engineers could actively participate in the acquisition process. Later, military officers were brought into the Logistics system, working alongside civilian engineers – people like Wesley D'Aranjo, an Air Force officer who became principally responsible for the acquisition of military equipment and weapon systems. With greater participation of military-trained and operationally experienced engineers, the whole assessment and procurement process improved greatly. All this helped to lend more credibility to the work of the Joint Staff.

The other thing that made the Joint Staff work was that the Air Staff, Naval Staff and General Staff supported the concept of the Joint Staff and worked well with the Joint Staff. Who gets what was decided by the Joint Staff, and when you control the purse-strings you get better cooperation. So our control of the budget was an effective tool. I was fortunate. I am not a brilliant guy, but I was adept at getting good people to work with me and I knew how to deploy the right person for a particular job. So, I had very good officers in the Joint Staff who were able to execute all that we needed done.

We had very tough and forceful Air Force and Navy chiefs at that time – Michael (Mike) Teo and James Leo. But they deferred to me because I was older and more senior. Mike was a good fighter pilot and a good commander, with very much a fighter pilot's personality and flamboyance. That was something I accepted, even encouraged. But Mike would always push for the Air Force to get more than others because they considered themselves special. For instance, Mike insisted that his helicopter pilots supporting our Army training in Brunei could not sleep in the field camp but had to sleep in air-conditioned rooms in the rest-house "because if they don't get good sleep, they can't fly safely". I said that was rubbish. But we met half-way; we air-conditioned some rooms in the camp where the pilots could sleep the night before they flew. These were the small things we had to work on with the different Services.

Joint Staff meetings with the Service Chiefs were very fiery. Boey Tak Hap, and later Ng Jui Ping, Mike Teo and James Leo fought like cats and dogs. I used to keep quiet and listen, then stand up and silence them, and pronounce the decision. That had been the way I handled the army commanders when I was CGS, because the different formation commanders would also fight fiercely for their cause when they attended General Staff meetings. When we put good commanders, good officers together, it was only natural that they would fight for their rights and for their formation and men. I recognised that and allowed the fights. While I had a view on what we should be doing, I wanted to let them express their views and to discuss, while steering them to what my staff and I thought was a good solution. But whenever I felt that someone had a valid point, I would accept the views and accede. When they had said enough and I had heard enough, I would ask them to shut up and go and do such and such. Chances were that they would be in agreement by that point. It was the same in the Joint Staff. That was how I used to do it. Money was always one of the main issues because if you decided to buy a squadron of aircraft, you could forget about raising divisions for the Army. The cost comparisons were like that.

My way of apportioning responsibilities among the Services was to say that anything one inch in the water was Navy, anything on hard land was Army, anything one foot above the ground was Air Force. For example, all military trucks on the ground, whether in air bases or wherever, were bought and maintained by the Army General Support and Maintenance Base. Helicopters in support of the Army were manned by the Air Force with the budget coming from the Army. Maritime air patrol aircraft were for the Navy and paid for from the Navy's budget, but piloted and managed by the Air Force with Navy people manning the equipment and sensors in the aircraft. Fast landing craft and fast jet boats in support of the Army were manned by the Navy and paid for by the Army. That was the basis on which we decided.

The SAF was too small to be completely self-sufficient within each Service. At one time there was talk about having an army aviation arm like in the US. In Australia they had started with the army operating helicopters and light fixed-wing aircraft. The rationale for having army aviation was inspired by the experience of the Americans in the Vietnam War where there was a great need for dedicated air support. In the early days of the Vietnam War, when the US army asked for air support, the air force had its own priorities, so the army did not get what it needed. And lives were lost. The thinking was that they could not depend on somebody else to provide the support they needed. But I said we were too small and it did not make sense for the SAF. I always told the RSAF not to forget that the Army paid for the helicopters and their primary role was to support the Army.

We also had an issue with field air defence artillery (ADA) units. These started out under the Army, which wanted the ADA unit to be with the division when it moved so that it could support the division. But the RSAF did not like the Army controlling air defence weapons because they feared that trigger-happy soldiers could shoot our own aircraft. This was a very long battle. In the end I decided that air defence units would come under the RSAF but specific ADA units would be dedicated to support Army divisions, so the affiliation and command and operational control were determined. But the rules of engagement would be defined by the Air Force. This was the period when we had to work very hard to ensure that the SAF could fight as a joint force. We knew that if we did not do so, we would not be able to fight effectively.

The next step was to have joint exercises conducted by the Joint Staff. We had joint exercises where the Chiefs of Army, Navy and Air Force participated with their respective staff. These were conducted in our Command Post to keep the facilities there well oiled, exercised, and warm. The exercises used to go on for one week to 10 days. We had decided to build our Command Post because we realised the need for such a facility. The command structure of the SAF was eventually made complete with the establishment of the post of Chief of Army. Ng Jui Ping, who was then the de facto Army chief as DCGS, became the first Chief of Army, with the General Staff as the Army staff.

If you ask me what my most important accomplishment in the SAF was, I would say that it was the establishment of a proper command and staff organisation. First the General Staff and then the Joint Staff. And single Service headquarters for the Army, Navy and Air Force. To fight effectively, we would have to fight as one – that is the most critical quality of a strong military force. So we needed to have a proper command structure for the SAF to be an effective armed forces and credible deterrent. Fortunately, we have not had to test this out in combat operations, but it has worked very well in complex humanitarian assistance and disaster relief missions. When the SAF conducted Operation Flying Eagle to help Meulaboh in Aceh, Sumatra, after the devastating Boxing Day Tsunami in 2004, it was a joint operation with the three Services working in a tightly coordinated response that was impressively swift and effective.

XVII

THE WILL TO FIGHT

*The best technology in the world does not
replace the soldier with the rifle who is motivated
to fight and to stand his ground.*

NOT LONG AFTER the Vietnam War, Dr Goh Keng Swee arranged to approach the US Department of Defense for a briefing on the US military's experience in Vietnam. He wanted to find out what had gone wrong for the Americans there and what lessons we could learn from their experience. He had hoped that the Americans could come to Singapore so that a bigger group of SAF officers could benefit from the briefing, but the US asked us to go over instead. I led a team of 35 officers – majors, captains and lieutenants – who were potential future leaders of the SAF. We went to the John F Kennedy Center in Fort Bragg, North Carolina. Officers from the Army, Navy, Air Force and Marines who had served in Vietnam, as well as Central Intelligence Agency officers who had conducted special operations there and Pentagon officials came to brief us. After the briefings in Fort Bragg, we went to Fort Belvoir near Washington DC to have a hands-on look at some of their engineering equipment. We also went to the Pentagon for some meetings and spent almost a week in Washington.

At Fort Bragg, the Americans organised a seminar on their operations in the Vietnam War and the lessons they had learnt. There were talks on counter-insurgency operations, starting with their experience in the Philippines against the Hukbalahap insurgency to their operations in Vietnam, and these were very comprehensive. The Americans had at first tried to transfer some of their experiences in the Philippines to Vietnam, but that did not work. They had studied the Malayan Emergency and General Sir Gerald Templar's strategy against the Communist Party of Malaya, and tried to use the "new villages" concept which had been used in Malaya to keep the people in and the communist insurgents out, but the Vietcong kept coming back. Though the Americans had placed great emphasis and effort on civil affairs, they had problems winning the hearts and minds of the people. And in their military operations, they found the Vietcong very determined and elusive.

Against the North Vietnamese Army, the Americans employed more conventional warfare where they brought in air power, armour, artillery, helicopters and heavy fire power. They wanted to cut off the supply routes to the South, but the North Vietnamese stealthily went through the Ho Chi Minh Trail. The Americans had many innovations in their use of military equipment and weaponry, but their enemy was just as innovative and very resilient. The Americans told us that from the strategic perspective, the Vietnam War was lost in the living rooms back home more so than on the ground – because they were using conscripts and it got harder and harder to justify politically what they were doing in Vietnam. They were fighting a very unpopular war and the media coverage back home fanned anti-war sentiments. Their every move in the battle-fields of Vietnam was beamed on television right into homes across the US. Scenes of their soldiers being killed and wounded wore down the American people psychologically.

When the SAF team returned, we prepared a report and conducted briefings and seminars. That was a good starting point, and our Army, Navy and Air Force had useful material to chew on. One big lesson we took away was that if you did not have the support of your people, the morale of your troops would plummet. Another lesson we learnt was that it was far more difficult to fight a war in somebody else's land. The Americans were facing an enemy who were defending their homeland. In contrast, the US troops were not very committed. And their ally, the South Vietnamese, generally lacked the will to fight. In military terms, the Americans were far superior in weapons, logistics and technology – but they lost to the small men with the straw hats and AK-47s. It was not that the Americans were not good soldiers. But they were fighting a war where other factors were stacked against them. The key takeaway for me was that when you fight, you have to fight for a cause, for your country, your own survival. This is most pertinent to the SAF which is by and large a conscript armed forces.

It was an eye-opener to learn how the Americans with all their military might had difficulty taking on the Vietnamese foot soldiers. The Americans sprayed chemicals to defoliate the jungles and, in the process, poisoned people and killed animals and plants. But that did not help them much because the whole of Vietnam was a big forest. This was jungle warfare, not conventional warfare. But the Americans were used to fighting conventional warfare and did not adapt sufficiently, unlike the British in Malaya. The scale was also very different, the battleground in Vietnam being so much bigger than in Malaya. When the British closed off the villages in Malaya, they choked off the supplies for the communist insurgents from their Chinese sympathisers in the villages, but closing off a hamlet in Vietnam did not stop supplies from coming in from elsewhere. Also, the Vietcong were after all from the people.

All that we learnt was very helpful and we became more acutely aware of the need to build up the SAF quickly and to work out what we had to do to strengthen it. We wanted to make sure that we could handle some of the problems faced by the Americans in Vietnam. We would have to equip the

SAF and prepare our troops properly to enable us to operate in our region because the terrain in Vietnam was very similar. With the help of the Israeli advisers, the SAF had been looking at conventional warfare. We would also have to prepare ourselves to fight in the jungle. That was why it was important that we went to Brunei and have jungle warfare training facilities there.

We were able to pick up how the Americans used helicopters, and their innovations in weapons and other military equipment. Learning from their experience, we went to get more helicopters, both for troop-lift and gunships. We were looking at mounting guns in our UH-1H helicopters. We found that the US Army made frequent use of waterjet boats in the rivers with shallow draft, so we bought some and learnt from the riverine operations that the Americans had conducted in Vietnam. We concluded that we would have to get as much training opportunities and equipment from the US as possible.

There was then a shift for the SAF from the British model to focusing on American military equipment. The Americans agreed to sell us more equipment. The SAF had started off with British second-hand equipment and then we had some French hardware. When American equipment became accessible, we went for that. Dr Goh asked us to prepare two shopping lists of "must-have" and "good-to-have" military equipment and weaponry. The US also gave us more training slots and we could send more people there for training courses. Our trainees came home with lots of American training materials which we studied and adapted. So, we moved to more American-style training and American equipment.

Besides learning from the American experience in Vietnam, we also learnt from the Japanese experience in the Malayan Campaign in the Second World War. Dr Goh wanted to know why the Japanese were so successful when they were so heavily outnumbered. In the early 1980s, I led a small SAF team to

Tokyo where we met some of the Japanese officers who were in the staff of General Tomoyuki Yamashita, who commanded the Japanese forces in the invasion of Malaya and the Battle of Singapore. Not many of Yamashita's staff were still alive by that time. The most important person we met was General Ichiji Sugita, Yamashita's intelligence chief, who was in his late 70s. In the famous photograph of the British surrender in Singapore in 1942, Sugita is the man with a thick moustache standing next to Yamashita. We also met the staff from operations and logistics. One particularly interesting officer we met had been involved in the preparatory phases of the invasion of Malaya, when Japanese troops trained in Hainan and Indochina before mounting the invasion.

We were closeted in a room in Dai-ichi Hotel for close to 10 days. We sat with them and went through the whole process of their thinking, their planning, their preparations, and the operation itself, from the landings in Songkhla and Patani in southern Thailand and Kota Baru in northern Malaya to their invasion of Singapore and the Allied surrender. All in 70 days! We were interested in the reasoning behind their decisions. Their plan was driven by their mission to reach Singapore as swiftly as possible and cut off the British before they could react. They did not have sufficient troop-carrying vehicles, so they commandeered whatever means available – civilian trucks and even bicycles – for their infantrymen to travel fast. Instead of waiting for special river crossing equipment, they improvised by cutting down trees and bamboo to build bridges when they had to cross rivers. They used light tanks very effectively, when it was thought that the terrain in Malaya did not favour tanks.

They did not face much resistance until they reached Negeri Sembilan and Johor, when they met the Australians and Indians in Gemas, Muar and Batu Pahat. But they soon overcame that. The Japanese deceived the Allied forces into thinking that the secondary attack via Pulau Ubin was the main thrust when their main attack was actually the crossing to Singapore's north-west coast. The surprising thing we learnt, which not many people knew, was that they had run short of supplies and especially ammunition by that time. They knew the British in Singapore had a fortress and they were outnumbered by the Allied forces. Furthermore, the Japanese did not want to be mired in street fighting in built-up Singapore. So Yamashita "played poker" with the British commander General Arthur Percival. He demanded that the Allied forces surrender immediately – and Percival folded.

The briefing by the Japanese was another revelation for me, and I found it valuable. Dr Goh had wanted us to find out how and why the Japanese were able to defeat the British. I concluded that it was sheer determination and aggression. Looking at the character of the two leaders, Yamashita and Percival, I saw that the fighting spirit of the Japanese was far superior. They had determination and they had guts. It is no wonder that Yamashita was labelled "Tiger of Malaya". On the part of the British, it was almost a defeatist attitude. That was why only the Australians and the Indians in Johor had put up some degree of resistance. By that time, the British were quite demoralised. The *Repulse* and *Prince of Wales*, their two capital warships, had been sunk off the east coast of Malaya. They had no air cover and the Japanese were bombing Singapore. The British soldiers were young and not battle-hardened, and Winston Churchill and Whitehall would no longer support their war effort here because they needed the resources for the fight in Europe and Africa.

The thing that stood out from these two learning exercises – from the Americans on the Vietnam War and the Japanese on the Malayan Campaign – was that the victors had the will to fight. The Japanese were determined to fight, as were the North Vietnamese and Vietcong. In Vietnam, the Americans were so obviously superior in their equipment and their technology. Even when the North Vietnamese regular troops came south towards the end of the war, they came with tanks that were clearly inferior to the American armour and firepower. The best technology in the world does not replace the soldier with the rifle who is motivated to fight and to stand his ground. I once watched an IDF video which proudly declared that the secret of their success was not their weapons but the spirit and passion of their soldiers. That is what I firmly believe too. I suspect the SAF sometimes thinks I am shouting too loudly, because its mantra is "technology, technology, technology".

XVIII

SCHOLARS AND WOMEN

I always believed that I could be successful only if
I was willing to have good people around me, and I could
work with them and use them to support me.

IN THE EARLY DAYS of the SAF, developing military professionalism and gaining the respect of the civilians was a priority for me. Thus, I had no problem with the SAF scholar system which was introduced by PM Lee Kuan Yew and Dr Goh Keng Swee in the early 1970s. I was very receptive to the idea and saw it as a blessing because I knew that there was a place in the military for brilliant people. I had always been inspired by the German General Staff system where intelligent and bright officers were inducted into the staff to support the commanders who were from the nobility. The whole idea of the SAF scholar system was to bring in people with high potential and better academic qualifications to take the SAF to a higher level. But when the SAF Overseas Scholarship (SAFOS) scheme started, there was understandably some concern and disquiet among the officer corps as they did not fully understand the thinking behind it and perceived it as a threat to their advancement.

The first batch of SAFOS were Lee Hsien Loong, Boey Tak Hap, Lai Seck Khui, Liu Tsun Kie and Sin Boon Wah. We were looking for outstanding people, so we had been monitoring them since they were recruits and officer cadets. When they went overseas to university, we arranged for military attachments for them. When they returned, the scholars were sent to different arms. Lee Hsien Loong went to Artillery, Boey Tak Hap to Infantry, Lai Seck Khui to Signals, Sin Boon Wah to Armour, and Liu Tsun Kie to the Air Defence Radar Unit. In the units, these men were again closely observed. The third batch of SAFOS was, in my opinion, the most illustrious – Teo Chee Hean, George Yeo, Lim Hng Kiang and Lim Swee Say eventually went into the Cabinet; Peter Ho became Head of the Civil Service. That was a bumper crop.

I was very mindful that this system of giving scholarships to people with high potential and bringing them into the SAF must not destabilise and demotivate the non-scholars in the SAF. I was keenly aware that while scholars could add value and raise the level of the SAF officer corps, the SAF could operate effectively and run well only if we also had good ground officers to manage the units and lead the soldiers. I think the Minister was aware of this too. Unfortunately, some of the people in the Mindef hierarchy gave too much attention to the scholars, which did not help to assure the non-scholars.

We wanted to nurture all the brighter people in our talent pool and ensure that it was not only the scholars who would advance more quickly. To do this, the Wrangler scheme was introduced to monitor those we put on the fast track – both scholars and high-potential non-scholars. That mitigated the concern of the "farmers", which was the nickname given to non-scholars by some smart-aleck officers – a nickname which stuck. We also introduced a system of grading all our officers on the Wrangler scheme, scholars and "farmers", on their command and staff potential separately. We did this because we realised that some could be good staff officers but not good commanders, while some could be good commanders but not good staff officers. The ones who had high potential for both command and staff jobs were the ones who could rise very high. That was a good system because it enabled us to fit people into the right jobs. Not all scholars made it to high-level command positions, but they contributed as staff officers.

Over time we refined the scholar system. The scholars played a key role in the development of the SAF. They helped us gain respect for the SAF as professionals and helped us match up against the civilians. Managing the scholars sometimes gave me headaches because the spotlight unfortunately got to some of their heads. Dr Goh told me to watch them closely and read them the riot act if necessary. There was one scholar who refused to take the exam required for promotion from lieutenant to captain because a language test was part of this exam. He said he was a scholar, so he was good enough and did not want to waste his time studying for the language test. I called him up and told him in no uncertain terms that if he did not take the promotion exam, he would be a lieutenant for life, and I did not care if he was a scholar or not. The word got around. Dutifully, he took the exam.

Teo Chee Hean and Peter Ho were sent to the Navy, and they were not too happy at the time. But we needed very good people in the Navy. George Yeo, who was in Signals, went to the Air Force because the Air Force could do with some brainpower in the Air Staff. Over time, we also had scholars becoming fighter pilots. I even approved taking a bespectacled but physically fit scholar into the Commandos. Ng Ee Peng initially met resistance and had a tough time. But he persisted, attended Ranger and Special Forces courses in the US, and was eventually accepted by the commandos. Not surprisingly he was nicknamed the "Smart Commando". That was how we distributed them to make sure that all the Services and arms got an even share of the scholars. And that really elevated the SAF. The SAF would not be what it is today if not for the scholar system. It is of course very important that the non-scholars are not neglected and shunted aside. I was always very aware of that and I was glad Dr Goh understood that.

I openly tell everybody that I am a "farmer". This "farmer" was happy to explain to other "farmers" the reason for bringing scholars into the SAF. I could see the critical importance of drawing in the best brains and the scholarship system was the only way to do this. I said this to the non-scholars many times: "Don't think the scholars are bad for you, because they help to boost the SAF's standing and that is good for all of us." And in time, it became clear that our promotion system did not prejudice against the non-scholars. We had, and continue to have, generals who are non-scholars, who have done even better than some scholars. These included Patrick Choy, Colin Theseira and Chin Chow Yoon, to name a few. So the concern of the non-scholars slowly faded. There will always be "farmers" and scholars in the SAF.

A modern armed forces must have people who have deep knowledge of technology and a broad mindset. In the old German General Staff, the people commanding the forces were nobles but the people planning the battles were General Staff officers who were chosen for their intelligence. This system worked well and the Prussian and German armies were among the most successful in their time. Having studied the German General Staff in some depth, I was easily convinced that the SAF scholar system was good.

Times have changed. Today it is hard to find non-graduates in the SAF officer corps because of our education system. The gap has closed, which is good. But I always say that you need more than just brains to run an armed forces. When you have to go to war, you need people who can command, who can lead, and it does not matter whether they are scholars or not. Notwithstanding technology, in the final analysis, we need the soldier, the boots on the ground. That has always been my guiding principle. While I accept that scholars are important, we must never forget that the important thing is to have properly trained soldiers commanded by people who can lead. I was surprised when I met Zac Xu Peiwen, my grandson's Sergeant-Major in 3rd Guards. He is a regular, a Ranger-trained guardsman with a Bachelor of Science in Information Systems Management with a second major in Strategic Management from Singapore Management University (SMU). I asked my grandson what Zac was doing in the Army, and he said Zac was happy serving as a sergeant-major. He had received a scholarship to go to SMU while he was in service as a sergeant. You have a sergeant-major with a B Sc; it is a different profile now. But especially in the earlier years of the development of the SAF, we needed the extra boost and the scholars provided that.

I always believed that I could be successful only if I was willing to have good people around me, and I could work with them and use them to support me. That was why I had no problem working with the scholars and gave them the runway. I guided them, told them what was needed, accepted their mistakes, and stayed alert for any scholar trying to do one on me. I cultivated that into an art. To me, a good leader is one who can help others who are good to work with, and for, him. That has always been my belief and I always practised that. I may have ideas but there are other people with better ideas. I drew inspiration from Ronald Reagan. He was a Hollywood actor but became a very successful US President because he knew how to get the right people to work with him and for him. I had no problem doing the same thing.

Some years ago, the scholars commemorated a milestone anniversary in the Istana. I did not know about it as I had already retired. PM Lee Hsien Loong was surprised that I was not invited and I subsequently received an invitation. In his speech at the event, PM paid me a compliment when he said that the scholars had Winston Choo to thank for the success of the SAF scholar system because I understood and was patient with them. I felt honoured and gratified when I heard that.

I thought women also had an important role to play in

TOP *Visiting a defence exercise as DGS, 1974.*

BOTTOM *With Dr Goh Keng Swee, Minister for Defence, visiting a combat field hospital deployment, 1975.*

ABOVE *Helping Warren with
chin-ups, Alexandra Park, 1974.*

RIGHT *In our orchid garden
at Alexandra Park with Kate,
Karina and Warren, 1974.*

LEFT *Being piped aboard during a visit to an RSN ship, 1976.*

BELOW *First airborne course, 1976. From left: Capt Ratna (Pilot), Col Edward Yong, LTC Raymond Tan, Col Peter Lim, LTC Jimmy Yap, Col Winston Choo and LTA Ho Soo Jau (instructor).*

LEFT *My canary-yellow Chevrolet Corvair. Leavenworth, Kansas, USA, 1971.*

BELOW *FPDA military chiefs, 1980. From left: General Hashim Mohd Ali (Malaysia), General Richard Vincent (Britain), Lieutenant-General Winston Choo (Singapore), General Peter Gration (Australia) and Lieutenant-General John Mace (New Zealand).*

FAR LEFT *Visiting my sponsors, Don and Mimi Maahs. Leavenworth, Kansas, USA, 1978.*

BOTTOM LEFT *Calling on Israeli PM Yitzhak Rabin, Tel Aviv, Israel. 1977.*

LEFT *With ACGS (Ops) Col Lee Hsien Loong at an SAF Small Arms Competition, 1983.*

BELOW *Observing armour training at Shoalwater Bay, Queensland, Australia. 1984.*

FAR LEFT *Graduation at Duke University, with Kate, Karina and Warren, 1982.*

ABOVE *Congratulating a new officer at a commissioning parade in SAFTI with Minister for Defence Goh Chok Tong, December 1983.*

TOP RIGHT *With Malaysian CDF General Tan Sri Ghazali Seth, who was Guest-of-Honour at the 1 SIR Battalion Anniversary celebration, 1985.*

BOTTOM RIGHT *Meeting Queen Elizabeth II, Singapore, 1985.*

TOP LEFT *Audience with President Suharto of Indonesia, 1986.*

BOTTOM LEFT *Being conferred the Darjah Paduka Keberanian Laila Terbilang by the Sultan of Brunei, 1987.*

BELOW *After the Investiture of the Distinguished Service Order (DSO) to General Benny Moerdani of Indonesia (left), June 1987.*

ABOVE *Leading in the taking of the SAF pledge with service chiefs. SAF Day Parade, 1988.*

TOP *With President Wee Kim Wee, SAF Day Parade, 1988.*

BOTTOM *General Tan Sri Hashim Mohd Ali, Malaysian CDF (centre), visiting the SAF, 1988.*

LEFT *With General Try Sutrisno, Commander, Republic of Indonesia Armed Forces, during his visit to the SAF, 1988.*

ABOVE *Kate congratulating me on my promotion to Lieutenant-General, 30 June 1988.*

LEFT *Warren at his commissioning parade, December, 1989. He received the Sword of Honour.*

the SAF and I tried to promote their status. In the early days, the women belonged to a separate corps. I used to encourage them to have get-togethers to develop their esprit de corps, and I asked them to invite me and the Air Force and Navy chiefs so that we could demonstrate our regard for them. The women could not be in combat roles in those days. I made them weapons trainers, and they were excellent at that. First, they did not get restless and want to move on after a while, unlike the men. The women were also patient and could adapt better to repetitive work. Hence they made very good and effective instructors. Most important of all, their presence had a salutary effect on the trainees. When my son was an officer cadet in 1989, he had a female instructor teaching him how to fire the anti-tank rocket-launcher. When I asked him about the training, his answer was, "Waah, Pa, this sergeant – power! She's so *kilat* (sharp, on the ball) that we're embarrassed when we *kena* (got) whacked for screwing up!" Women can be very assertive.

When we upgraded our AMX-13 tanks and put in a new fire-control system, I went to test it out. I got into the commander's hatch. The instructor was in the gunner's hatch. Then the instructor's voice came through my headset – an unusually high-pitched voice, I thought. When I was ready to fire, I looked down and saw a pair of small, slim hands loading the 75-mm round. I fired off three good shots, got out and asked to speak to the instructor. The instructor came out, took off the helmet, and the hair cascaded down. A female sergeant. It was a complex fire-control system and she took somebody like me, who had never fired the system before, through it systematically and clearly to fire off three rounds and make three hits. She could do it because she was a very efficient instructor. Moreover, it was not easy to load 75-mm rounds in the tank; it required strength and technique. We also deployed women as tank driving instructors.

I always appointed women as my Staff Officers to set an

example, because I wanted to encourage and promote women in the SAF. I insisted that they do parachute jumps because I wanted to show that they were capable of doing things that some people presumed only men could do.

I am glad the SAF is now deploying women in jobs that were closed to them in the past. There are women commanding army combat units such as artillery battalions. Now we have a few female fighter pilots. One of our first female pilots, Koh Chai Hong, was the top trainee in aerobatics in her batch and wanted to go on to fly a fighter. The RSAF said no. She was very upset and wanted to take it all the way up to the Minister. Dr Goh told me to talk to her, so I interviewed her. She was so worked up that if my table had not been that huge old British table, I think she would have reached across and beaten me up. She was so adamant that she wanted to fly a fighter.

I remember asking her, "Chai Hong, can you kill?" She replied that in a fighter, if she pulled the trigger, she would not be able to see who she killed, so she could kill if she had to. I said that she would be flying as a wingman to another pilot and, whatever she might say, it was a man's instinct to protect the woman. So, her partner could be killed, as he would be looking out for her and not do what he should be doing. That set her thinking. Eventually she grudgingly accepted that she could not go to fighters. The Air Force had also told her that her legs were too short to reach the Skyhawk pedals. At that time, the RSAF was not ready to have female fighter pilots. Chai Hong later became a flying instructor, and a very good one too. Just before I retired, I teased her that I would post her to fly the F-16. Her reply: "You didn't want to offer me when I wanted it. Now I am too old."

We sent our women to OCS in SAFTI and they trained alongside the men. I once discussed this with an American general who was impressed that we had female cadets in OCS long before they had women in their West Point Military Academy. I said that credit had to be given to the women themselves. They wanted to be trained just as rigorously as their male counterparts. I used to say that the women were serving in the SAF and doing a man's work, so we should support and recognise them if we thought they were good. I fought for them to be promoted and I hoped to see a woman rise to flag rank. But the Mindef leadership was not ready to accept a female general for a long time. I tried but the answer was always "not yet". It was only in 2015, 40 years after I became CGS and long after I retired, that we had our first female general with the promotion of Gan Siow Huang to brigadier-general. When she was promoted, I said to her, "May I shake your hand? At last I can see my wish come true!" I am so pleased to finally see women in the top ranks of the SAF.

I was also concerned that our women, especially the officers, might find it difficult to get married. I respected the choice of those who preferred to be single. But because of the gender stereotypes in those days, I did not want it said that female SAF officers would surely end up on the shelf. I used to interview our female officers and encourage them to socialise. I also wanted to help them in their grooming. So I brought in Carrie Models, a top modelling agency of that time, to teach the female officer cadets etiquette and posture, how to dress and apply make-up. I was questioned about this, and I said that our female officers should carry themselves like ladies. I even directed that their mess kit be designed to be more elegant and less military-looking. I always believed in the axiom that women are the fairer sex but not the weaker sex. There was good reason to make them fairer, but that would not make them weaker.

I let the women move into the Tanglin Officers' Mess when they expressed interest, and they took up one floor. I said there would be no curfew, and the women and men could visit one another if they wanted to – they were old enough. Dr Goh told me that I was very brave, and my reply was that if anything was going to happen, it would happen even if the women did not stay there. He laughed and said I was right. That turned out to be a good match-making unit as many marriages came out of Tanglin Officers' Mess.

XIX

MAKING FRIENDS

*There was an important need to make friends
beyond our neighbourhood, for both strategic reasons
and practical objectives...*

I WAS ALWAYS keenly aware that it was important for the SAF to develop good relations with foreign counterparts. After all, our early development had been possible only with the help of friends. It was also a priority to have good and friendly relations with our two big neighbours, although it was a historical fact that we had become an independent country under difficult circumstances with those same neighbours. We were also acutely aware of our geographical disadvantages. So, there was an important need to make friends beyond our neighbourhood, for both strategic reasons and practical objectives like securing access to training facilities and to military equipment and knowhow.

We had realised very early on that the limitations of our small territory meant that we would never have adequate training facilities in Singapore. This was one of our biggest challenges – and this would be one of our biggest weaknesses if we could not find solutions. We fostered military cooperation in the form of training and exercises with all our ASEAN partners when the organisation comprised the original five members. The degree of collaboration varied though. It was clear that doing much more with Malaysia, beyond the multi-lateral exercises in the FPDA, was not possible given the circumstances of how we had been thrust into Separation.

We went to Brunei and the Bruneians agreed to our request to conduct jungle training there. As PM Lee Kuan Yew and the Sultan of Brunei had a very good relationship, it was settled at that level. At the working level, my links with the Bruneian officers who had been my juniors at FMC moved the arrangements along more quickly. They were already senior commanders and senior staff officers. I was a colonel and they were lieutenant-colonels by then. Later, we also conducted army and navy exercises with them.

Then we went to expand our training in Thailand beyond the commando training which I started back in 1973. The Thais were very friendly and helpful to us. I think they saw the value of working with us. Over my 18 years as CDF, I dealt with and developed close relationships with many Royal Thai Army chiefs. The Thais subsequently allowed us to use a dedicated training area in Kanchanaburi where we could conduct training for various arms of our Army. This was very generous assistance from them.

Our Air Force went to the Philippines and the Filipinos too were very accommodating, allowing us to train at Clark Air Base. With Indonesia, we held joint exercises. In the early years we never trained there because of political sensitivities. Later, through General Benny Moerdani, the Commander of the Indonesian Armed Forces and eventually the Defence Minister, we managed to jointly construct an air range for the two air forces in Siabu near Pekanbaru in North Sumatra. By then I had a comfortable relationship with the Indonesian military leadership and General Moerdani saw this facility as a mutually beneficial arrangement. I officiated at the opening of this air range jointly with General Try Sutrisno, who was then my Indonesian counterpart.

Taiwan became very important for the SAF's training

from those early days. PM Lee and President Chiang Ching-kuo of Taiwan had a good relationship and the Taiwanese understood our great need for training areas. There was an agreement in principle to make training facilities available to us, and I led a small team there to assess the various sites. We wanted to train as many arms of the Army as possible, so I looked for facilities for armour, artillery and infantry, which all required large training areas. The person whom I worked with and who facilitated our training requirements was the Head of Operations of the Taiwan armed forces, General Hau Pei-tsun. He was much older and more senior in rank to me, and I found him to be fatherly and easy to work with. Our relationship lasted through the years when he was the Chief of the General Staff and later the Premier of Taiwan. The last time I met him was when he came to Singapore to pay his last respects to Mr Lee Kuan Yew. I sent him off at the airport. He was very spritely even though he was 95 years old. I was saddened to learn of his passing in March of 2020 at the age of 100.

On that first visit, we went from the north to the south of the island. The Taiwanese were so generous. They made available all the facilities we needed – barracks for our soldiers, garages and other facilities for our vehicles, and training areas. One of the camps was small and old, but we were happy to take whatever was offered. That camp could not be expanded – so some of their troops left to make room for our troops. I was very surprised to see that another camp offered to us was brand new. They had been planning to move some of their units in there, but General Hau told me that they decided that we should have it. I remember the officer who showed us around said to me, "Sir, new, new, very new." When I went to check out the toilet and bathing facilities, he said, "Sir, modern sanitation." But what I saw in the toilet was a big drain running through, with partitions at regular intervals. He proudly told me that they turned on the tap twice a day and let the water run. They were obviously practical people who built functional and adequate facilities; there was no need for frills. I agreed that it was modern and thanked him. I was really so grateful to them. We did not have many problems reaching agreement on the key issues regarding the use of their facilities, although there were still many details to be resolved.

That was a tremendous experience and exposure to diplomacy for me, especially in learning how to give and take in negotiations. It was also very useful experience in practical operational thinking and working out the whole logistics train. We had to arrange everything, including how to feed our men, and how to ensure that purchases of food and other supplies were properly accounted for. Before the agreement kicked in, we sent a batch of armour trainees there, one objective being to find out possible problems and pitfalls. An interesting and unexpected discovery we made was that when our soldiers were at the airport departing for home, there was a bunch of young girls in tears saying goodbye to them. That was a potential problem! So we decided on controlled R&R (rest and recreation) for our men at the end of the training programme. Even then, there was a limit to what we could do and control. There was another, more positive, discovery – our soldiers had a taste of life in the rural, less developed parts of Taiwan, and that made them appreciate the comforts in Singapore which they had taken for granted. I clearly remember some men among this batch of armour trainees kissing the ground at Changi Air Base when they arrived home on the Charlie-130 aircraft.

People often say, join the navy to see the world. In the case of the SAF, you could also join the army and the air force to see the world. We were training in Brunei, Taiwan, Thailand, Australia, New Zealand, the US. I always made it a point to visit our men in training whenever I could, not only in Singapore but also overseas. Unless you were there on the ground with the men, you would not fully understand their problems. When I went on these visits, I did not only sit down with the officers but often spent time in the training area talking to the soldiers. I enjoyed doing that. It was important for me to have a good sense of the value of the training and how well the training was conducted, so that I would know if we were moving in the right direction. With the RSN, I tried to get them to allow me to sail with them on their ships. I remember once, sometime in the 80s, I went on an LST (landing ship, tank) for, I think, a Starfish exercise with the FPDA navies and I was given a cabin. I opened a locker and found women's clothing inside. I summoned the captain of the ship: "You have women?" "Yes, sir. We have women in the Navy sailing on board our ships and this cabin is for the female officers." It was then that it struck me that we had come a long way and we now had women serving on board our ships. As for the RSAF, I visited their training deployments overseas in Arizona in the US, and in Australia.

So I travelled extensively to visit our training exercises overseas and, importantly, to touch base with the officers and officials in the host countries. It was necessary for us to show that we valued the training opportunities and appreciated the help that they were giving us. We should never take the training opportunities and our relations with the hosts for granted. I was often travelling as much as twice a month and my wife was a "widow" because I was away so often. I brought Kate on official visits only when she was also invited. But that came later after it was established in our system that when I travelled on an official invitation which included my wife, her ticket would be paid for. The first of such visits were to New Zealand and Australia. Later on, we went to the US together.

I sort of stumbled into military diplomacy. In the early days, there was no defence relations policy set-up in Mindef. The Minister himself dealt with this and he set the directions.

When Dr Goh Keng Swee told me to go overseas and meet counterparts and make friends, I followed his orders. In those days, it was go, go, go and make friends. We had deliberate plans for developing some of the relationships, but many evolved naturally over time.

The military had a very important role in the government and politics of countries in our region and it was useful for the SAF to develop good relations with them at the level of the armed forces. In Indonesia, Thailand and the Philippines, the military was politically powerful. In Malaysia, the armed forces did not have the same political clout, but the military-to-military relationship was an important and useful channel for us. This was especially beneficial when my counterpart had the ear of the political leadership.

My first official visit overseas as DGS was to the Philippines. The Armed Forces of the Philippines (AFP) invited me and gave me my first overseas award, The Legion of Honour (Degree of Commander). That was when I first met General Fidel "Eddie" Ramos, who was then Chief of the Philippine Constabulary. He later became Chief of Staff of the AFP, and 18 years later in 1992, he was elected President of the Philippines. My counterpart then was General Romeo Espino, a very nice gentleman. He had a serious case of asthma but was still a keen golfer. When we played golf, he was accompanied by an aide lugging an oxygen tank. The AFP looked after me extremely well. On that first official overseas trip, I learnt how to conduct myself – be friendly but not too forward, and don't say too much or appear overly enthusiastic.

My second overseas trip was to South Korea, where I was invited for their Armed Forces Day parade and celebrations. They were still under martial law then. That trip was memorable in another way. I travelled alone and flew there via Hong Kong on Cathay Pacific, as there were no direct SIA flights then. I had put on my uniform during the flight so that I would arrive properly attired. When the plane landed in Seoul, there was an announcement for all the passengers to stay seated. A colonel came on board. I was seated in economy class, right at the back. He saw me in my uniform, came up to me and said, "Colonel Choo, come with me." All the passengers must have been wondering, "Who is this fellow?" I reached the door of the plane and there, on the tarmac, was a Guard-of-Honour! All the passengers were still stuck in the plane. I was mortified. At that time, we did not have an embassy in Seoul. The self-appointed "Singapore representative" was the SIA Manager Eddie Ong, who was just about to set up office there. Eddie said to me, "Aiyah, Colonel, you make us very *malu* (ashamed). Why did you fly economy?"

That visit to South Korea was another eye-opener for me. I saw that with martial law, the military was indeed powerful. My hosts put me in a car escorted by a jeep in front and another behind. Then I witnessed something that shocked me. A car overtook our convoy and the jeep came up from behind and stopped the car. One of the soldiers pulled out the driver and slapped him. I was aghast. The military parade was huge and very impressive, but I knew that it was something that we would never need to build up to. For my return flight, Eddie Ong bought me a first class ticket. He insisted. It was the first time in my life travelling first class. When I came back, I related this to Dr Goh. He laughed so hard; I had never seen him laugh so loudly. He called the finance officer and told him to reimburse SIA for my ticket. And he put out a note that "From now on, DGS will travel first class."

Subsequently, I always travelled with a small delegation, right up to the time I retired. These trips were not only for my official business but also for the exposure of SAF officers and their development. I also used the opportunity to assess them. That was one reason why some officers avoided travelling with me. The other reason was that I jogged every morning and they had to wake up at 5 am to run with me, sometimes after a night of heavy eating and drinking.

On a trip to Israel, a Captain Lee Hsien Loong was one of the officers who accompanied me. We were there to see the Israeli Air Force's command and control system. We transited in Athens, arriving there at 7 am. As the connecting flight was not until about 4.30 pm or 5 pm, the SIA Manager in Athens offered to drive us in his new Audi to visit Corinth. On the way back, the brand new car broke down – and we had a flight to catch! There was a help phone on the roadside, but no one could speak Greek. After what seemed like a very long time, we managed to get some help and made it to our connecting flight in the nick of time. I learnt a lesson – never take side trips when you are on an important mission. When I accompanied PM Lee Hsien Loong to Israel in 2016, he said in a speech that he was glad to be there because the last time he was in Israel was about 40 years ago when he accompanied me – "the Chief of the General Staff then, who is now my Ambassador to Israel."

Moving beyond the Southeast Asian countries, we started working on building deeper relations with Australia and New Zealand. They had been part of the Commonwealth forces stationed in Singapore before Independence and continued to have air force components and troops based in Singapore as part of their contribution to the FPDA. The Australians and New Zealanders participated actively in the FPDA and were important to us. We were also looking at them as possible partners for training. Once, I was away for almost two weeks on a combined visit to the two countries. My Australian host, General Peter Gration, provided an aircraft and flew with me all over Australia. It gave me an opportunity to see various possibilities for training areas in Queensland and other Australian states. General Gration and I maintained a close relationship and he was most helpful when I went to Canberra as Singapore's High Commissioner after my retirement from the SAF. The New Zealanders also provided an aircraft and brought me from North Island to South Island. I built a pretty good rapport with the New Zealanders and Australians, and continued to visit them and maintain contact.

I realised that we had to go even further. At that time the Americans, especially from the Pacific Command (PACOM), were interested in engaging us. We had visits from the Commander-in-Chief of the Pacific Command (CINCPAC) and their component commanders from the Pacific Navy, especially the Seventh Fleet, the Pacific Air Forces (PACAF) and Pacific Army (then called the US Army Western Command). We had an army-to-army exercise in alternate years, mostly at command post level without troops. The army reserve units in Hawaii were involved and that allowed us to also involve our reserve officers. Gradually, we had exercises with all three services of PACOM. Our more valuable interactions were with the Seventh Fleet and PACAF because they were of great help to our Navy and Air Force. For instance, our A-4 Skyhawks were originally carrier-based aircraft, so the naval logistics support for our Skyhawks was very important. With the Pacific connection, we were able to achieve quite a lot because of their assistance, such as getting additional courses for our people. It was like building an old boys' network; I could pick up the phone and call some of the top people. This became very useful for us to get training, and various kinds of assistance and support.

Our relations with PACOM, headquartered in Hawaii, helped to build up the relationship between the SAF and the US military. The people in Washington DC were too far away and hardly visited Singapore. I developed a very good relationship with Admiral William Crowe when he was CINCPAC. I first met him in Washington when he was Director of East Asia and Pacific Region in the Office of the Secretary of Defense and played a key role in the programme to brief us on their Vietnam War experiences. He eventually became Chairman of the Joint Chiefs of Staff. He held this apex post in the US armed forces when I made my second official visit to the US in 1988. He told me his staff had looked through all the rules and regulations and they had no other award for a foreigner except The Legion of Merit (Degree of Commander), which I had received during my first official visit in 1978, so he was giving me that same award a second time. I was told that it was rare that a foreign officer was given this award twice.

One visit I made to Turkey was quite unexpected. I jumped at the invitation when it came as it was an opportunity to expand our network of friendly countries. That visit to Turkey was enlightening. The Turks had one of the largest armed forces in their region. When the Commanding General showed me the map of Turkey, I realised they needed such a large force because they had borders with eight countries, and not all their neighbours were necessarily friendly. Another informative trip was to Kuwait and Saudi Arabia after the end of the first Gulf War. It was an opportunity to engage Arab countries in the Middle East. My team and I saw the burning oilfields and remnants of the withdrawing Iraqi army from Kuwait all the way to Iraq. It was a display of the value of a United Nations-sponsored alliance and what a mighty force led by the US could do.

Another significant visit was to India. Up to that point we had very little contact with the Indian Army but they invited me. Accompanied by my wife, I led a delegation of some 10 officers there. We spent almost 10 days travelling all over India visiting army bases and units and saw first-hand how professional and combat-experienced they were. During this visit I had the opportunity to renew my relationship with the legendary Field Marshal Sam Manekshaw, famed for delivering India one of its most remarkable victories over Pakistan in 1971. I had been invited to give a dinner address to the Defence Services Staff College in Wellington, Tamil Nadu, where he lived. Sam had invited me to his home and was happily chatting with me, which resulted in the students and instructors at the staff college having to wait an hour for me. Sam had insisted that "the boys" could wait.

It impressed me greatly to see how the Indian Army was so steeped in military tradition. This had been partly inspired by the British Army in the days of the Raj and evolved over the years. It helped explain the high degree of professionalism in the Indian Army and how it had remained so strongly apolitical. That visit led to a return visit by Indian senior officers, which in turn led to more exchanges and training opportunities with the Indian Armed Forces. Today the SAF is training in India.

By taking every shot at making friends and reaching out to more and more friendly countries and armed forces, we have extended the range of training opportunities for the SAF and surmounted land-scarce Singapore's limitation in military training areas. It was no wonder that making friends and visiting friendly armed forces was always a key secondary role for me.

XX

BUILDING TIES

We may not be born diplomats, but we learn to be good at diplomacy. The line I always took was: "I am not a diplomat; I am a soldier. If I make mistakes, forgive me."

WE KNEW that we needed a credible armed forces for effective deterrence should anyone have any notions that our little red dot would be easy meat. But we also consciously invested great effort to make friends both near and far. That combination of deterrence and diplomacy was the best way to enhance Singapore's security and ensure our survival.

After travelling to and engaging many countries, I realised that we did not have anything going with Malaysia. Although I had friends from FMC, they were not senior enough at that time, being mostly colonels. But that changed later, as many of them rose to senior positions in the MAF, including Ismail Omar, who became CDF, but only after I had retired from the SAF. We needed to find some activity which was non-threatening and comfortable for both sides to engage in. As golf was a popular sport played by both SAF and MAF officers, we thought that a golf exchange would be good for breaking the ice and bringing both sides together in friendly exchanges. Dr Goh Keng Swee thought it was a good idea and supported it. In retrospect I realised why, when I was appointed DGS, Dr Goh had ordered me to learn to play golf when he found out that I was not a golfer.

It started as an event between the two defence ministries, and not SAF-MAF per se. It was a mix of Mindef civilians and SAF officers with their Malaysian counterparts. The Malaysians were comfortable with that. The golf convenor for the Malaysian side when we started the exchange was Brigadier-General Hashim Mohd Ali, who later became CDF. I was the main convenor for Singapore. I had the good fortune to work with him to get the games going and, through golf, the two of us developed a very strong relationship and became lasting friends. I realised that he too shared the desire to develop this bond between our officers. The annual games alternated between Singapore and Malaysia. We tried to make the golf game not too competitive. I told our golfers to be friendly and not take it too seriously. But if the Malaysians wanted to bet, we would have to bet. It was not too hard for our golfers as they were so used to wagering over a golf game. In the early years, some of our golfers asked me, "So how? Do we win or lose this year?" I said we should just play our best and see what happened. Over time we became comfortable and were not hung up about beating each other at golf. I said that we should leave diplomacy to the lunches and dinners.

We went to golf clubs all over Malaysia, while in Singapore we played at different courses. We always started with a dinner the night before and there would be two golf games, lunches and another dinner over two days. That provided the opportunities to mix and socialise. Both sides found this to be a good model. As not all were golfers, we included badminton and table tennis in the annual games so that more officers could participate. I could see that these games were working and achieving the aim of allowing officers from both sides to get to know one another and develop a cordial relationship. People became less suspicious of one another and were less guarded.

We used the same golf model with Indonesia. But the

exchange became a bit more elaborate. They had music and singing on top of the games and meals. Unfortunately, we were very bad at singing. The Indonesians could all go on stage to sing, effortlessly and very well, whereas I had to "arrow" our people, designating the singers. I thought it odd that our officers could not sing whereas the Taiwanese could. So it could not be that we did not have "singing genes" unlike our Indonesian friends. Then I realised that the difference could be this thing called karaoke. We found out that in Taiwan they had a karaoke machine in all their units, so perhaps this was how they learnt to sing so well. So I bought 40 karaoke machines from Taiwan and gave one to every camp. Then our people became less self-conscious and a little better at singing. Otherwise, it was always the same people singing for the SAF at these functions.

When I saw that golf was a good catalyst for developing relationships between our officers and the Malaysians and Indonesians, and enabled us to better understand and be comfortable with one another, I suggested to my Thai counterpart that we adopt this model, and he gladly agreed. But the Thais came with a much larger delegation, normally 50 officers, so we had to increase the budget to host them. We also started a golf exchange with Brunei but that was on a smaller scale.

At one point in the early days, there was some talk about whether there was a need to build some kind of defence pact among the five original ASEAN members. But there was already the FPDA, which involved Malaysia and Singapore, while Thailand and the Philippines were members of the US-led military alliance, the Southeast Asia Treaty Organisation (SEATO). The Indonesians were not keen at all; they had always thought that the FPDA was directed at them as the threat. I promoted the idea of joint training and joint exercises. I said that we should consider that rather than a pact, and this was better accepted. At that point, the SAF was already having training and exercises in Malaysia, Thailand, Brunei,

Philippines and Indonesia. Malaysia used to say that they had a common border with every ASEAN country, which is true. I said that Singapore also had a common thing, which was that we trained and exercised in every ASEAN country. That helped the process. People were comfortable with the concept of a network of training exercises. ASEAN military heads were meeting to talk about training and exercises, and not about a defence pact or anything like that.

I established strong personal relationships with many military leaders among our ASEAN partners. The key relationships were with General Hashim Mohd Ali in Malaysia, and General Benny Moerdani and later General Try Sutrisno in Indonesia. With Thailand, the people at the top of the Royal Thai Armed Forces and Royal Thai Army changed quite rapidly but I was fortunate to develop good relationships with many of them, including General Kriangsak Chomanan, General Prem Tinsulanonda and General Chavalit Yongchaiyudh, all of whom became Prime Ministers later. And in Brunei, General Mohammad Daud, General Sulaiman Damit and General Ibnu Apong – my juniors in FMC – had risen to the top of the Royal Brunei Armed Forces and defence establishment. With the Philippines I had always made an effort to reach out and maintain a warm personal friendship with military leaders like General Renato de Villa and General Fidel "Eddie" Ramos.

Our political leaders encouraged the development of these relationships. PM Lee Kuan Yew and Dr Goh Keng Swee felt that we could make use of these relationships if any issues arose between Singapore and these countries. The defence channel could be a useful, even important, channel between two countries when dialogue was difficult at the political level. So, from time to time, I had to arrange special meetings with my Malaysian and Indonesian counterparts to discuss specific issues. With Thailand and Brunei, there was no such need as our political relations were generally warm and smooth and we did not face sticky issues.

One notable issue that arose between us and our immediate neighbours was the visit of Israeli President Chaim Herzog to Singapore in 1986. There was an outcry from Malaysian politicians, including threats to cut off the water supply to Singapore. There were also strong reactions in Indonesia, but not to the same degree as Malaysia. I was sent to speak to my counterparts in Kuala Lumpur and Jakarta with the message that while the politicians spewed their rhetoric, the military should stay out of the fray and not upset the status quo. We had to keep our cool. From time to time, other sensitive issues cropped up between us. A few times, the Thais very kindly offered to host my Malaysian and Indonesian counterparts and me in Bangkok, providing us a venue so that we did not have to meet in Kuala Lumpur or Jakarta. We went there to have dinner and play golf. This was ostensibly a social gathering, but it had an important agenda. This was a very valuable channel as we were comfortable and had the confidence to speak freely in private. When I came back from my meetings with the Malaysians and Indonesians, I would be debriefed by the Minister and sometimes by the PM himself. Once PM Lee told me, "You should have said this." He was badgering me; I was frustrated and blurted out, "PM, if I can think like that, I would be PM." He looked at me and laughed.

I told my ASEAN friends, from Malaysia, Indonesia and Thailand, that we should meet without any agenda, because we should not be meeting only when we had problems. They agreed and we took turns to host. We would let our hair down, talk about wine, women and song, and not talk about problems. Those informal meetings became institutionalised and we were joined by other ASEAN military chiefs. We would always find occasions to meet, such as the Thai King's Birthday celebrations, Malaysian Armed Forces Day, Indonesian National Day or the Air Show in Singapore.

General Benny Moerdani, who was then very powerful

under President Soeharto, came to give a talk to the Temasek Society in the late 1980s. This is an SAF forum for our officers and civilians to discuss strategic and professional military issues. General Moerdani told his SAF audience that between dealing with an enemy threatening Singapore and one threatening Merauke, which is in Indonesia's easternmost Papua province, they would move their armed forces into Singapore. They would react if things were not right in Singapore because Singapore was closer to Jakarta. The message was clear: the Indonesian armed forces would move into Singapore if they thought there was a need, whatever they might construe that need to be. I stood up and said, "We appreciate what you said, Pak Benny. But you will come only at our invitation." Benny smiled.

President Soeharto had given the same veiled threat when I called on him. He gave me a long lecture and the phrase that struck me was "*kurung dan bunuh musoh-nya di-dalam kandang*" – confine and kill the enemy in the cage. I had asked for interpretation although I understood everything he said. He meant that they could move into Singapore to contain any perceived threat to Indonesia.

The Indonesian mindset really struck me. I told the SAF, "Don't think that things are all hunky-dory." It was good that they felt comfortable enough to reveal their real thinking, because that allowed us to have a good fix on them. It was the same with General Hashim who used to lecture me, expressing very strong views. With him being Malaysian Prime Minister Dr Mahathir Mohamad's brother-in-law, I took what he said even more seriously. I also found that I could be very candid with him. We have, to this day, a special and close personal friendship which I value greatly. We have been meeting well beyond our retirement. Similarly, I greatly value the special personal relationships I have developed with every one of my ASEAN counterparts and treasure every opportunity to meet even in our golden years. Some of them made an effort to visit me when I was unwell, which I truly appreciate.

I would not say that I am a born diplomat. But over the years, with more exposure, experience and practice, I learnt how to relate to people from all over the world. In the beginning, I was the youngest among all my counterparts, so I was sensitive to that and always willingly played the role of a humble younger brother. That way, I did not come across as offensive or a threat. I found this approach to be a good one and I honed it as I went along. In Southeast Asia especially, being perceived as modest and humble can take you a long way. It came easily to me; I just had to be myself. You can be humble and still stand your ground and speak up when you must. I had no qualms conversing in a mix of English, Malay, and Indonesian – *bahasa campur* (mixed language) – if it helped to get the conversation going. The thing was to reach out and make people feel at ease with you and in that way build a high level of confidence and comfort. Thereafter, things become easy. I must have done something right as I have received decorations and awards from all the original ASEAN members.

I always considered my role in nurturing defence relations to be one of my key functions because I believed that the role of the military is not only to prepare for war but also to keep the peace. And one way to contribute to keeping the peace is to build strong ties with other armed forces. To me, the military leadership has a duty to develop such relationships. We may not be born diplomats, but we learn to be good at diplomacy. The line I always took was: "I am not a diplomat; I am a soldier. If I make mistakes, forgive me."

XXI

VALUE YOUR PEOPLE

*If you want your men to serve you well,
to follow you in peace as well as into battle, you
must value them and look after them well.*

AN EXCELLENT armed forces must have, above all else, excellent leadership. The most basic quality of a good military leader is a sense of purpose and duty. He must transcend self-interest and serve the higher purpose of the military, which is to defend our country and secure our sovereignty. A military leader's purpose and duty must be the cornerstone of his military life. That was my guiding principle once I decided to be a soldier: the military was now my life, and this was my duty. Professional competence and proficiency are also fundamental if you want to be a good leader. You must know your job. That is why I always worked hard to learn all that I needed to be a good soldier, starting as a cadet and then in all my training courses. I made sure that I absorbed the professional knowledge that was needed for me to stay on top of my responsibilities and gain the respect of those I led. But these qualities – a strong sense of duty and professionalism – are only basic requirements.

The most important quality of a military leader is the ability to get people to follow him, in peacetime and into battle. Whether he can command men to face great odds – and even the possibility of death – will determine whether he succeeds in a mission, whether he wins or loses a battle. And if you want your men to serve you well, to follow you in peace as well as into battle, you must value them and look after them well. That was the code I lived by.

People debate about whether the men or the technology is more important. I have always said that technology gives you the value-add that makes your forces more effective. It can offset our disadvantage in numbers. But ultimately, it is the soldiers, the sailors, the airmen who win or lose the battle. If you do not have competent and committed soldiers, all the technology in the world will not help you. In a battle, technology can help to bring you there and keep you there, but victory or defeat still requires capable and motivated fighters. And they can be so only if they are well trained and well led.

A good leader must have a genuine concern, even love, for his people. I always looked at the individual as valuable and treated him with respect. When the SAF started, Singaporeans were generally far less educated than the present generation. We had the Hokkien *peng* (literally a Hokkien soldier, referring to one who was not well educated). We had to use a mixture of English, Hokkien and Malay to communicate with them. It was important to get through to them and not look down on them being poorly educated or even uneducated. I found that once you got through to them and handled them right, and they respected and trusted you, they were excellent soldiers. Respect and trust could not be demanded by a commander but had to be earned – which was possible only if he respected and showed trust in them in the first place.

I used to remind my officers that they were leaders only because of their men. If they had no men, what were they a leader of? They had to have a deep and genuine care for their men's welfare – this was all important. It was not just big things but also small things, like finding out more about them and their families. You had to engage them because only then could you know if they had problems and help them where you could. But while it is good for your men to be comfortable in your presence, they should not become overly familiar. There must be proper respect for authority, and saluting and salutations are essential. Respect for authority coupled with able leadership are the necessary ingredients for maintaining command and control in the heat of combat.

I insisted that my officers made sure that their soldiers were properly kitted with uniforms and equipment. Now, on enlistment they get one big duffel bag, called an Alibaba bag, with everything inside. In those days you had to go to the quartermaster store and draw one item at a time. I used to stand there and make sure that my soldiers had everything they needed. That's a basic thing – you make sure your men have every item they are supposed to get. Even though these days everything is in the kit bag, the commander can still show his care. And even though food is now catered, it does not mean that you cannot make that extra effort to ensure that your men are eating well. As a cadet, I had been served in the cadet dining room, and as a young officer in 1 SIR the food I ate was different from the food the men ate – and I thought that was not right. After 1965, the food for the officers and men came from the same serving point in the cookhouse, but they sat at different tables.

As a CO going for my meal in the cookhouse, I would first walk around to make sure that the men were eating properly before I sat down to eat. It was the same thing out in the field. I did not eat until I had made sure that my men were eating and the food was all right.

When I visited units in training, I would first observe the behaviour of the CO and officers. I would be very upset if I saw them eating before their men. To me, the commander's concern for his men's welfare was key. So, it was not just to see how they trained but also to see how leadership was expressed through concern for the men's well-being. In defence exercises for instance, the hardest part was digging trenches. I expected commanders to dig alongside their men when they were not busy with their other duties.

It was very important for me to engage my men and show that I respected them and that every one of them mattered. Soldiers, like anyone else, want to know that they are valued and not regarded as a mere digit in the bigger scheme of things. With this in mind, I always had an open-door policy from the time I was a CO. I allowed my soldiers to come directly to me if they had a problem. As CDF, I did not discourage soldiers from coming right up to me at Mindef. But I always made sure that I did not disrupt the chain of command. I listened to the soldier's problem and then I told him that I would speak to his CO, who would get back to him. Then I called up the CO to tell him that his soldier had seen me about such-and-such a problem, and he should sort it out. This served two purposes: the man knew that he had been heard, and the CO knew that someone at the top could hear about what was happening in his unit. I also had my informal channels. For instance, my staff car drivers were one of the best sources of information. Some people did not agree with my open-door policy, but I believed that it was the right thing to do.

One day, I walked into my office and there was a very pretty girl in my waiting room. When I asked my Personal Assistant who that girl was, her reply was, "That's not a girl." He was an NSman, a telephone operator at Changi Air Base. He had been beaten up and he took advantage of my open-door policy to see me. I asked him to come in; frankly, I was curious. He said the commandos had beaten him up and the reason was that "I like them, Sir, because they are so strong. I try to talk to them, but they get very upset." I told him, "Don't approach them. You are only asking for trouble." The commandos were based in the vicinity of Changi Air Base. So, I instructed the base to keep him safe and have him posted out, away from the "strong" and tempting commandos. I knew that we had to adjust the way we trained and disciplined soldiers as the profile of the NSmen changed. My leadership style had to be dynamic and evolve as my soldiers evolved. That's why when old soldiers grumble to me that we used to be very tough in our training and discipline and now we are treating our men like kindergarten children, I would point out that our soldiers now are unlike our soldiers in the past. Their family and education backgrounds are different because of Singapore's development. In the early days of the SAF, we just followed the old British style of leadership and training. That approach was to first break the men in because many came from the farms and villages and were not well educated. They were treated roughly and made to do things that they did not like to do. The aim was to make the men obey orders without question, so that when they were ordered to charge up the hill to face the enemy – which went against people's natural instincts – they would do so without question. That was the unthinking soldier approach; drill them to follow orders unquestioningly. There were elements of this approach even when I was a cadet, such as the ragging system which was aimed at wearing us down to make us conform.

To me, a good leader can see change and see the need to adjust accordingly. The unquestioning do-or-die approach worked only when the soldiers were rough and tough, uneducated and uncomplaining. And only if society at large accepted that what the Army was doing was right and for the best. As our country developed, we needed to move on from thinking that our soldiers can understand only the language of the fist. They are much better educated these days and more exposed to the world at large. Almost all our soldiers now have qualifications beyond secondary school. They will not react well to harsh and unfair treatment. And, more and more, I see parents taking a keen interest in their sons' National Service, which is a good thing. So over time, we had to tone down the traditional emphasis on spit-and-polish and harsh discipline, and build cohesion, resilience and obedience in our soldiers through other means.

The foundation for this must be excellence in training, with competent officers leading their units by example. I expected officers to handle their men firmly but with respect. They could be more informal and relaxed without being overly familiar. To me, the way to bring out the best in our soldiers was not to adopt an attitude of "I am the leader and you are the subordinate and therefore you do as I say". A good leader should be receptive to questions and suggestions from his subordinates and must be able to provide satisfactory answers and solutions to problems. Of course, there is a time and place for this – definitely not just before we mount an attack! And if I could not provide an answer or solution immediately, I would try to do so when possible and when the situation permitted. I thought that the men we led deserved this. And that the Army would benefit from this. If our soldiers could understand the bigger picture and their own role, they would accept orders better and carry them out intelligently. Led in this way, our soldiers would be even more valuable assets. This would hold true too for relationships between senior and junior officers.

The SAF called this People-Oriented Management for want of a better term. It has always been very clear to me that a military leader is not a manager. The difference between leading and managing is that you lead people and you manage resources. And though we said "people-oriented", this was not a liberal approach where discipline was relaxed and training and work standards were compromised. People-Oriented Management was a philosophy of command that placed the soldier as the most important asset in the SAF and deserving of his commander's genuine care and concern. The way for a commander to express this was not by being nice to his soldiers but rather to inculcate in them good discipline and equip them with the skills to fight well and survive in combat while treating them with respect. Discipline was fundamental, and if there was a breakdown in discipline in one's command then it was a failure of leadership.

It is not incompatible to care about the soldiers' welfare and also be demanding in discipline and training. I did not compromise. A good leader must never compromise. He has to be firm and demand high standards in training and discipline. That to me is welfare, because if your men are not properly trained and they have to go to battle, then you would be exposing them to unnecessary danger. As the saying goes, the more you sweat in peace the less you bleed in war. Soldiers who break rules have to be punished. I did not compromise discipline to show that I was caring, because I think that the best way to be caring is to enforce discipline.

Sometimes I had to make tough decisions. There was a very good commando who just could not stay out of trouble. When a discipline problem was brought to my attention, I supported his unit's decision to demote him from sergeant to corporal to lance-corporal. When he improved, he was promoted back to sergeant. Then he was demoted again because he got into trouble again. He was aware that I was fully briefed on his case as I made it a point to talk to him whenever I visited the Commandos. Even after we both retired, and to this day, he sends me good wishes every Christmas and New Year. I had to make similarly tough decisions with officers too. For instance, if there was mass food poisoning in a camp, the CO was automatically removed. It was a tough decision if he was not directly liable. Still, he had to bear responsibility for such a serious problem. That way, you sent a clear message to other COs that they had to attach the highest priority to food safety for their men.

One very tough decision I had to make involved a lieutenant-colonel who was a long-time friend; we had been together in 1 SIR when we were both lieutenants. He was a good CO but he had a stubborn streak. He was due to go overseas for training and his passport had expired. But he refused to pay $15 to renew it, on the grounds that if the Army wanted to send him overseas, the Army should pay for the passport renewal. I called him up and I explained to him that a passport was a personal document which he could use for his personal travels as well. He said that on principle, he would not pay for the renewal. I told him that on principle he had to, and I gave him $15 to renew his passport. "No, I don't want your money, Sir!" he said. So I told him that I was giving him an order, and if he did not get his passport renewed, I would have to punish him. He refused, so I had him removed from the SAF. We remained good friends even after that. He said to me, "You had to do what you had to do, and I had to stand my ground." I once had a colonel demoted to his substantive rank of lieutenant-colonel for making a serious mistake in the National Day Parade, even though he had been my senior.

A good leader must be willing to make hard choices. In the passport case, my heart ached because he was a good friend. But if I had let him off, I would not be able to stand my ground to discipline other people and the whole disciplinary system in the SAF would break down. This is where leadership comes in. On one hand, you must make sure you look after and value the individual, because the men are the backbone of the whole system. At the same time, you must be firm and demanding to maintain the integrity of the unit and the SAF. I used to accept invitations to attend get-togethers of the NCOs who came from the SAF Boys' School, even long after I retired from the military. At one of the gatherings, two of them came to me and told me that I had been a tough commander and they were afraid of me. I said I never expected to be feared. They elaborated that they were afraid of me but they respected me, adding that "We need commanders who are like you." That was good to hear, but I was taken aback to be told that I was feared. That was not what I aimed for in my leadership style. A few retired warrant officers at the gathering, on overhearing the exchange, explained that it did not mean that they were frightened of me but that I commanded respect. If that was so, then it was not bad.

While the emphasis was always on good performance in work and training, I also insisted on good turnout and bearing. This was not only for form but also because it helped ingrain self-discipline. In my view, sloppiness in dressing and carriage would be reflected in sloppiness in work performance. Moreover, sloppy soldiers degraded the SAF's image and standing. The negative impression they left by displaying poor discipline would negate the big effort that we had put in to strengthen the SAF's image and standing as a professional and combat-effective armed forces and a credible deterrent force.

I always thought it unfortunate that our people did not attach enough importance to the image our soldiers projected, unlike some of our regional counterparts who try to project machoness. When we mounted a Guard-of-Honour for foreign dignitaries at the Istana, I used to make sure that our soldiers were tall and not bespectacled. But I guess it is a losing battle; when you have limited manpower, you can't be picky. I had asked that the peak cap be designed so that our soldiers would stand erect with chin raised; the peak came down at an angle that forced the soldier to raise his head, otherwise he could not see where he was going. That was the design of the peak cap I wore as a cadet. First impressions are important. I was always very particular about projecting the right image for the SAF. Once a senior officer turned up at an embassy function in mess kit without his cummerbund. I told him that he should go home and put it on. He had not even realised that his cummerbund was missing! So he went home, put it on and came back. Some people said I was too extreme. But I was not satisfying my own quirks. This was about protecting the profile and stature of the SAF.

XXII

WALK WITH YOUR MEN

*I wanted a deeper understanding of what my men
went through by having my own direct experience....
All this was important to be a true military leader.*

I STRONGLY BELIEVE in leadership by example. If an officer wants the respect and trust of his men, he has to lead by example to gain this respect and trust. This is particularly important in the SAF because, even from our earliest days, our officers are not much older than the men they command. They may be better educated and may have attended a few more military courses, but no soldier would accept their leadership for those reasons alone. An officer must walk with his men, train with his men, and share the risks and discomforts of military life with his men. At the most basic level, an officer has to demonstrate professional competence and physical fitness because this is what we demand of everyone in the SAF. Those who lead have to demonstrate these qualities to an equal, if not higher, degree than their men. Otherwise, they have no moral authority to expect their men to respect and trust them and follow them into battle.

I expected high standards from my officers because only then could they demand high standards of their men and be respected. In field training, I expected my officers to wear their helmets, carry their rifles, camouflage themselves, move tactically and take cover – just like their men. I did not think much of officers who behaved as if they were invisible to the enemy and invincible. I had witnessed some of my British commanders dressed comfortably while their men were in combat battle order, not bothering to wear helmets and carry rifles, and I thought that was wrong. When the men went on endurance marches, when they carried full-pack loads, I expected their officers to do no less. I expected officers to do PT (physical exercises) together with their men, take the same tests and pass the IPPT (Individual Physical Proficiency Test), no matter what their ranks and appointments were. In personal discipline, I expected officers to observe the same standards that they required of their men. Only then could the officers hold their heads high and demand high standards from their men. Otherwise, the men would see through them.

The bond between officer and soldier is a human one which does not come automatically by rank but must be forged. This bond, just like the bond between comrades in arms, must be deep and strong if our soldiers, sailors and airmen are to risk their lives for one another. The process of bonding people together in this way is as much an emotional as a rational one. It is the outcome of soldiers living and working together, going through hardships and danger together. The means of achieving this may have modified over time, but one basis for developing tightly knit units which will never change is leadership by example.

I lived by this doctrine. This influenced my decision to take the parachute course when we launched the course in the SAF. Parachuting may no longer be a favoured manoeuvre in modern warfare, but it remains a very useful means of training soldiers to overcome fear. It is especially necessary for a military leader to go through this. No rational person will jump out of a perfectly working aircraft. But in the army, if he has to, he will put on a parachute and he will jump, notwithstanding his fear. I did not entirely lose the fear when I jumped, right up to my twelfth and last jump. Clarence Tan (the first Chief Commando Officer), who had done over 2,000 jumps, told me that even on his last jump, the fear was not entirely gone. I wanted to set the example by demonstrating the importance of being able to overcome your fear, to promote that ethos. The parachute wings is a badge of honour. Your soldiers will think: "This fellow is okay." If you want to command respect and lead, you have to project that. That was why I always considered an officer favourably for command if he had jumped and qualified for the parachute wings. In those days you needed 12 jumps to qualify.

It was 1974 and I was CGS when we started the parachute school. When the Minister and Permanent Secretary heard that I was joining the course, they both told me I was mad. I explained to Dr Goh Keng Swee what I saw as the benefits – I wanted to set an example, and also to try out the training system in the parachute school. He understood. I was one of the six colonels and lieutenant-colonels who took that first course. We were the only trainees. We insisted that our ranks did not matter; we were trainees and we should be treated as such. The course commander, Ho Soo Jau, was an excellent commando lieutenant assisted by a New Zealand instructor as consultant, and the other instructors were commandos who had been trained in the US. Our commando instructors were outstanding and very professional. I still meet some of them.

That being the first parachute course, we were the guinea pigs. It was physically and mentally tough, more so because we were doing our regular jobs at the same time that we attended the three-week course. During the two-week ground training phase, we started with a run at 6 am and carried on traning until 1 pm, after which we went back to our respective duties. We did quick repetitions for the many drills; there was hardly any time to catch our breath. As there were only six of us, the cycle repeated very quickly. During the morning runs, people were wheezing, and sometimes someone would go to the drain and throw up. The ground training was very hard, repetitively launching from raised platforms and hitting the ground. It was especially painful if you did not land properly. I lost more than four kilograms in the first three days, mostly from perspiring so much. For the jump phase, we started at 1 pm and continued into the night for night jumps. Standing at the door of the plane, watching the red light go off and the green light come on to signal you to jump out – that always set off an adrenaline rush.

The plane took off from Sembawang Air Base and did a circuit, flying over Choa Chu Kang cemetery. It was bad enough standing at the aircraft door. Looking down at the cemetery made me feel worse. I was always the first jumper. When I asked the instructor why, his answer was, "Because you are the heaviest." It was actually not true because there was someone else bigger and heavier than me. The tough training brought out the best in people. A good example was Lui Pao Chuen. He was not a combat-trained soldier and he was less fit, so he suffered. But he had so much tenacity and I really admired him and took my hat off to him. He went through the training successfully and proudly wore the parachute badge.

My first jump was a "night" jump because I closed my eyes when I exited the plane. But the first jump was not the most frightening because you did not know enough to be very frightened. The subsequent jumps were more frightening because then you knew what was coming. I tried to break the tension when I collected my parachute by asking the rigger: "Corporal Seetoh, are you sure the parachute is okay?" Her reply was: "Sure, Sir. If it's not okay, if it doesn't open, come back and complain."

You had to be very focused before you jumped. The fear would creep in and you had to overcome it. More so as an officer, you could not turn back and say that you did not want to do it. Once you jumped, you forgot the fear because you had to concentrate on the drill, going through the processes you were taught. We jumped from the rear of the Skyvan and the slipstream lifted you up after you exited, which was a very nice feeling. But not if you are twisted in the airstream. During one of the jumps, the Skyvan was flown by a female pilot who knew I was always the first one out. I suspected that she naughtily waggled the plane as I jumped, causing the rigging lines to get twisted and making me work hard at untwisting to set myself right.

The night jump was a wonderful experience because you were floating in darkness. It was an exhilarating feeling until you realised that you would be hitting the ground soon, but you did not know when because you could not see the ground in the pitch darkness. It was dangerous as you would tend to reach out with one foot, and landing on one instead of both feet could break your leg or ankle. This almost happened to one of the trainees. When you carried an equipment bag, you let the bag loose on a line about five metres long before you landed. The bag would hit the ground first and when you heard the "plop", it was your split-second warning that you would be landing very soon. But if you did not carry equipment, you did not have the sound to alert you and you had to estimate. If you were not alert enough, you would land with a thump. On one of the night jumps, after I landed and was wrapping up my chute, I heard a voice in the dark: "Sir, how are you?" It was Clarence Tan. I asked how he knew it was me and he replied that he could hear me land!

I wanted to learn to fly a helicopter, but I could not spare the time needed to qualify. However, I managed to experience taking the controls of a helicopter in flight. I was not qualified to pilot an aircraft, but I flew in every type of fighter the RSAF had, starting with the Hunter, the F-5, the A-4 and the F-16. My first experience was in the Hunter fighter aircraft. They gave me one of the best Hunter pilots, Harry

Lim, and we flew for an hour. When we got back, the base commander climbed up the ladder, looked into the cockpit, and asked, "Harry, why is CGS not sick?"

Even on my last flight, before I retired, the RSAF was still trying to make me sick. That last flight was in our training aircraft, the Marchetti S.211. What an adrenaline rush that was! Koh Chai Hong, who was then an instructor, flew us out of Tengah Air Base, circled around, did a touch-and-go at Paya Lebar Air Base and landed in Seletar Air Base. In the air, Chai Hong did all manner of aerobatics – perhaps to remind me that I did not accede to her request to be a fighter pilot years ago. She asked if I would like to do a loop. I said I would do a loop if she did one to show me how. She did, and then I took over and did one. I did a barrel roll and other man-oeuvres. When we were positioned to do the touch-and-go at Paya Lebar, she said, "Over to you." I could not land but I could take off, which is easier. Then we landed in Seletar, and they had a bottle of beer and a water hose waiting for me. They hosed me down, and I drank the beer. RSAF chief Mike Teo told Chai Hong that she had failed because I had not soiled my seat. It was not for want of trying by her!

There was another memorable flight in our Skyvan, the plane I used to parachute out of. We wanted to see whether the Skyvan could make it to Brunei without refuelling. The pilot had a reputation of being a cowboy. He got up from his seat, said to me in the co-pilot's seat, "Over to you, Sir", walked out of the cockpit and was gone for about half an hour, leaving me to "fly" the aircraft. When we neared Kuching, he said we had to refuel. There was nobody at the air base there to help us even though we had made arrangements. Fortunately, I met an army officer whom I knew from my FMC days and he helped us. We sat in the mess while waiting for the Skyvan to be refuelled. But when it was time to go, we could not find our pilot; he had vanished. He appeared after some time with some earthen jars which he had gone to town to buy. "Sir, don't get angry that I disappeared. I let you have one of the jars." He was a good pilot but a maverick. Those were the characters I had to handle in the Air Force. Mike Teo always used to call me "bird shit" because I had jumped from a perfectly serviceable aircraft, parachuting out of the Skyvan.

When Teo Chee Hean was the Chief of Navy, he wanted me to experience naval combat diving and to award me the Naval Diver badge. So he arranged for me to go through a short, modified diving course, and was there to pin the badge on me after I did my final dive.

I flew, I sailed, I dived, I parachuted, I drove tanks. I did everything that I was allowed to do because I wanted a deeper understanding of what my men went through by having my own direct experience. Before I was DGS, I had operational combat experience during Konfrontasi, attended as many courses as I could so that I could say I was well trained, and had even charged up hills in several live-firing exercises. In my view, all this was important to be a true military leader.

XXIII

EDUCATING A FARMER

*[The course] helped me to order my thinking, ask the right
questions and know where to look for answers. It had
the salutary effect that Dr Goh, in his wisdom, felt I needed.*

IN THE EARLY DAYS of the SAF, many officers had joined
the military without a university degree. I was one of them.
Dr Goh Keng Swee wanted to give these SAF officers the opportunity to pursue a university degree and raise their level of
education. But he knew that it was not possible for us to study
full-time; we could not be released for three or four years at
a stretch. He was also uncertain if people of my vintage were
up to it. I was already CGS then. Would it be possible for me
to do a full-time job and go to university at the same time?

Dr Goh tasked the Education Department in Mindef to
look for a solution. They approached Singapore University
(SU, now the National University of Singapore or NUS) to
consider running a course which would at least qualify us for a
diploma. But SU was not willing to make special arrangements
to accommodate our requirements. Mindef then had to go
further afield to overseas institutions. An approach was made
to the Head of the History Department in Duke University,
to find out if Duke would consider taking in adult students
for a short course for a diploma. Duke counter-proposed a
programme that would offer a Master's degree not leading to

a PhD, with the pre-requisite of a certain number of credits from the undergraduate courses in SU. To do the SU courses, we had to have A-Levels or equivalent qualifications such as a teaching certificate, and be prepared to study part-time over three years.

There were 10 of us at the start, doing History 101 in SU. I took the courses on Chinese history, Japanese history, American history and military thinkers in the first year, attending the lectures and tutorials together with the young undergraduates. Before the first year was over, half the group had dropped out. By the second year, only three of us were left – Ng Jui Ping, Kwan Yue Yeong and me.

It was a gruelling regime. When we did not have lectures and tutorials, we were doing our regular work in the office. We had no time to queue for books on the required reading list, called "red spot" books. So we got hold of a medically downgraded NSman who was posted to Mindef and deployed him to stand in line for the "red spot" books we needed. It was difficult to share one book among the three of us so the NSman photocopied the relevant pages for us. I spent no small amount of money on photocopying.

My days were fully occupied with work and the university, how much time at the latter depending on the time-table. In the evenings, I often had official functions. After getting home at 10 pm or so, I would catch a few hours of sleep, wake up at 1 am to read my books and write my essays until 6 in the morning, go for a run, and then start the day again. It was like that from Monday to Friday. It was very hard on my family. Nobody could come near my study – not my children, not even my wife. She came in only to bring me food and drinks. What kept me sane was church and golf on Sundays. I would play golf no matter what, because that was the only thing that took my mind away from my punishing routine. This went on for three years. It was physically, mentally and emotionally very stressful for me, and no less difficult emotionally for my family because I had no time for them at all. My children complained that I was grouchy, sometimes impossible.

Some young men, NSmen, looked at us sitting at the back of the lecture hall and one brave guy finally came up to me and asked, "Sir, what are you doing here? Are you spying on us?" I told him, "I have no time to spy on you. I'm a student." He looked at me in disbelief. I assured him that I was a student, but it was clear that he was doubtful. Sometime later, when we were lining up to go into the hall for the exams, the same student saw me and exclaimed, "You're taking the exam!" It was only then that he believed that I was a student.

The officers who dropped out during the first year must have decided that the huge strain on them and their families was not worth it. But I carried on because it was my nature to tough it out and complete whatever needed to be done. Also, this was Dr Goh's project and it should not fail. In my heart of hearts, I was not convinced that getting a Master's degree would be of any significant benefit to me; I was already CGS. But what Dr Goh said made sense – it would lend me credibility. Not only in Singapore society, which set a very high value on university qualifications, but also when meeting foreign counterparts, many of whom would be university graduates. So I stuck at it. And when I attended the tutorials, I realised that our work experience made us better students than our young classmates. We looked at historical events with greater maturity and did not merely depend on what we read, so we had more depth in our discussions. I appreciated that the value from a university education was learning to look at things more deeply and analytically and not take things at face value.

After securing the required credits from SU after three years, we sat for the Graduate Record Examinations (GRE), the standardised tests for admission to American graduate schools. Preparing for the GRE was itself a challenge. We had to be tutored and did several test exercises before we were ready for the exam. Again, when I walked into the hall at the Singapore American School, I drew some curious stares from the other candidates, all of whom were very much younger than me. Only after meeting all the requirements were we able to set off for Duke University in Durham, North Carolina. That was 1981. We could bring our families, which made me extremely happy. This was heaven-sent after the previous three gruelling years, especially as it would be the first time since I became DGS in 1974 that we could be close together as a family for an extended period. Karina was then 13 and Warren 11. It was quite an adventure for us.

As this was the first time we were staying overseas as a family, setting up home was quite a task, but an exciting one. We stayed in a motel while we looked for a house. We had to buy a car, get driving licences and make arrangements for the children's schooling. Kate and the children took it all in their stride and we settled in with minimum fuss. We managed to get a comfortable two-bedroom townhouse apartment not far from the university. I was ready to be a full-time student again.

The classes at Duke were interesting. I did German history to write my thesis on the German General Staff. But I discovered that the primary sources for that were mostly in German. As I was also doing American history, I geared my paper towards looking at whether the American military had considered adopting the German General Staff system. The Americans did study the German system but eventually did not adopt but adapted it instead. Jui Ping, Yue Yeong and I were in the military history group, the oldest students in the class; the rest were mostly in their early twenties. There was one student who had been in the course for five years. He played football for Duke and the professor called him a "professional student".

There was a cultural shock from being a very mature student in a university campus. I had to learn how to use the library. In Singapore, we had no time to go to the university library and our NSman did what was needed for us. Duke had a very good library. As a graduate student, I had a dedicated carrel. This was just next to the open carrels where a young girl, one day, kept popping bubble gum as she did her work. I could almost keep time with the regularity of her pops. I was irritated, but she was oblivious to my glares. Finally, I spoke up and asked her to please stop, but she ignored me. When she still refused after I asked her again, I told her that if she did not stop, I would take that gum and put it in a place she would not like. Then she looked at me and asked if I was a professor. When I said I was a student, she exclaimed, "But you are so old!" It hit me then that I was not a spring chicken.

I tried to behave like a student. No one except a couple of my lecturers knew that I was a soldier. I would go to the union house for coffee and a hot dog or burger, and engage the young people. I wanted to know more about the typical American college students. They would ask about Singapore, and I was able to get some insights into their lives, their concerns and challenges. I had the impression that American students, especially undergraduates, were playful, carefree and did not take their studies seriously. But after interacting with some of those kids, I realised that most of them were serious about their studies. They played hard but they also worked hard, in part because Duke was an expensive university and not easy to get into.

I was grateful that I finally had time to relax. It was a great time for bonding with my family. Kate and I would sit in our backyard and trim each other's hair. Longer hair was acceptable among the students and my hair grew beyond the SAF regulation length for the first time in my life. In the evenings after my studies, I would go out to play with my son and the neighbourhood children who came around. Many of the children in our neighbourhood lived with a single parent, in most cases their mothers. There was a little boy who was very appropriately named Brad, because he would stamp his feet and cry every time he missed catching the ball and then refuse to pick it up – a brat indeed! After some time, I got him to behave and before long, every now and then, Brad would come knocking on our door and ask Kate, "Is Pops in? When can he play with me?"

During the school breaks, I brought my family to travel around the east coast of the US, and once we took a trip to Disney World in Florida. My children enjoyed their time in the US. Warren, who was quiet and reserved, blossomed, partly because the American school system encouraged independence and he enjoyed that. Karina won prizes for social studies and English at the end of the school year, and when she walked up to receive her prize, the audience was aghast that a foreign Chinese girl had won the English prize. She also topped her grade. Both my children took a nationwide assessment exam and were in the top 10 per cent. It was wonderful exposure for them. It was not so easy for Kate though. Not only did she have to look after the children and cook and clean for us, she also had to type my essays, term papers and thesis – on a second-hand mechanical typewriter with two fingers and lots of correction fluid. There were no word processors then and an electric typewriter was too expensive.

I found the courses I took interesting and enlightening. The professors were engaging and understanding. My faculty adviser was a reserve US Air Force major-general. He was the only one besides Professor Ted Ropp, who had organised the course for us, who knew that we were serving SAF officers and especially that I was the CGS and a major-general as well. I took the opportunity as a full-time student to immerse myself in university life and took my studies seriously. I wanted to make the most of my shot at attending Duke University and earning a Master's degree. I worked hard at doing well and completed the thesis and requirements for a degree in two semesters. This presented a problem as my children had not completed the school year, so I attended the summer semester, auditing some very engaging courses.

The time in Duke was a good break after the three hectic years studying part-time at SU. At least I did not have to get up in the middle of the night to study. More importantly, it helped me to order my thinking, ask the right questions and know where to look for answers. It had the salutary effect that Dr Goh, in his wisdom, felt I needed. After I returned, I could hold my head a bit higher. Not that it mattered much, but I felt that I was only half a "farmer" now. It was good because by that time in the early 1980s, more and more of the people joining the SAF were graduates. Most of my younger officers were graduates. So that was a useful uplift for me.

XXIV

PREPARING FOR
CIVVY STREET

*I had done a top-notch programme to prepare for
the business world and it underscored the seriousness
of my preparation for my new phase in life.*

IN EARLY 1991, I was given notice that I would be handing
over the post of CDF in one-and-a-half years' time. I was
ready for it. In fact, I had been thinking about this since my
return from Duke University in 1982, as by then I had served
almost 10 years in the top post. But Minister for Defence Goh
Chok Tong thought I should carry on.

As the years went by, I increasingly felt that I might be
overstaying. The SAF had matured sufficiently and there were
capable officers senior and experienced enough to assume
the top posts. We were ready for change. I used to joke that
I had to look out for the bucket that some impatient officer
might place at the door to my office, hoping for me to kick
it. Holding the top post for too long would impede the progress of younger officers. Although there were service chiefs
and other top positions in the SAF they could aspire to, I
was mindful that some of the officers, especially the SAF
scholars, were getting restless. There was no formal succession
plan, although names of possible successors had been tossed
around. I was relieved that at last a successor was found and
the time had come to prepare me to leave the SAF.

I was told that Mindef had arranged for me to attend an executive programme in Harvard University. Once again, I was bound for the US, a decade after I attended Duke University. I seemed to be in the US every 10 years for studies: 1972 at the Command and General Staff College in Leavenworth, Kansas; 1982 at Duke University in Durham, North Carolina; and now, 1992 in Harvard University in Cambridge, Massachusetts. It was ironical; I had joined the military in part because I did not care much for studying, but I found myself studying one course after another throughout my SAF career. I was sent to Harvard for its Advanced Management Program (AMP). It boosted my morale to know that Mindef was doing something to prepare me seriously for my separation from the SAF and a second career. I think the practice of sending our top military officers for such executive management programmes to prepare them for a career after the SAF began with me.

So off to Harvard I went for the winter AMP course in early 1992. It was for three months. I was sent a bunch of books and a long reading list ahead of embarking on the programme, but I had no time even to touch the books and read the case studies. Nonetheless, I thought I should at least do something to prepare myself as I was serious about starting right and being able to get the best from the programme. I asked around for advice from people who had done the AMP and narrowed down to looking at accounting as I was not well versed in it. So I reached out for the accounting book, had some coaching, and did the exercises at home before I left. On the plane from London to Boston, I looked around the cabin to see quite a few passengers reading the same books I had been given before I left. A number were Singaporeans, one of whom being Boey Tak Hap. He told me not to worry as he had been told that nobody read the books before they got to Harvard – whereupon I closed the book I was attempting to read and enjoyed one more movie.

I landed smack in a rainy Boston winter with the other

Singaporeans. I was fortunate to be met at the airport by a young lady from the Economic Development Board (EDB) office in Boston. It was bitterly cold and we were dying for any kind of hot food. We were grateful to be taken to Chinatown for hot Vietnamese *pho* – a bowl of noodles never tasted so good. Then we were ready to take on Harvard Business School. My room was like a tiny ship's cabin, so small that I could almost touch the opposite walls when I stretched my arms out. I could lie in bed and reach out to turn on the computer on my desk. There were eight of us from different countries in a cluster of two rows of rooms facing each other with a common lounge area. The cluster was called a can (slang for toilet), so called because in the old university hall the eight students had to share one toilet. Now we each had an en-suite bathroom. The can was arranged such that a mixed group from different countries and backgrounds were put together. I had a Korean, an Englishman, a Frenchman and four Americans as can mates. It was important to get on well with the people in our can as we had to not only live together in such close quarters but also work and study together.

The AMP participants hailed from all over the world. Most were top executives, and they came from a wide spectrum of industries. There were also senior officials from government agencies and the military. Of the six from Singapore, three were from government and three from the private sector. There were also many women living in the hall, and I was quite taken aback but also amused when we were issued a pamphlet drawing our attention to sexual harassment and abuse as well as what was considered acceptable conduct and behaviour in the living accommodation and the school. That set the tone for us throughout the three months.

The course was mainly based on case studies, with a few lectures thrown in. Every evening we had to read and discuss a few cases with our can mates, and the next morning we would go to another can to discuss with a different group of people.

Then we would go to class and go through the cases with very good professors. I learnt very quickly how to survive the course. I prepared well so that at class I could be among the first to make a comment or give an answer and be left alone after that. Another thing I figured out was to read the cases judiciously. Having to read two cases and prepare for the discussions would keep you up all night if you were to read the cases from cover to cover.

What was wonderful and most valuable about the programme was the opportunity to learn from one another. As all the students had a great deal of business experience, the real learning came not so much from the cases themselves but from how the cases were treated by the participants. Among the case studies were two on SIA and Portnet, a Port of Singapore Authority computer system for efficiently handling ships coming into Keppel Harbour. The Singaporean students were very proud, knowing that only the best were selected as case studies in Harvard.

Because the course was so packed, I set a strict routine for myself. I was up at 6.30 am and did not get to bed before 1 am because there was so much reading to do. Lunch was usually a group affair in the dining facility. For dinner, I would pack a soup, a banana and a bag of potato chips back to my room to eat while I read the cases. That was my diet throughout the course. I managed to keep up my fitness regime as I could go to the gym most evenings for a fitness class; it was too cold and the snow too deep to jog. The classes were attended mostly by young people and I ended up being among the few oldies. Fortunately, when the weather improved, I could jog along the Charles River, which was more refreshing. Still, it was quite distressing when the very much younger undergrads kept overtaking me throughout my run.

We worked through the week from Monday to Saturday morning, wore a suit on the weekdays and dressed informally on Saturdays in a sports jacket with a tie. We could send our clothes to the laundry, but this took about a week so most of us did our own washing. It was rather surprising that many of my classmates did not know how to operate a washing machine or how to iron their shirts. These were presidents and chief executives who knew how to run large companies but did not know how to wash their clothes. I offered to help them. I taught them small tricks to save time ironing, like pressing only the collar, front and cuffs of the shirt as the suit jacket would hide the rest of the creases. It was fun to teach these captains of industry basic skills on how to take care of themselves. In the course of doing this, we became friends and I was able to pick up useful lessons from their experiences in running businesses.

A huge value of the AMP was the networking with senior people from business and government from around the world. We were thrown together in the cans, at group discussions, in class, and at social outings. As part of the practice to encourage mixing and socialising, each member of a can had to take a turn hosting the other members to a meal. This could be expensive for those of us who did not have the benefit of an expense account. On weekends, we went out to Cambridge where there were many things to see and do, and it was reasonably affordable. A few of us stumbled on a very interesting pub. It had about 350 brands of beer from all over the world and the challenge was to drink every brand by the end of the course. I did not make it. I was dismayed though, that Tiger beer was not one of the brands available. When I got home, I alerted our brewery to this shortcoming.

One great feature of the programme was that they arranged for our spouses to join us in the last two weeks. They could not stay with us in the school; it would have been impossible to have two of us in the little cabin anyway. So I booked Kate into a hotel in Cambridge. To make the programme for the spouses interesting, they were given two case studies to read before they came, and they were treated to the same form of group discussions followed by classroom sessions. This was a very good idea as the cases chosen were interesting and contemporary and it gave the spouses a sense of what we had gone through.

There was no exam at the end of the course. We had a final dinner celebration in Boston. This was a black-tie event, and I decided that I would proudly wear my mess kit and show off the SAF at the dinner. I had arranged for my uniforms to be sent to Harvard as I was scheduled to make my farewell calls in Washington DC and Honolulu after the AMP. The US Air Force officer also came in his mess kit and the two of us cut quite dashing figures that evening.

In Washington DC, I called on General Colin Powell, who was then Chairman of the Joint Chiefs of Staff, and a few others. I stopped over in Tucson to spend a few days with my son who was studying at the University of Arizona. Then it was on to Hawaii, where I called on the CINCPAC, the Pacific Fleet Commander and the other chiefs in PACOM. The final stop was in Taipei to make my farewell calls, one of which was on General Hau Pei-tsun who was then Prime Minister. When I got home, it was too close to the date for my retirement for me to make farewell calls on many of my counterparts elsewhere. I had hoped to go to Australia and New Zealand, but that was not possible. I managed to make fleeting calls on most of my ASEAN counterparts. Fortunately, even after my departure from the SAF I was able to find opportunities to call on and meet my other ASEAN friends.

Although I had experience serving on the boards of Singapore Technologies and other government-linked companies before going to do the AMP, the stint at Harvard gave me better insights into the world of business, broadening my exposure to business strategies and management practices. It also allowed me to build a good network of business contacts from around the world. Like my Master's degree from Duke University, the Harvard AMP was a boost to my confidence.

No less important was that it showed that I had done a top-notch programme to prepare for the business world and it underscored the seriousness of my preparation for my new phase in life.

XXV

FAREWELL AND
A NEW BEGINNING

It was not that I did not want to leave. I was ready.
But after 33 years, more than half of my adult life,
I could not help being overcome by emotion.

I WAS MENTALLY PREPARED to step down as CDF. When the time came, I had no qualms about leaving the SAF. I also told myself that I was only separating from the SAF; this was not retirement. I was 50 years old and retirement at the age of 50 did not seem right to me.

As I listened to the experiences of my counterparts in other countries who had retired, I knew I was going to be fine. They told me, for instance, that they did not even know how to buy postage stamps or how to pay their utility bills as most of these things had been done for them. They were warning me that since I had been CDF for so long, I would be even worse off than them. Fortunately, I had never led a sheltered life. When I was CDF, I ate at hawker centres, did things for myself without expecting others to take care of things for me. I was a regular Singaporean guy. Once I queued for *popiah* (fresh spring rolls) at a hawker centre and the stall-holder did not believe his eyes. He looked at me and said, "Hey, you look like Winston Choo!" I said, "Yes, I am." "Really, you are Winston Choo?" "Yes, I am Winston Choo," I repeated. The customer in front of me turned round, looked at me and laughed. I asked the *popiah* seller why he did not believe me and he said, "No lah, Winston Choo won't come here and buy *popiah*. People will come to buy *popiah* for him." When it came to my turn, I said, "I don't want to take out my IC to show you that I am Winston Choo. I have no brothers who look like me." When Kate, who had gone to buy something else, joined me at the *popiah* stall, she laughed and told the stall-holder, "This is my husband, and I am Mrs Winston Choo." This little encounter confirmed in my mind that people have expectations of you which may be very wrong.

When I retired in June 1992, I was honoured with a very big parade. It was organised by the Signals formation and held in SAFTI at Pasir Laba Camp. It was almost like an SAF Day parade. There were contingents from various arms of the Army, Navy and Air Force, armoured vehicles, artillery vehicles, signals equipment vehicles, and other weapon systems, and all three Service chiefs and their senior officers were there. This was the first time we had a farewell parade for the defence chief. When I took over from Kirpa Ram Vij, it was just a hand-shake, and when I walked into his office he had already left. We had not yet instituted change-of-command parades.

Nowadays it is the practice to hold a change-of-command cum farewell parade. I thought this was more meaningful because it was not merely bidding farewell but also handing over your duties to your successor while you moved on to do something else. I also thought it was important to openly show appreciation for the outgoing chief just as I had been cheered at my farewell parade.

I attended the Change-of-Command Parade for the ninth CDF, Lieutenant-General Perry Lim, which was the first I had decided to attend since my retirement 26 years earlier. I stood up to applaud him when he was walking back after inspecting the Guard-of-Honour. Apparently it hadn't been done before. Perry sent me an email shortly after that. He said, "I would like to express my heartful thanks to you for leading the standing ovation…. It made the day even more special and unforgettable for me." Some of the senior officers who were there told me that I was starting a precedent. "No, no. Don't you think he deserves a standing ovation? After all, he has served honourably and well as the Chief," I said.

In my speech at my farewell parade, I highlighted the progress of the SAF and what I believed was important for the SAF to always keep in mind. I emphasised the key role of our people even as we continued to acquire excellent hardware in the development of the SAF. I reiterated that how the SAF projected itself as a deterrent force depended on how our men projected themselves, in the way they behaved and dressed. I stressed the importance of the spirit and camaraderie within each Service and the SAF as a whole. Our Army had attained a level of excellence, our Air Force was second to none in the region, and our Navy, though small, was potent and packed a powerful punch. And the sum of the three Services made the SAF even stronger than its parts. It was also important how the SAF interacted with the other armed forces in the region. The better we knew and understood one another, the more we were friendly and cooperated with one another, the less likely we would end up having to fight one another. That was my defence diplomacy pitch and my parting words.

I had prepared the speech, but I had not prepared for the emotions that overwhelmed me as I spoke the words out loud. It was just as difficult during the interview with the media after the parade, and my daughter told them, "I hope you understand; it's hard for him." It was not that I did not want to leave. I was ready. But after 33 years, more than half of my adult life, I could not help being overcome by emotion. At the end of the parade, the men lined up along the road and clapped as I rode by in a Land Rover on my way out. The song that they played to accompany my ride was "The Way We Were" sung by Barbra Streisand. I was very touched. At the gate, I got into my staff car for the last time and went home.

That night, I was hosted to a dinner at the Dynasty Hotel, now the Marriott Tang Plaza Hotel, by then-Defence Minister Yeo Ning Hong. The senior officers and their wives were there. The Minister gave a speech and I responded. I thanked him for his kind words, but I was most touched and grateful for the praises he gave to Kate for being a supportive wife and for all her service to the SAF over the years. But the next day was difficult. It was the first of July, SAF Day. For the first time, I was driven to the parade in a civilian car. Frankly, I had thought that they would let me retire after SAF Day. But the Minister thought it was best to let my successor start on SAF Day. I did not argue that point although it was a blow to me. At the reception, President Wee Kim Wee gave me my valedictory letter. Then it hit me – that was the final send-off.

What would I do after I left the SAF? I discussed it with my wife. I was thinking of getting a job outside the government. How much I was paid was not the issue. I just needed to do something. There were a couple of offers, but I was not in a hurry to accept. I told myself not to jump into anything, but to take my time and find my way around. Just days before I left the SAF, PM Goh Chok Tong had invited me to the Istana for lunch. He asked if I would like to head a statutory board. It was not something I saw myself doing, so I said no. I said to him, "It's been 33 years, maybe I should take a break." But though I would have appreciated a clean break, I sensed at that time that to make a complete break from the establishment would be a wrong signal. So I took the offer to become Chairman of Chartered Industries of Singapore (CIS). I thought it was good for the Government to be seen to be looking after me. In any case, CIS was something familiar to me because the SAF was at that point its biggest customer.

My move to CIS was one that had no precedent. How would they remunerate me? With Mindef's penchant for equity and such, they worked out my salary in a way that I neither gained nor lost. CIS paid me the difference between my monthly pension and my last drawn salary, so that in effect I received what I was paid as CDF. It was clever but I did not think it was very fair. Some people thought I was short changed. My pension was something I earned for my past service and should not have been a factor. If I was given a new job, I should be paid the worth of that job. Still, I did not quibble. My approach to life has always been to be content with what God gives me. And I was happy that CIS provided me a car and a driver.

I was with CIS from July 1992 to February 1994. The biggest mindset shift for me going to CIS was that I was now the vendor whereas I used to be the customer. I was now on the other side of the relationship. I once used to call CIS to come and see me. Now I had to go to my customer. It was a learning process for me. Although I had prepared myself mentally for the change, there were some finer aspects that I had to learn. I had to remember that I was no more the Chief commanding more than 250,000 regulars and reservists. I now had 3,000 people working under me, mostly civilians though some were, like me, formerly from the SAF. I also had to remind myself that I should not be giving orders but making requests. For instance, I used to tell my Personal Assistant, "Send for So-and-so." Now I had to say, "Can you find out whether So-and-so is free to see me."

Being on the other side, I had to hold meetings with people who used to be my subordinates. Once I chaired a meeting with RSAF officers to discuss some issues about ammunition. The Head of the Ammunition Division in CIS was a very heavy smoker. The ban on smoking in government buildings was already in force and an aggrieved RSAF lieutenant-colonel asked, "Why are we smoking here?" I kept quiet, and he turned to me and repeated his question, "Why are we smoking here, Mr Chairman?" I told him, "This is a commercial establishment. This is the CIS building, not the

Ministry of Defence. We have always smoked here. But if it bothers you, we won't do it." "But do you know who your owner is?" he retorted, "The Government owns this place." What audacity! So I said, "Yes, but this is still a commercial establishment. If it distresses you though, I will tell them to stop smoking." The word got back to the bosses in the RSAF. A senior officer rang me to apologise. But I was not upset because I realised that it was something that came with the switching of roles. The difference between customer and vendor was very stark.

There was also the reversal of viewpoints. The SAF was CIS's only significant customer. We were producing small arms ammunition but we were not using the whole capacity of the lines because the demand from the SAF alone, without overseas sales, was not enough. It was expensive to maintain the production line, but it was Mindef's requirement that we maintained it as a strategic capability. So I tried to negotiate with Mindef to pay for the maintenance of the production line and I found myself being thrown the same arguments I used to make when I was CDF. I did not succeed and had to make the very painful and unpopular decision to downsize the ammunition division. I cannot remember exactly how many people were retrenched but it was a sizeable number. I tried to soften the blow by getting some of them transferred to the other CIS companies, and giving early retirement to others. But I could not help everyone, so it was quite a blow. It was not the first thing I wished to do in my new role, but it had to be done to keep the business viable.

Notwithstanding the adjustments I had to make, CIS was a very useful transition to the private sector for me. It was a civilian organisation but dealing with military things and many people there were ex-military personnel. It was a nice half-way house. CIS made ammunition, artillery weapons, armoured vehicles, anti-aircraft guns. There was a logistics arm and an international marketing outfit. Even the mint was part of CIS, to my surprise. I used my military knowledge to translate into handling what were called sub-units; now they are called subsidiaries.

We had to look for opportunities to grow the business, so I travelled quite a bit. The Soviet Union was particularly interesting. We were in Moscow after Gorbachev instituted Perestroika to restructure Soviet political and economic policies. I discovered that they were ready to sell almost any weapon and military equipment. If I wanted a T-72 main battle tank, I could get one if I could bring it home. I could buy night-vision devices off the shelf. Out of curiosity, I asked about buying an AK-47 rifle in a shop selling military memorabilia and the man led me to the back of his shop, took out a box with an AK-47 still nicely wrapped up inside. The Russians were very keen to sell. They had beautiful factories which were no longer running because the Soviet Army was scaling down.

I had a taste of how they negotiated deals in Russia. You started at 9 in the morning, drinking vodka right up to lunch time, then you drank vodka during lunch until 4 pm when lunch ended. Later, at dinner, you drank vodka again. The Soviets had good weapons, but it was not easy for us to adapt them for the SAF's use. They had a very good man-portable anti-aircraft weapon system which I tried to interest the SAF in so that CIS could do the deal. Another country I visited with a similar problem was South Africa. It had one of the best arms industries during the days of apartheid. When we were there, it was post-apartheid and their arms industry was downsizing. They too had very good arms factories but no work.

CIS had to try hard to sell our products overseas. But it was difficult to compete with the Chinese and South Koreans on small arms ammunition because they were heavily subsidised by their governments while we were not. We could not match their prices. There were also weapons we were producing under licence from others, such as the AR-15 rifles from Colt, which we could not sell to others. CIS resorted to designing our own assault rifle, the SA88A, a worthy product which we tried to market overseas. As CDF, I had made the Istana guards carry them as an endorsement of a local product. CIS had designed and started producing the Ultimax light machine gun even before I became its Chairman. It was a very good weapon and was already adopted by the SAF. But again, it was hard to sell overseas. Our best advertisement came from a *Time* magazine cover showing Philippine General Fidel "Eddie" Ramos and Secretary of Defense Juan Ponce Enrile with the Ultimax slung over their shoulders during the People Power Revolution in Manila. But I don't think we have sold many Ultimax guns to this day. One difficulty with selling arms and military equipment is that countries mostly make their decisions not on the merits of the equipment, but on political grounds or to favour their own manufacturers.

The arms industry is a tough business. I was involved in it for one-and-a-half years and had first-hand experience of this. I cannot say I had a glorious and successful time in CIS. But it was excellent exposure, and a good transition for me to the commercial world.

XXVI

THE RELUCTANT DIPLOMAT

*"Yes, SM. Everything turned out well. But now I will have
to pick up the pieces after you!" ... He looked at me
and laughed, "Ah, that's the job of the High Commissioner."*

EVER SINCE I stumbled into diplomacy when I was ADC to
President Yusof Ishak, I found that somehow or other I could
not run away from being a diplomat. As DGS, CGS and then
CDF, it was a job requirement to be a diplomat, or at least
to behave very diplomatically and represent the SAF and our
national interests. Right from the start, I had to deal with
the advisers and consultants from various countries, the commanders of the Australian, New Zealand and UK forces here,
and the heads of the FPDA. And soon I had to start making
friends with my counterparts in the region and beyond in
search of training areas and common security interests.

That was always rather ironical to me because all I wanted
was to be a soldier; being a diplomat was the last thing on
my mind. So when the prospect of being a full-time diplomat
was offered to me – when I was approached to be an Ambassador
– I demurred. I was first offered the post in London; I said
no. London was a popular destination, and I did not want to
spend half my time at the airport receiving a constant stream
of people from Singapore. I also turned down Bonn; my ex-
cuse was that I did not speak German. The third offer, I

am not sure on whose instructions, was made by Lim Siong Guan, Permanent Secretary of Mindef. I was asked to go to Australia as the High Commissioner. Knowing my aversion to airport duties, Foreign Affairs Minister Prof S Jayakumar made a deal with me. His instructions were that I would not have to go to the airport in Sydney (in those days there were no direct flights from Singapore to Canberra) to receive anyone except the President, Senior Minister (SM) Lee Kuan Yew, PM Goh Chok Tong and any minister who had official business in Sydney. I did not even have to receive him, the Minister for Foreign Affairs. By then, I thought it would not be wise for me to say "no" a third time. I could not find any more excuses. Australia was near enough and I was familiar with the country having been there on vacations and official visits as CDF. Kate and I also had relatives living in different parts of Australia. By that time, my daughter had already graduated and started work while my son was studying in the US, so it was just the two of us, Kate and me. Thus, very reluctantly, I said yes, and we packed our bags and went to Canberra.

Once my mind was settled on going, I looked forward to taking on the job of High Commissioner to Australia. (In a Commonwealth country, the diplomatic mission of another Commonwealth country is called a High Commission, not an Embassy.) I was not worried or apprehensive. The only difficult thing was to go house hunting as the High Commissioner's residence in 8 Mugga Way was slated to be demolished and rebuilt. I never imagined that one of the job specifications for the High Commissioner was to be a clerk-of-works. The house we rented was a 15-minute walk from 8 Mugga Way. Kate and I, together with our adopted child Benji, a border collie, would walk there every morning and evening to monitor its progress. Sometimes we would not see anyone for days. That was when I learnt that Australian workmen had days off for all kinds of reasons, including rostered days off. Together with public holidays, it could add up to four days of no work at a stretch. But the quality of their work was very good.

Then there was a snag in the valuation of the work variations; the difference was about A$60,000. The architect disagreed with the amount and refused to sign off on it. So I had to intercede, and I reasoned with the builder to take what I had calculated to be a more reasonable sum of slightly less than half the amount, and not go to court as it was not in his interest to pay exorbitant lawyers' fees. He accepted my reasoning, shook my hand, and said, "I am giving you a bottle of whisky." I said, "No. Come Christmas, you bring the bottle of whisky to my home and we will drink it together – you and your workers will drink the bottle of whisky. I will not take it now." I wanted to get out of my rented house quickly as it had taken close to two years to rebuild the residence. We moved into 8 Mugga Way even before the main door was installed.

My induction to being a full-fledged diplomat was quite painless. I was fortunate because I had friends in Canberra. On the first weekend after my arrival, my Defence Attaché, Colonel Tan Hung Kee, organised a barbeque in his home and invited all my old friends. They included those who had retired to Canberra: ex-CDF General Peter Gration, the serving CDF Admiral Alan Beaumont and ex-CGS Lieutenant-General Laurie O'Donnell who was then also President of the Royal Canberra Golf Club – a very important man to know to get into the club. It was a good introduction. They told me I should know two things about Canberra: I would freeze to death and I would be bored to death. How wrong they were.

Even before I could settle into the house we rented, my first task was to prepare for SM's visit. We were still living out of our suitcases as my *barang barang* (belongings) were still on the high seas. I had been told about his trip during my pre-posting briefing back in MFA and was given a list of his preferences to note. I was not expected to survive because I was not a career diplomat and SM Lee was tough to handle.

The High Commission in Canberra was very small and I had a new team. But I was not daunted as I had worked under him since my days in the Istana and I thought it could not be any more challenging now.

While my wife was trying to settle into our rented home, I spent the next week or so travelling to all the cities in SM Lee's itinerary – starting in Canberra and going on to Sydney, Melbourne and Perth – to make sure that everything would be in order for his visit. It was necessary to recce the different venues for his programme and his accommodation. I had to look at such things as the room temperature and firmness of his mattress, and ensure that there was an exercise machine and no fresh flowers in the room because of his sensitivity to pollen. I had to check on the pollen count in the various cities and inform his office. The visit had to be planned and conducted with almost military precision to make sure that there would be no hitches. One important requirement was the need for good communication among the High Commission team. We had only two mobile phones and we needed two more. With the multi-city itinerary, someone needed to travel ahead to the next stop to ensure that everything was in order for the delegation's arrival and programme. MFA HQ did not approve the purchase. I went ahead anyway and told HQ to charge the cost to me if they wished. In the end, they paid for the new phones.

It was good that the Australians were not very protocol conscious. Although I had not yet presented my credentials to the Governor-General, I was given access to all the government departments that were involved in SM Lee's visit. It was not difficult to deal with them as they liked you to be frank and forthright. I also found that the way to handle them was to give them back as hard as they gave you.

SM Lee was due to fly into Sydney, and I was shocked to find out that the Australians had not provided a security officer for him. They did not see any security threat to him

ABOVE *Receiving Maj-Gen Pehin Mohammad Haji Daud, Commander of the Royal Brunei Armed Forces, 1988.*

RIGHT *Being conferred the Darjah Yang Mulia Setia Mahkota by the Yang Di Pertuan Agong of Malaysia, Sultan Iskandar, 1989.*

RIGHT *Being conferred my
second Legion of Merit
(Degree of Commander) by
Admiral William Crowe,
Chairman of the Joint Chiefs of
Staff, Washington, USA, 1988.*

LEFT *ASEAN Military Chiefs, 1990. From left: General Hashim Mohd Ali (Malaysia), General Renato de Villa (Philippines), Lieutenant-General Winston Choo (Singapore), General Sunthorn Kongsompong (Thailand), General Try Sutrisno (Indonesia) and Major-General Sulaiman Damit (Brunei).*

BELOW *Getting ready to fly in the S.211 with Captain Koh Chai Hong, 1990.*

TOP RIGHT *My can mates at the Advanced Management Program, Harvard University, 1992.*

BOTTOM RIGHT *With Singaporean course mates at Harvard University, 1992.*

ABOVE *My family at my farewell parade, 30 June 1992.*

TOP RIGHT *An emotional moment at my farewell parade, 30 June 1992.*

BOTTOM RIGHT *With service chiefs at my farewell parade, 30 June 1992. From left to right: Brigadier-General Michael Teo, Lieutenant-General Winston Choo, Major-General Ng Jui Ping and Rear-Admiral Teo Chee Hean.*

TOP LEFT *Kate and I with SM Lee Kuan Yew, Mrs Lee and George Yeo at Melbourne University, 1994.*

BOTTOM LEFT *FMC Intake 4 get-together in Cebu, Philippines, 1997.*

BELOW *Kate and I with Australian PM Paul Keating and Mrs Keating. Canberra, Australia, 1994.*

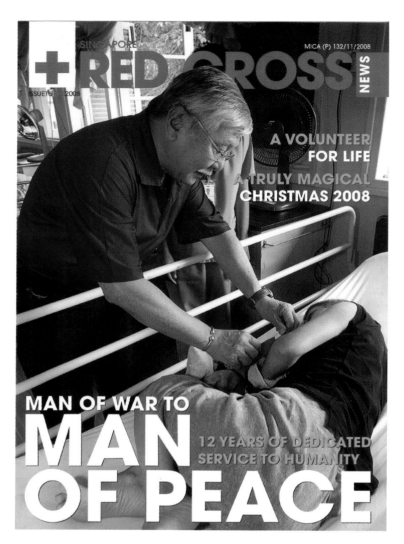

ABOVE *My visit to the Red Cross Home for the Disabled was featured in* Red Cross News, *2008.*

ABOVE *Saying hello to a future NSman and his family during the reception after the SAF Day parade at SAFTI Military Institute, 1 July 2009. Looking on was MP of Tanjong Pagar GRC, Indranee Rajah.*

RIGHT *With my grandchildren on holiday in South Island, New Zealand, June 2008.*

LEFT *With General (Retd) Hau Pei-Tsun, former CGS and Premier of Taiwan, 2015.*

ABOVE *Being conferred the Distinguished Service Order by President Tony Tan Keng Yam, 2015.*

LEFT *With Brigadier-General Gan Siow Huang, the SAF's first woman general, SAF Day, 2015.*

ABOVE *At the Istana in Brunei with Generals Mohammad Daud (Brunei), Try Sutrisno (Indonesia) and Hashim Mohd Ali (Malaysia), 2016.*

LEFT *With PM Lee Hsien Loong at the Dome of the Rock, Temple Mount, Jerusalem, during his official visit to Israel in 2016.*

ABOVE *The Choo clan, 2020. Seated from left: Dana, Winston and Deanne. Standing from left: Ethan, Karina, Kate, Warren, Su-Yin and Daniel.*

RIGHT *Three generations of soldiers. My son Warren was an officer in 3 Sig Bn, while my grandsons Ethan (left) and Daniel (right) were in 6 SIR and 3 Guards respectively.*

now that he was no longer Prime Minister. I went right up to the Secretary-General of the Department of Foreign Affairs & Trade (DFAT) and threatened to cancel the visit if they did not deploy a security officer for SM. They managed to get him one but when I went to the airport, the security officer was nowhere in sight. As we walked to the arrival gate, I asked the protocol officer and was told, "He's coming. He went to watch a football match." The security officer did not appear until after SM Lee had gone into the VIP lounge. That was how I realised that I could not be a pushover when dealing with the Australians – I would need to be firm and put my foot down when necessary. On another occasion, when then-President Ong Teng Chong visited Adelaide University to attend an alumni gathering, the Australians did not want to give him the due VIP treatment, saying that he was on an unofficial trip. They did not allow me to receive him at the airport arrival gate but I just walked into the security area to the arrival gate anyway.

SM's trip was my baptism of fire. I remember he sent a copy of his speech to the Asia Society of Australia for my comments. I said to myself, "I just arrived here. What value can I possibly add to his speech?" I went through it anyway and made only one comment. I suggested that he delete his remarks about the Australian trade unions and their strikes. I said things had changed and the relationship with the unions was better. But when he arrived, the first thing he saw from his hotel window overlooking Darling Harbour was a strike. I told him that since I arrived in Australia, I had never heard of one. "How long have you been here?" he asked. I said the strike he saw was an aberration. "Okay," he replied, "I won't mention it."

I was bracing myself for things that could go wrong. That evening, at a private dinner in the hotel, SM asked for a good Australian beer. Being new in town, I had no idea what to order. I had seen many advertisements for Tooheys Blue, so I ordered one for him. He took a sip and put it down. "This is not beer! This is bitters." I ended up drinking it and ordered him a Foster's lager, which I had on standby as I knew it was his regular beer. Then as we were about to start dinner, he asked for a good Australian white wine. I was not going to bungle again. I got hold of the sommelier, gave him 20 bucks and told him, "Bring a good white wine or I'll have your head!" When SM tasted it, he said, "This is good. You know your wines, Winston." I said, "No, SM. I paid the sommelier $20 to bring this wine." He laughed.

I was relieved that his visit to the University of Melbourne to receive an honorary doctorate was uneventful. When he asked for my opinion, I said he should go even though there had been protests by faculty members calling him a dictator and such. I pointed out that since the university council had decided to confer on him the award, he should go and receive it, and he agreed. As it turned out, there was no protest or anything of that sort when he went there. The media, though, made a big to-do over it. It was the same in Canberra where he gave a talk at the Press Club. The journalists gave him a hard time, badgering him on why he had called Australians "white trash". SM replied, "I don't remember ever using that term." He really gave it back to them and I was hoping that things would not get out of hand. That was when I saw first-hand how adept he was at handling the media. I also learnt about consistency. He was very consistent throughout the trip; he did not deviate but kept to the same line everywhere he went.

On his last stop in Perth, we had a private dinner. I had booked a room in a French restaurant. As was the practice, I had sent the menu to SM's room for Mrs Lee and him to order their meal in advance. Before they arrived, Minister George Yeo, who was accompanying SM on the visit, asked me whether we could get any *kuay teow*. I found out that he could not go too many days without Asian food. To our delight, the coffee house in Hyatt Hotel served *char kuay teow* and soon we were ordering Hokkien *mee* and other Asian dishes. When SM and Mrs Lee came down and saw what we had ordered, they said, "Why can't we have that too?" So I went to the coffee house to make the order. As for the French dishes which SM and Mrs Lee had ordered, the rest of us shared them.

When I sent SM and Mrs Lee off at the airport, he said to me, "Things went all right. The Australians looked after me quite well, made sure I ate the right things, the hotel rooms were okay." Then Mrs Lee interjected, "What Australians? Winston was the one. You think the Australians looked after all these things for you?" I thought it was very kind of her to intercede. Then he said, "Well, I think the visit went well. The Australians were quite receptive." I said, "Yes, SM. Everything turned out well. But now I will have to pick up the pieces after you!" He asked what I meant. I told him, "The media will go to town, if they have not already done so." He looked at me and laughed, "Ah, that's the job of the High Commissioner." I was thrown into the deep end of the pool, but contrary to the prediction of the staff officers in HQ I did not drown.

SM Lee's remark was not frivolous at all. I found that engaging the media was very important and I was kept busy dealing with them on many occasions. My first encounter with very bad press was over Michael Fay, the American boy who was caned for vandalism in Singapore. The news was all over Australia. Not long after we arrived in Canberra, when Kate and I were at the Department of Transport to get our driver's licences, the officer at the counter said to me, "Oh, you are the Singapore High Commissioner. You are barbarians." I said, "I beg your pardon. What right have you to call us barbarians?" "Why did you beat the poor boy?" he asked. I told him bluntly, "He got less than what he deserved." The Australian media had published a supposedly eye-witness account by a US marine of a "public caning" at the Padang. According to him, the Singaporean crowd watching was baying for blood and at every lash they surged forward and cheered. I wrote in to clarify but the press refused to publish my letter. Later, I learnt to get around this by paying to have my letters published as advertisement.

We were vilified in the media over other issues such as the Flor Contemplacion case, when the Filipina domestic helper was hanged after being convicted of murdering another Filipina and a four-year-old boy. The Filipinos in Canberra picketed outside our High Commission in protest. I never knew that there were so many of them around Canberra. Then, when Christopher Lingle, the American university lecturer who left Singapore under a cloud, wrote some very disparaging things about Singapore that the Australian media published, I spent a lot of time trying to get my response published. It was to no avail until I threatened to buy advertisements. But what they published was a heavily edited version of my letter. Again, I had to buy advertisements when the media refused to publish my responses regarding Tang Liang Hong, who was giving talks in Australia together with a few other dissidents who had congregated in Sydney.

When the Australian Broadcasting Corporation (ABC) asked to interview SM Lee in Singapore, saying that they wanted to find out about the economic situation in Asia, I thought it was quite harmless and SM agreed. I was horrified when I read the transcript of the interview. After two or three questions about the Asian economy, they began asking him about Tang Liang Hong, his comments about crime in Johor Baru, and other controversial topics. SM Lee jumped at it and said, "You want to know the truth, let me tell you the truth." The next thing I knew, I was trying to stop ABC from publishing the interview. I was told by HQ to say that the Tang Liang Hong case was now in court and it would be sub judice and contempt of court if they published the interview.

ABC replied that their lawyers said it was not, and so they would publish.

I was woken by a phone call at about 4 am (1 am Singapore time). SM's security officer was on the line telling me that SM wanted to speak to me. I told him to let me go and wash my face first before putting SM on the line. When SM came on, he said, "Ah, Winston, how are you? What time is it?" I said, "4 am." "Is that so? I guess you should be awake anyway." SM called me almost every other day about the ABC's insistence on broadcasting what he had said about Tang Liang Hong in his interview. Once, I was in my office with my Counsellor Tan York Chor sitting in front of me. SM wanted to speak to the editor of ABC. I said he should not; it was my job to speak to him, and if anything went wrong he could blame me. York Chor was surprised to learn that I was speaking to SM and exclaimed, "Wow, you speak to him like that!" As it turned out, I got ABC to agree to feature the interview in their Australian service but not in their Far East service. The next thing I did was to ask the Malaysian High Commissioner not to report the ABC interview, where they had pressed SM on his remarks about crime in Johor Baru, back to Wisma Putra (the Malaysian Foreign Ministry) lest tensions flared up again. Fortunately, we were good friends, and he agreed to let it lie.

I almost got into trouble because of Pauline Hanson, an anti-Asian politician from Queensland. She had opened a Pandora's box and racist sentiments flared up. Some of our students in Toowoomba in northern Queensland were actually stoned by some local people. The SAF was training in Shoalwater Bay and we had our soldiers in the nearby town of Rockhampton. A young lieutenant coming out from church was beaten up. Even in Canberra, there were cases of Asians being beaten up.

A journalist from ABC wanted to interview me, supposedly to talk about an upcoming bilateral meeting. This was an initiative I had helped to get started, called the New Partnership which involved the Ministers of Foreign Affairs, Defence, and Trade from both sides. I agreed as I thought it was a good thing to publicise this important development in the bilateral relationship. Also, I had been cultivating this journalist. After a couple of questions on the bilateral meeting, he asked me about Pauline Hanson. He was trying to get me to criticise Prime Minister John Howard and the Australian Government for not doing enough to put her down, but I would have none of it. Then they misquoted me. On the prime time 7 o'clock news that night, a headline read: "Singapore High Commissioner warns of economic reprisal over Pauline Hanson." To make matters worse, other Australian print media picked it up and posted the story all over the front pages the following morning. Fortunately, I had my First Secretary with the tape recorder throughout the interview and I made a transcript of it.

The next morning when Foreign Minister Prof Jayakumar and his Cabinet colleagues got off the plane at Canberra, the first thing he said to me was, "Winston, what have you done?" I said, "Minister, let me explain", and gave him the transcript. "Oh, they misquoted you. As expected," he said. I told him that the media would be hounding them for the next two days, and I suggested that he need only say that he had nothing further to say; his High Commissioner had said it all. Prof Jayakumar thought that was a good idea. I would not say that you should not trust journalists, but you must be very careful. That was the lesson I learnt from all this.

XXVII

JUST DOING MY DUTY

I think in the final analysis I was not too bad a diplomat.
I was comfortable with people and related well to them.

THE JOB OF a diplomat was not all about picking up the pieces. I was kept busy on several fronts and was travelling sometimes as frequently as twice a month to cities all over Australia. The High Commission in Canberra also had to help our EDB and Trade Development Board deal with economic and trade issues and enquiries, and I was often invited to speak on such topics. Having learnt from SM Lee about being consistent, I used the basic speech I had prepared, and updated the data whenever I had to speak on business opportunities in Singapore. The other thing that often took me on the road was visiting Singapore students. I made it a point to meet them and to attend their university gatherings if they invited me and I happened to be in Sydney or Melbourne.

One thing that worried me was their susceptibility to being seduced by the Australian lifestyle. One student told me how he would look out of his apartment on a Thursday afternoon and see his neighbour cleaning his boat, getting ready for the weekend. On Friday, his neighbour would come home in the early afternoon, hitch his boat to his car and take off to the lake. How nice such a life was. I tried to get them to see the bigger picture. Some Singaporeans there had shared with me their dismay about the glass ceiling they had encountered. They had chosen to live there but they were not all that happy. I tried not to rub them on that point; if that was the life they had chosen, so be it.

I had to be careful not to say things which could unwittingly upset them; I had, on more than one occasion, been misquoted. Once I told some Singaporean students studying in Canberra that perhaps they had decided to study there because they wanted the exposure or perhaps because the university course they wanted was not available in Singapore, but whatever the reason, they should make the best of their time in Australia. I was misquoted as saying that they were studying in Australia because they could not make it back home. It was reported to MFA by my successor that I had said this to the students and upset them.

I was very open when dealing with Singaporeans in Australia. Every state had a Singapore club; it was called the Singapore Club in some states and the Temasek Club in others. I was warned that they did not welcome the High Commissioner as they thought he went to spy on them. Perth had many Singaporeans, and I had several close friends there. I told them, "Look here, I have neither the time nor the inclination to spy on you. What makes you think that you are so important that we would want to spy on you?" I felt bad saying that. But because they were my friends, I thought I could be more frank with them.

When SM visited Australia, I asked the Temasek Club in Sydney whether they would like to meet him and host him to lunch. They did, and SM agreed. He took my advice not to scold them and he was very nice when he met them. He said his colleagues had told him that it was good for him to reach out to Singaporeans overseas. It was a very pleasant, cordial lunch. When some of the club members came to talk to him, he asked them the usual friendly questions like how long they had been there and what they were doing. The word came back that he had interrogated them! When PM Goh Chok Tong visited Australia, I asked the Singapore Club in Brisbane whether they wanted to host him, and they said yes. I suggested that PM Goh address the issue of National Service in his talk. Some Singaporeans in Australia had left Singapore without registering their sons for NS, and those whose sons did not serve NS now found that their sons could not return to Singapore without getting into trouble with the law. PM Goh was very straightforward with them. He talked about the importance of NS and told them, "If you are a draft dodger, then you will be treated as a draft dodger." I made a copy of his speech and circulated it to all the Singapore clubs across Australia so that I did not have to keep repeating the answer every time I was asked this question.

I discovered that although our relationship with Australia was good, it was very much based on personal links among people in the establishment. Though many Australians knew Singapore well, there was no institutional memory at the official level. So I proposed to MFA Permanent Secretary Kishore Mahbubani that we establish something to institutionalise the relationship. We worked with Michael Costello, who was DFAT Secretary-General, and launched the New Partnership, which later became the Singapore-Australia Joint Ministerial Council (SAJMC). This brought together the Foreign, Defence and Trade Ministers in an annual meeting co-chaired by the Foreign Ministers and alternating between Canberra and Singapore. In conjunction with the New Partnership, we had the Singapore Australia Business Alliance Forum (SABAF) which brought together Australian and Singapore businesses and was co-chaired by an Australian businessman and a Singapore businessman. We timed the launch of the New Partnership and SABAF for PM Goh's official visit, and it was he who gave the name SABAF. He preferred "forum" instead of "council" which was commonly used in similar arrangements which Australia had with other countries.

I managed to get MFA to fund Singapore's National Day celebrations. At that time, only embassies in ASEAN countries were given a budget for this. I had to *tumpang* (piggy-back) on the Defence Attaché's SAF Day celebration. I lobbied hard and eventually got MFA to agree. The inaugural National Day celebration in Canberra in 1996 was memorable. The Anglo-Chinese Junior College choir was there and sang "Majulah Singapura" and "Advance Australia Fair". The diplomats and other guests were very impressed by the choir, which I had invited as they happened to be in Sydney for the 4th World Symposium of Choral Music. I said I could not pay for their trip to Canberra, but I could feed them. I felt so proud. I was doubly proud because we had scored a first in having then-Deputy Prime Minister Tim Fisher as our Guest-of-Honour. Until then, the Guest-of-Honour at the national day celebrations of other embassies was always the DFAT Director of Protocol. I believe we were the first embassy to have someone from the Cabinet – and it was not only a Minister, but the Deputy Prime Minister. I had developed a good relationship with Tim Fisher as he had served with the Australian Army in our part of the world. So when I tried my luck and invited him, he readily agreed. It was truly a feather in our cap.

I had to visit every state to make my introductory calls on the State Governors and Premiers. Australia is a big country so that took a lot of my time. I was fortunate that some of the Governors were ex-military men and already knew me. One of them was General Sir Phillip Bennett, the Governor of Tasmania. I first met him when he was the Commanding General of the 1st Division in Queensland and later when he was the CDF, so I knew him very well. He invited me, Kate and my First Secretary, Henry Tan, to stay in his official residence, Government House, as his guests instead of staying in a hotel, which was an unusual honour. Hobart Airport was very small and you picked up your own luggage from a small baggage trailer loaded with bags from the aircraft. We looked around but nobody was there to receive us. So I asked Henry to call the protocol officer, who asked in disbelief, "General Choo is still waiting for me? It can't be. I have him in my car with me." When Henry insisted that I was at the airport waiting for her, she burst out, "Oh dear! We must have made a grievous mistake."

Eventually she came and took us to Government House. Sir Phillip and Lady Margaret were waiting at the doorstep. Lady Margaret apologised profusely for the officer's mistake. It turned out that she had picked up a Korean general who had grey hair like me. Then I recalled that he and his wife had been sitting across the aisle from us in the plane. They had disembarked ahead of us and when the protocol officer asked if he was General Choo, he apparently said yes. There was no conversation in the car until they drove into Government House, whereupon he exclaimed, "What a glorious hotel this is!" Sir Phillip told me that when the car pulled up, he had remarked to his wife, "Winston has grown so old." I didn't have as much grey hair then.

At the banquet that evening, Lady Margaret told all her guests about the "stupid mistake" they had made. This leaked to the media and was reported in *The Sydney Morning Herald*. The story even found its way to the Singapore media. On one of my trips home, PM Goh asked me, "What are you trying to do, masquerading as a Korean general?" I was asked by a senior Australian official whether I wanted to lodge a formal complaint, and I said there was no need for that because it was a genuine mistake. The protocol officer thanked me profusely, saying that otherwise she might have lost her job.

Looking back at my tour in Australia, I must give credit to my High Commission staff. It was a very small embassy, even after I managed to add two officers. I had made a case for another First Secretary and MFA conceded. With all the SAF training in Australia and the Defence Attaché covering

New Zealand as well, it was too much for one person and I convinced Mindef to send an Assistant Defence Attaché. I put great emphasis on fostering teamwork, not only among my MFA staff but also with the other agencies represented in the High Commission. Every Monday, I chaired a meeting where everybody gave an update on their work. The exchange of contacts and information helped our small embassy work more cohesively and efficiently.

I treated my staff like family. They were mostly younger than, or about the same age as, my children. Kate felt good because our children were not there with us. Once or twice a month, Kate and I hosted a meal in the residence for all the staff – a lunch, high tea, or potluck dinner. We celebrated everyone's birthday. Kate was very good at making them feel at home. It was hard to be away from home especially for the unmarried staff. My Personal Assistant, Sheila Pillai, a vegetarian, always asked me when she came over, "HC, what have you cooked for me today?" And I would assure her that I had vegetarian food for her. Sheila was a tiny girl who had to depend on her colleagues to take her home, so she eventually learnt to drive and got a small Mazda. One day, I had a call from the police. "Oh dear! What happened?" I asked. The reply came back: "She is driving too slowly." I told the officer that it was better that she drove slowly and not like a maniac.

In Australia, I was concurrently accredited as Ambassador to Fiji. I told HQ that this was not practical. For one thing, it was not easy to travel to Fiji from Canberra. I must also confess that I was so busy making my rounds in Australia that I managed to make only one representational visit to Fiji. Fortunately, the Fijian Prime Minister Sitiveni Rabuka, who as an army officer had instigated a coup in 1987, was someone I knew as he had been in touch with the SAF through one of our officers who had attended a course with him. When I visited Fiji, I was well received by him. MFA later rightly decided to appoint a Non-Resident Ambassador to Fiji.

I was aware that I had been parachuted into the MFA system and, more than that, into Australia, which was a choice posting for MFA officers. I was the third SAF general to land in MFA in this way, after Mike Teo and Chin Siat Yoon. My posting to Australia had also resulted in the incumbent High Commissioner having his term slightly shortened. With this at the back of my mind, I always made it a point to tell the MFA people that I was not a career diplomat and was not there to compete with them or to take their job; I was just doing a duty that had been assigned to me. I think in the final analysis I was not too bad a diplomat. I was comfortable with people and related well to them. I had no regrets about going to Australia because I had really enjoyed my time there, learnt a lot, seen a lot, and made a lot of good friends.

I stayed six months longer than my three-year term because my successor was not yet ready to take over. I was anxious to go home because my son was getting married and we wanted to be back in time for his wedding. Kate had baked all the fruit cakes in Canberra for the wedding, and we were sending them back in batches through friends going to Singapore. While playing golf in Canberra, Prof Jayakumar had asked me to stay on for one more term in Australia but I politely declined. He then asked about Kuala Lumpur, saying that I was already well established and had many good friends there. That would have been the worst thing for me to do! He reluctantly conceded. Then he said he would leave me alone for three years and we would talk again after that.

XXVIII

TWELVE YEARS OF NATIONAL SERVICE

*Doing relief work was not all glamorous photo shoots
showing you inspecting new clinics and shaking hands with the
happy recipients. You needed to be not only diplomatic
but also street smart and creative and have your wits about you.*

IT WAS LATE 1996 and I was approaching the end of my posting as High Commissioner in Canberra. One day, I got a phone call from Dr Kwa Soon Bee, Permanent Secretary of the Ministry of Health. He said his Minister, George Yeo, thought that I should be doing something after my return and he had just the job for me. Disregarding my protest that I had lots to do, Dr Kwa said they needed a Chairman for the Singapore Red Cross Society (SRCS). I was taken aback and responded that I knew nothing about the Red Cross, which was a fact. I said jokingly that I knew how to make war but not peace. I told him to let me think about it and I would give a reply when I returned to Singapore. Minister Yeo also spoke to me, telling me that I was "just the man for the job". He made it clear that I would not be paid as this was a volunteer job. I said, "Never mind. Let me come back to Singapore first."

To my surprise, sometime in early December 1996, perhaps a month after the telephone call, I received a letter from President Ong Teng Cheong appointing me as Chairman of the Red Cross in Singapore. This was unexpected as I had not said yes, and I was not due back in Singapore until June 1997. So I had to run the Red Cross from Canberra, by phone and fax as we did not have a reliable email system then. By then, I had found out that the Red Cross was more than just boys and girls in white uniforms selling flags and waiting for people to faint on school sports days. Also, I sensed some wariness over my appointment because I was an army general. In a phone conversation, an official from the International Committee of the Red Cross (ICRC) asked me if I was still a serving general. I replied that I had retired and was now an ambassador, and assured him that there was no military influence and he should not be concerned about my appointment.

As soon as I got home, I plunged myself into finding out more about the Red Cross in Singapore. The first discovery was that it involved many government ministries and agencies, all of which had ex-officio representatives in the SRCS Council. There was the Ministry of Health, which was the supervising ministry, and also Defence, Foreign Affairs, Education, Home Affairs, and Community Development. They took turns to brief me on each of their interests in the Red Cross. The Permanent Secretary of Defence explained that Mindef's interest was in international humanitarian law and the Geneva Convention, which the Red Cross was responsible for. He added that the Singapore Red Cross had not done enough, so it was good that I was now involved. MFA dealt with the ICRC and was interested in conflict resolution, which the Red Cross was supposed to be doing. Education's interest had to do with the boys and girls in white, the Red Cross youth. Home Affairs was on the Council because the Red Cross assisted in local emergencies. The Ministry of Community Development focused on the home for the disabled that the Red Cross ran. I had so many bosses! When I met my number one boss, Minister of Health George Yeo, he gave me his vision for the organisation. His task for me was to elevate the profile and exposure of the Singapore Red Cross and do more work overseas.

I familiarised myself with the various activities of the Red Cross. They had youth and adult volunteers; they ran first aid instruction courses, an ambulance service, a home for the disabled, and the blood donation programme. I learnt how the Singapore Red Cross fitted into the international Red Cross system. That was very important given Minister Yeo's instructions to me. I also realised that the Singapore Red Cross was not an NGO (non-governmental organisation) but an arm of government established by an Act of Parliament. That was why the Chairman was appointed by the Government. I thought it was strange that the Government had so much say and yet they were not paying for the Red Cross. There was no government subsidy or subvention to the Red Cross except from the Ministry of Education, based on the head count of the youth members, and from MCYS based on means testing of the residents in the home for the disabled. The running cost of the Red Cross was all met through donations and contributions.

I had two immediate tasks. The first was to learn how to raise money. To do that, I needed to lift the profile of the Red Cross in Singapore as Singaporeans did not know much about it. My other priority was to expand and enhance the council. But before I could settle down, Minister Yeo, who had by then moved out of the Ministry of Health, suggested to me that we reach out and help Indonesia. The 1997 financial crisis had hit the region and the Indonesians were facing lots of problems. Drought and floods were beleaguering them at the same time, and they needed help with food and other essentials. So began my first effort at making a public appeal for money from Singaporeans. I managed to raise S$5 million within a week or so.

I thought that the best way to help the Indonesians was to work with the Indonesian Red Cross. So I went with a small team to Jakarta. We were met by the Vice-Chairman, a retired banker, who hosted us to dinner at the bankers' club where we were treated to fine wine and fine food. My volunteers were wondering, "Who is trying to help whom?" The Vice-Chairman said to me in Bahasa Indonesia, "*Bapak, lima juta kecil.* (Sir, five million is a small amount.) You give us the money, we will buy the things and distribute." I did not think this would go down well with Singaporeans who donated the money; they needed to know how we spent it. So I diplomatically told him that it did not make sense for us to give them the money to buy rice when they had a shortage of rice because of the drought and floods. It was better for us to bring the rice in from stocks bought by Singapore. When I made that argument, it was hard for him to disagree.

We then worked with the Secretary-General of their Red Cross, Pak Susanto, a retired Admiral who had a good sense of accountability. We packed boxes, each containing 2 kg of rice, 2 kg of flour, 1 kg of sugar, 2 litres of cooking oil and one tin of powdered milk. Every box had the Singapore flag, the Red Cross symbol, and the words "Contribution from the People and Government of Singapore" printed on it. Wherever we went, each family was given a coupon the night before we arrived, which they could exchange for the package. The coupons were given on the very eve of the distribution so that the villagers could not reproduce them. We brought our doctors along to provide medical treatment. We gave most of the elderly people Vitamin B injections, which they needed. Some were so thin that they had to lift their sarong and offer their buttock because they did not have enough flesh in the arm to receive the injection. It was heart wrenching for me and my volunteers to see this.

Through this exercise, Singaporeans became more aware of the Red Cross and its work. I purposely wanted the food boxes to be packed in Singapore because I could get more people, including schoolchildren, involved. It was a learning experience for our young and the not-so-young. We were also able to get help from Singapore companies such as Pacific International Lines and SIA to help us with the transportation. Most important of all, the Singapore flag on the boxes helped raise the profile of Singapore as a donor. The other spinoff was being able to work with Indonesian Government agencies. We needed them to help provide transportation and security, so I approached the Pangab (Commander of the Indonesian Armed Forces) General Wiranto. I told him that we needed his help, and subtly pointed out that it would also be beneficial to the image of the Indonesian Armed Forces (ABRI, now TNI) when they were seen bringing in the aid boxes to the villages. With ABRI's help, we were provided security and land transportation and could reach villages which were difficult to access. We made many trips over two to three months, to Central Java, West Java, Sulawesi, Nusa Tenggara and so on. I went on most of the trips. Wherever we went, the people there got to know about Singapore. Then suddenly we were more than just "a little red dot" to them.

It became clear that I needed to beef up the Red Cross staff and the organisation to support large-scale operations and overseas relief missions. For the Indonesian mission, I was the logistician, fund-raiser, book-keeper and the one ordering supplies. I had a very good Secretary-General, Geri Lau, but she needed more assistance. I decided that I had better bring in some muscles and went looking for retired SAF officers. The first person I brought in was Lim Theam Poh, my first Staff Officer when I was DGS. He was a tremendous help and worked with the Red Cross until 2016. I also recruited a good man, Gregory Yeo, who was a lieutenant-colonel from Logistics. Between the two of them, I was able to run the activities more efficiently.

I reorganised the HQ into management teams – Administration to handle finance and personnel; Fund-raising, which was a very important department because without them we would have to close shop; Services, which was responsible for blood donation, the home and the ambulance service; Volunteer organisation; and the Training Centre where we trained people in first aid and related courses. Later, I added a Corporate Communications department to work with the media to get good and sustained media coverage for our operations, support our fund-raising efforts, and raise the profile of the Red Cross.

Disasters seemed to follow me. There were earthquakes in Turkey, Gujarat in India, Iraq, Tehran, Afghanistan, Sichuan in China. North Korea was hit with floods, as was Myanmar from Cyclone Nargis. We needed a proper standard operating procedure. With the help of my two ex-military officers, we worked something out that guided our approach to relief missions. First, send in a small recce team to find out the problems and needs. Work as much as possible with the sister Red Cross Society in the destination country as that was where we could get the best support and accountability. Keep the key international Red Cross bodies informed on what we were doing because they were very sensitive about us driving on our own. The most important thing was to take a Team Singapore approach where the Red Cross tried to facilitate the work of the various NGOs in Singapore under one team and fly one flag – the Singapore flag.

When it came to mounting a donation effort to raise funds for relief efforts overseas, I worked out an arrangement with Bilahari Kausikan, then Deputy Secretary MFA, in which the Government would give the Red Cross seed money to raise an appeal for donations from Singaporeans. The money we collected would then be a donation from the Government and people of Singapore. This way, the amount of Singapore's contribution would be more sizeable than if it were to come only from the Government.

We took this approach when the 2004 Boxing Day Tsunami hit. The response from Singaporeans was overwhelming. Children were coming in with their piggy banks. Someone came with $250,000 cash in two paper bags. We needed to bring in extra manpower just to receive the donations and count the money. I discovered a new source of volunteers – the *tai-tai* (wealthy married ladies of leisure). When handling money, they were very reliable and willingly came and ran their own shifts. After $20 million was collected, I wanted to stop the donation drive as I was concerned that this was siphoning the limited pool of donation funds away from the other charities and NGOs in Singapore. When I sent out an open letter to express our intention to stop the collection, some people in the public reprimanded me, arguing that we should continue with the drive. Even after we stopped when we reached $40 million, people continued giving and we ended up with $95 million.

We were initially overwhelmed by the enormous emergency relief effort required in the three tsunami-hit countries that we were supporting – Indonesia, Sri Lanka and the Maldives. There was the need to collect and send emergency supplies together with relief and medical teams to the affected regions. Our staff were not organised to undertake the surge of work that this tsunami brought us. Fortunately, many retired SAF officers stepped forward and volunteered almost on a full-time basis to do the bulk of the work. This was helpful as we also needed to work closely with the SAF and coordinate with their relief efforts. The initial relief phase went on for weeks.

As with the disaster-relief aid we had provided to Gujarat, Tehran and elsewhere, we used the bulk of the money to build hospitals, medical centres, houses, and similar facilities where we planted a Singapore flag to show that it was a donation from the people and Government of Singapore. We had established a system which enabled us to react immediately to a disaster: we reached out with whatever relief supplies and assistance were needed in the emergency phase and then concentrated the bulk of our efforts on the reconstruction and rehabilitation phase which was more impactful and sustainable. The Singapore Red Cross also partnered some international

NGOs and government agencies in the affected countries to undertake large reconstruction projects, such as building thousands of housing units, hospitals, piers and other types of infrastructure.

Because Singaporeans had donated so generously to the Red Cross, we thought that we should make some of the funds available to Singapore NGOs which were reaching out to help the tsunami victims. With the Government's endorsement, we set up a Tsunami Reconstruction and Facilitation Committee to assess requests from these smaller NGOs for money and other assistance for their tsunami-related projects. I chaired this committee, which sat almost daily during the reconstruction phase of the tsunami relief effort. The members included Tee Tua Bah representing the Red Cross, a representative from MCYS and representatives of some leading NGOs. Zulkifli Baharudin, the Chairman of Mercy Relief, an important partner of the Red Cross in the tsunami relief effort, was an active member of the committee. After the committee approved, we would give these NGOs an initial sum for their projects, monitor their progress and, when each phase was completed, disburse the money for the next phase. Together, we built clinics, kindergartens, schools, orphanages and ecologically safe community toilets; provided clean water supply systems; taught better farming techniques; and handed out fishing boats, among other things, in Indonesia, Sri Lanka and the Maldives.

I visited some projects to verify the work done, sometimes flying in small aircraft where the seat belts were frayed and the buckles rusted, and landing on air strips where the pilot had to skilfully avoid potholes. The vigilant monitoring was necessary to ensure accountability and assure Singaporean donors. And when the reconstruction and rehabilitation phases dragged on, I managed to convince a retired SAF colonel, Chris Chua, to join the staff and take on some of the travelling to monitor the many ongoing projects. Chris became SRCS

Secretary-General in 2006.

Doing relief work was not all glamorous photo shoots showing you inspecting new clinics and shaking hands with the happy recipients. You needed to be not only diplomatic but also street smart and creative and have your wits about you. The Indonesians at one time wanted to tax us for all the relief supplies going through Medan. So I rang up Pak Kuntoro Mangkusubroto, the Director in charge of the reconstruction works, with whom I had a good working relationship, and said, "We want to help and you want to tax us. If you tax us, your people will get less." So no tax was imposed. And in Aceh, where we were building a hospital, our operations would be disrupted from time to time by insurgents from the separatist group Gerakan Aceh Merdeka or Free Aceh Movement (GAM). So we recruited GAM fighters to be our security unit and the disturbances ceased. Sometimes you have to think out of the box to get things done. But we were aware that this required us to be extra careful with the "friendly forces" and to constantly be on our guard.

While I had many good volunteers who did great work, there were also those Singaporeans whom we called disaster tourists. They sailed to Meulaboh in Aceh on the SAF's LST but made no effort to be punctual to catch the boat that left at 7 every morning to bring them for the day's work on shore. And it took five persons to nail one board, with one holding a camera. I thought they were wasting money, time and space. But we wanted to be inclusive and encourage volunteerism. The other problem was that while they meant well, there were many Singaporeans who ignored our appeal, because of practical and logistical reasons, for cash donations only. There was a woman who wanted to donate expensive evening wear. She scolded me when I said that we could not accept it: "Do you know how much this dress costs?" I told her that did not matter to the women in Indonesia; what they needed was something simple like a sarong. "What's wrong with you?" the woman said to me in a huff. Another donor lectured me: "Do you know a monk brings a bowl, pushes it out, and puts his head down. He doesn't bother what goes into the bowl. And here you are telling me not to put things in that you don't want." In this work you had to face all kinds.

Back at the Red Cross HQ in Singapore, we changed how we managed the membership system and expanded volunteer membership by creating what we called Chapters in tertiary institutions like the polytechnics and Institutes of Technical Education. We were thus able to plug the gap in Red Cross youth membership which had stopped at the junior colleges. We tried to make volunteering in the Red Cross more meaningful. The adult volunteers could opt not to wear the uniform and could choose what they would like to volunteer for – blood programme, disaster relief operations, or other specific activities – and be trained accordingly. When flag day came around and students volunteered to sell flags, I had to recommend to schools that their students be awarded CCA points only if their tins were filled, as many just stood around comfortable street locations chatting with one another instead of approaching people for donations.

Another change I initiated together with the Permanent Secretary of the Ministry of Health, Moses Lee, was for the Red Cross to take on the role of promoting the blood donation programme and bringing in donors, while the Health Sciences Authority collected the blood and was responsible for its safety. The Red Cross did not have enough volunteer doctors who could spare the time to go through the extensive training programme to qualify to do bleeding. It was also a challenge for the Red Cross to build up the capability to ensure the quality of the blood products. This was a happy resolution as the Health Ministry was assured of the quality of the blood and the Red Cross could still be very much involved in its traditional role in the national blood donation programme. Also, the Red Cross was reimbursed by the Health Ministry for the cost of the promotion and recruitment drive, which was a significant change.

Not many Singaporeans knew of the existence of the Red Cross's home for the severely disabled. It was important to raise awareness of our home not only to raise funds for its running cost but also to get volunteers for the home. For a start, we encouraged volunteers to go and just sit with the residents, many of whom had been abandoned there by their relatives and needed human interaction. As more people came to know about the home, we had volunteers who organised programmes for the residents. Now we have a new home for the disabled in Lengkok Bahru.

Although my work at the Red Cross was an unpaid, often full-time job, many people thought I received a salary. In fact, on top of my contribution of time and energy, I was a regular donor. And from time to time, I used my Krisflyer frequent flyer points to travel on Red Cross business. At the height of the scandal involving the National Kidney Foundation, we received calls from the public asking how much people in the management were paid. So we gave them the numbers. They did not believe that the Chairman did not receive any salary, accusing us of lying. Someone asked about the car I was driving and was told it belonged to me and not the Red Cross. The next question was "How many Mercedes have you got?" One of my managers had a sense of humour and replied, "We've got quite a few Mercedes. All ambulances."

I stayed as Chairman for 12 years – longer than I had bargained for. It was only when I found a successor who was acceptable to the Government that I could step down. I had brought in Tee Tua Ba, a retired Commissioner of Police and Ambassador, to be a council member. After two years, I broached the subject of him taking over. He was reluctant and I had to get the help of President S R Nathan to persuade him. Happily, Tua Ba agreed to do it, and in 2008 he took over.

My 12 years of "national service" were really interesting,

satisfying and fulfilling. There was meaning in what I was doing. When PM Goh Chok Tong joked about turning me from a man of war to a man of peace, I had replied, "You need a man of war to do the work of a man of peace." Indeed, it was my background, my military training and understanding that enabled me to be effective in the work of the Red Cross. I had not expected that there would be so much work, but I would like to think that by the time I left, we had made a lasting impact on the communities we served, and more people knew of the Singapore Red Cross not only in Singapore but also internationally. The Singapore Red Cross was chosen to host an Asia Pacific Red Cross regional conference shortly before I stood down, and that was a success. Today, Singapore Red Cross members are sought after to sit in various international committees of the Red Cross. Indeed, I believe that we had succeeded in placing the Singapore Red Cross on the map of the international Red Cross movement.

XXIX

LONG-DISTANCE DIPLOMAT

*The joke was that on my first representational
trip to Israel as Ambassador, I had started a war
and brought down a President.*

IN MARCH 2000, almost exactly three years after our conversation on the golf course in Canberra, Foreign Minister Prof Jayakumar appointed me Non-Resident Ambassador (NRA) to Papua New Guinea (PNG). I was less than thrilled as I had expected a more exciting place like a European country. But MFA assured me that PNG would be very stimulating, and it certainly turned out to be more thrilling than I had bargained for.

Although I had a taste of being a non-resident envoy with my concurrent accreditation to Fiji when I was in Canberra, being a full-fledged NRA was quite different. I found the job of NRA in some ways more challenging than being a resident Ambassador. There were occasional representational visits, but I was largely operating remotely from Singapore. It was critical to build a good network of contacts and I had to work hard to be effective. I thought the expected minimum of two representational visits a year was inadequate, so I sometimes made more visits. Being a novice NRA, I was fortunate that my predecessor, Lee Chiong Giam, a seasoned diplomat, had represented Singapore's interests in PNG for a long time and had laid a very solid groundwork. Also, there were not many major bilateral issues that required urgent attention. So, PNG was not a bad place to start as an NRA.

However, the logistics presented some challenges. There was then no reliable direct commercial flight to the capital Port Moresby. I would usually fly by SIA into Brisbane, sometimes staying overnight, before connecting to Port Moresby by Qantas or Air Niugini. MFA sent different officers to staff me on my visits. Some were fresh recruits or new to covering PNG, so I ended up providing them background information instead of the other way around. Whenever I raised this with MFA, they would flatter me by saying that they always sent the young ones to be trained by me because I was an experienced diplomat. To which I responded in Dr Goh Keng Swee fashion: "Rubbish!" Indeed, I ended up training them, but I must say that it was interesting and fulfilling. I recall vividly a young, petite lady staffer who, lugging her heavy laptop, could hardly walk – I ended up carrying it for her.

In those days, personal safety was a serious issue as PNG, particularly Port Moresby, could be a dangerous place. Unemployment was above 50 per cent. People from the provinces and highlands converged on Port Moresby to look for jobs in vain, resulting in rampant problems of drugs, alcoholism and a high crime rate. It was not safe to walk in the streets. And it was difficult to move around as taxis and rental cars were very unreliable.

There was not enough current material and media reports about PNG to keep me well informed and updated on the political situation there. The politics was very fluid and the records in MFA had to be constantly updated. So it was a priority for me to develop good contacts who had political connections and knowledge of the domestic politics. PNG then was very unstable and there were frequent changes of political leaders. The Australians had taught them democracy too well and they were adept at bringing down Prime Ministers and governments, made worse by Members of Parliament being able to jump across the aisle without losing their seat. I relied on two main sources for information, a former PNG High Commissioner to Australia and the Australian High Commissioner in Port Moresby, both of whom I got to know during my posting in Canberra. Our Honorary Consul-General was a Singaporean running a very successful business there, but he was frequently out of the country. He was competent in his consular responsibilities but did not have the connections or the insights we needed. There were a few other Singaporeans, mostly small businessmen, but they had only a shallow understanding of the domestic politics.

I knew I could not carry on like this if I wanted to be more effective, so I went on a search for a good Honorary Consul-General. A name that kept popping up was Sir Henry Chow, a well-established businessman who was a fourth-generation Chinese born in PNG. The incumbent Honorary Consul-General threw cold water, saying Sir Henry would not be interested. So I devised a plan to meet him and make my pitch. When I heard that he was travelling to the UK via Singapore, I sent a message through a business contact to invite him to extend his stopover in Singapore. I arranged to put him up at the largest suite in the Raffles Town Club, got a Rolls Royce to pick him, his wife and grandson from the airport, and hosted them to a fine dinner. Kate was with me. At the end of the dinner, I popped the question about becoming our Honorary Consul-General. He said, "I used to do a lot of business in Singapore. And I know important people in Singapore, like Sim Kee Boon." I said, "Good. You are just the man." And he agreed. Sir Henry served as our Honorary Consul-General in PNG well beyond my term as NRA to PNG. When he became ill, he had his son continue as our Honorary Consul-General.

Sir Henry was a wonderful representative for Singapore and my life as NRA to PNG improved dramatically after his appointment. He alerted me to political issues and possible changes, which made me more effective in my job. When I made my representational visits to Port Moresby, he took care of me from the moment I arrived – driving his car to pick me up at the airport – to the day I left. He arranged all my appointments and he drove me to every one of them himself because he did not want me to use rental cars as they were unreliable. He had good contacts and knew people from both sides of the political divide, so I had good access. One of the first things he did was to arrange for Kate and me to have a private dinner with the Prime Minister, Michael Somare, and his wife, together with him and his wife. Until then, I had never been able to secure a meeting with the Prime Minister.

Sir Henry also held dinners and parties in his house for the Singapore community and invited some political people whom he thought I should meet. His wife, Lady Colette, was a wonderful hostess who looked after us very well. With her, Kate could visit places of interest around the country because she had a vehicle and security protection. The Singapore community there was happy because they could meet more often and I could do more for them. I got to know many of them at Sir Henry's parties. Through him I was given opportunities to see more of PNG which gave me a better sense of the country. I served six memorable years as NRA to PNG and enjoyed my assignment there.

About a year or so after my appointment to PNG, just as I was settling down, MFA asked me to take on a concurrent appointment as NRA to South Africa. It was important as Pretoria was a listening post for Sub-Saharan Africa. While Pretoria was not as dangerous as Johannesburg, it was still not safe to walk around on your own. I said to MFA: "Another dangerous place. What have I done to deserve this?" Their cheeky reply: "We send soldiers to dangerous places."

One mitigating factor was that I could fly directly from Singapore to Johannesburg, which took nine hours. We also had a High Commission, with a proper staff and a Consul-General, Bernard Baker, who acted as High Commissioner when I was not there. He and the High Commission staff did most of the work; I was only the icing on the cake. Bernard was well connected and an effective Consul-General. Nonetheless, as Bernard himself acknowledged, the NRA helped to open doors to people whom he, not being the High Commissioner, could not reach. My presence enabled the High Commission to reach out to a wider range of South African bureaucrats and Ministers whom we would normally have difficulty getting access to. My visits usually lasted a week and a half. It was always a full programme making representations and meeting people. It was a pleasant posting, and I enjoyed my tenure. It was safe if you were not too adventurous, and I had the opportunity to see the beautiful country and meet interesting people. I was NRA to South Africa for a little over four years, from July 2001 to October 2005 when I was replaced by a resident High Commissioner. This was good because a resident High Commissioner in Pretoria would better represent Singapore's interests in an important African country and have the time to travel to the other southern African countries.

Even as I was serving in PNG and South Africa, I was quietly hoping to be assigned to a country in the northern hemisphere. I thought that Israel might not be too bad a posting for me because of my long military relationship with the Israelis. Sometime in 2005, I got a pleasant surprise when MFA told me that they were considering appointing me as NRA to Israel and, in preparation for that, I was to join Senior Minister (SM) Goh Chok Tong's delegation for his visit there. At that time, our Ambassador to France was concurrently accredited to Israel. The Israelis were not happy with that arrangement. Understandably so, as the Ambassador could not dedicate much time to Israel because of his primary focus on France and a couple of other European countries where he was also accredited to. What Israel wanted was a resident Ambassador in Tel Aviv but Singapore was not ready to set up a full embassy. Instead, we offered Israel a dedicated NRA who would have no other diplomatic assignments. My name was put up and the Israelis accepted as they knew me well from my SAF days. Five months after that May 2005 visit to Israel, I stood down from my NRA appointments to South Africa and, a few months later, to PNG, in preparation for my assignment to Israel.

I went to Tel Aviv in July 2006 to present my Credentials. That first official trip to Israel as NRA was quite unforgettable. After presenting my Credentials I called on Shimon Peres, whom I had met when he was Defence Minister. Although he was then not holding any official position, he was still an important and useful person to meet. When I was in his office, he took a phone call and I saw his face change. He hung up, looked at me, and said, "Not good news. We have just gone to war." The second Lebanon War had broken out. Not long after that, there were many war planes flying over Tel Aviv and the army was mobilised. Kate was with me and we were worried whether we could get a flight home. As it turned out, we managed to make our way home on our scheduled flight. When I got back, SM Goh asked me, "What did you do? You started a war?" I said jokingly, "No, I didn't start a war. I went there to approve their military plans."

I presented my Credentials to President Moshe Katsav. He had a reputation. Before the presentation ceremony, the protocol officer briefed Kate and me on the proceedings. Kate would be brought into the residence where she would meet the President while I inspected the honour guard. The protocol officer warned Kate to be careful – the President would hold her hands and move very close to speak to her and he would not let go of her hands, so she had to be prepared to pull them away. Kate wondered if the protocol officer was joking. After the event, Kate told me, "Ya, he wouldn't let go!

He came very close." Less than a year after I presented my Credentials, Moshe Katsav stepped down from the Presidency under a cloud. He was later charged for rape and sexual harassment and handed a seven-year prison sentence. I was teased that on my first trip to Israel as Ambassador, I had started a war and brought down a President.

I did not find Israel as dangerous a place as some people made it out to be, because I was quite familiar with it. I did not have worries about our security, and Kate was happy to move around on her own as she had done many times in the past. Unlike South Africa, we had no diplomatic mission in Israel. But we had Shuki Glietman, who had been our Honorary Consul-General for many years. He was very established, having served as secretary-general in a government ministry and as the Chief Scientist. He had a good understanding of the domestic political situation and could recommend the right Ministers to approach who would be helpful on specific issues. He also had useful links in the business community, particularly with people in R&D and technology. He took his work very seriously, but he did not have the kind of access that I had hoped for. So I had to capitalise on my SAF connections to meet influential people and ex-military officers with strong political connections. I also had the good fortune of support from retired SAF officers who had settled in Israel for work. This was very helpful for somebody with no *kaki tangan* (people to assist me) in-country.

These Singaporeans who were there with their families were also very kind to us for they would invite us to their homes for meals, not only when restaurants were closed during religious holidays but also most of the time that we were there on representational visits. It was also through them that I was able to reach out to some of the friends I had made when I was in the SAF. In Israel, many high-ranking military officers ended up in politics. So I had friends who became Ministers, even Prime Ministers, which was very useful. It was difficult to get access to people through their Foreign Ministry because their ministries did not work well with one another, so I had to use my own resources to get to some of the important people I wanted to meet. Once, a Foreign Ministry officer called me on my mobile phone and was very surprised when I said I was having a glass of whisky with Ehud Barak, who was then the Defence Minister. I guess my good connections with the Israelis, especially with their defence people, was one of the reasons why MFA sent me there. I was always aware that I was there as Ambassador and had to be careful not to be seen as a defence representative. I also made it a point to promote bilateral interactions and cooperation in other areas, such as R&D and technology, education, and culture.

I found the Israelis somewhat like the Australians. They were informal but could also be difficult and demanding. For instance, they would try to dictate the programme I was planning for a ministerial visit, and I had to stand my ground and insist on our desired programme. One thing they were not happy about was our insistence to call on the Palestinian National Authority. It was our policy to be even-handed, so I had to be firm to safeguard our national interest. There were times when the Orthodox Jews, who had become very influential, mandated that their officials could not meet foreign guests who arrived on the Sabbath. But our Ministers could not be dissuaded from arriving on a Saturday. Fortunately, my contacts from outside the Foreign Ministry could help with airport clearances and the like. It was also a challenge arranging to meet people in both Tel Aviv and Jerusalem, linked by a highway often clogged by heavy traffic, and I had to make sure the arrangements took this into account. Sometimes I had to play hardball with the Israelis when arranging a programme, and the MFA colleagues who accompanied me on the recce visit wondered why I was so undiplomatic. But I knew that if I did not insist, my principal could well be saddled with an unacceptable programme. When the officials were being too difficult, I sometimes went over their heads to a higher authority. I found it useful to say, "I am not a diplomat. I am a soldier. I just want to get things done."

After 14 years as NRA to Israel, I felt that I had done enough. I have had memorable encounters and handled difficult and delicate issues. Our relationship with Israel was special but also a tall order to manage, having always to be nurtured while ensuring that we maintained our principled position. I am proud and honoured to have been given the opportunity to serve as Ambassador to Israel. I had always admired the Israeli people and treasured our special relationship. I am delighted that I was able to facilitate the milestone reciprocal visits by Prime Minister Lee Hsien Loong to Israel in 2016 and Prime Minister Benjamin Netanyahu to Singapore in 2017. I finally stepped down in July 2020. I can now tell MFA, "No more; I have done my share. Don't *kacau* (bother) me anymore!"

Though I never had the ambition to be a diplomat, I ended up spending 26 years as one – almost as many years as I was a soldier. It was very fulfilling, and a privilege to continue serving my country in that role.

XXX

THE GIFT OF MY LIFE

It moved me most deeply when my children said,
"Pa, you may not have the Army anymore, but you still have us,"
and Kate said, "Yes, you still have me."

WHEN I LOOK BACK at my life, I do not think I could have asked for more. My Christian upbringing at home, in ACS, in the BB and in church has taught me to put my trust in God and be grateful to Him for the many blessings in my life. And there have been many wondrous gifts. The biggest gift of all from God has been a very special woman – Kate, my wife and life partner. To me, ours is a relationship made in heaven.

From the time we first met, I knew that this was someone special whom I wanted to be with. I was then in the BB and she was in the Girls' Brigade in Prinsep Street Presbyterian Church. I was 13 and she was 12. I found her very likeable and very kind, with never a nasty word for anybody. There were other boys who had a keen eye on her, so I had competition. But our upbringing was such that we would not imagine going into a serious relationship at that age. In those days we did things together as a group of friends, whether it was church activities, picnics, or house parties. We remained as good friends, although I always had her on my mind. When I was a cadet, we would meet when I came back to Singapore from time to time, but as good friends.

It was after I graduated from FMC that I started to date Kate. I remember it was 7 November 1961. It was a funny kind of date. My elder sister was getting married to Kate's youngest uncle, and the two of us were running wedding errands together. After that we started dating seriously. The relationship survived my frequent absences – away on courses and training, on operations, and then in the jungles of Sabah during Konfrontasi. Both of us did not know whether I would be coming back alive from Sabah. Even after we were engaged on 5 June 1965 and planning to get married, she accepted the postponement of the wedding plans when I became ADC to the President and took the disappointment stoically. She patiently tolerated the changes that came along with my life as I did not have much time for her. Her parents sometimes wondered what was going on.

When we finally could get married after I left the Istana, Kate faced the prospect of not having a church wedding. She was raised an Anglican and was looking forward to getting married in St Andrew's Cathedral, where we worshipped. She could not imagine anything other than a church wedding; it meant a great deal to her. Even so, she accepted it when I said that we should get married in the Registry of Marriages first. My plan was to get a marriage certificate so that we could be allocated married quarters by the SAF. We wanted to start our married life in our own home instead of having to live with her parents or mine until we found our own place. It was unusual then to get married in the Registry first, but for us it was the practical thing to do.

We hit a snag when Reverend Anthony Dumper, the Dean of the Cathedral, threatened not to solemnise our wedding. He was very unhappy that we had gone to get married in the Registry of Marriages before the church wedding. He questioned why we had gone to the Registry when he could marry us in church. I explained our reasoning and the church finally agreed. We had our church wedding on 3 December 1966. So we have two wedding dates, the other being 6 October 1966, when we got married in the Registry of Marriages. As far as Kate is concerned, our wedding anniversary is 3 December, but I said that legally it is 6 October. Being the good wife she is, she conceded. And that is the date that we always celebrate, as we did on our golden wedding anniversary in 2016. But come 3 December every year, Kate never fails to wish me "Happy Anniversary".

After marrying me, Kate had to face many disruptions in our lives and handle things on her own, as I kept moving to new postings, going away on courses, and travelling on official visits. Even for the births of our children, Kate had to manage on her own as I was not around both times. Then there were the difficult three years when I had to bury myself in my university studies and assignments, and she had to keep the children away from me as I shut myself in the study each night. She took every disruption, every challenge, and every burden in her stride without even a whisper of complaint.

Kate played the role of the CO's wife extremely well because she saw this as her duty. The challenge was exponentially bigger when I was appointed DGS. Just as it had come as a bolt of lightning for me, it was an equally huge shock for Kate when she was told of my appointment. My DGS duties and overseas travels kept me away from her and the family most of the time. She was literally on her own, raising the children single-handedly. She willingly gave up teaching, something she loved very much, so that she could look after the children and run the home. When I was asked to look into setting up an Officers' Wives Club, Kate willingly and generously took on the job to initiate this. She clearly understood my objectives for the club. She had always shared my belief in the importance of wives and husbands supporting their spouses in the military and being by their side so that they could undertake their tasks with confidence. Kate was a natural, and capably took on the challenging task of rallying the wives from different backgrounds to be members and to serve in the club. She carried no rank, but I can say that if I had three stars, she should have been given four. She was very successful in the Wives Club mostly because she was approachable and the wives saw her as one of them. She did this for 18 years, happily and most ably. A handful of the old members, whose husbands have already retired, still meet regularly with her. They include some wives of CDFs who came after me.

When I stepped down as CDF, Kate was again there by my side and sharing in the emotions of my leaving the SAF after more than 30 years. It was as touching a moment for her and the family at my farewell parade as it was for me. I was not the only one who had tears. It moved me most deeply when my children said, "Pa, you may not have the Army anymore, but you still have us," and Kate said, "Yes, you still have me." We took our change in lifestyle with no discomfort or problem. Kate took on the tasks of overseeing the rebuilding of our home, and the packing and moving out of our quarters, uncomplaining and loving as ever, seeing it as her karma. Then, before we could settle down in our new home, we had to pack our bags and go to Australia when I was appointed High Commissioner. And all Kate said was: "If you must, take it and we will go to Canberra together."

As a diplomat's wife, Kate was wonderful. She ran the residence in Canberra with aplomb and gave it a Singapore character, going out of her way to prepare Singapore meals whenever we hosted. Many of my diplomatic colleagues and Australian officials looked forward to being invited to the Singapore High Commissioner's residence. Our Ministers and other Singapore visitors were treated to whatever Singapore dishes they desired; *chai tow kueh*, *chwee kueh* and *roti prata* flowed out of Kate's kitchen. There were no instant mixes in those days; everything had to be prepared from scratch. Kate was like a mother to the embassy staff and a grandmother to their children.

Most importantly, Kate kept our family and me spiritually strong. I must admit that I had not always been devout, nor had I led an exemplary Christian life. But she never faltered and she ensured that we kept our faith. This was especially so after our first grandchild came along. That was when I said to myself that the backsliding must stop and it was time that I return to God, not only for my own salvation but also because my home must be a sanctuary for my children and my grandchildren, and it must be a Christian refuge.

The biggest test of our faith came when I was struck with cancer. Let me share my walk with God during that trying time. It began with a sudden very high fever, a week after I returned from a business trip to the UK. I was diagnosed with pneumonia. Because I had blood in my sputum, the doctors did a scan and, in the process, spotted nodules in my thyroid and a swollen lymph node, although they were not looking for anything in these areas. It was God's will that these were discovered. Then the doctors poked a needle into three places in my thyroid and lymph node, without anaesthetic, to do a biopsy. Because the cancer in my thyroid was different from the cancer in my lymph node, they sent me to an ear, nose and throat (ENT) specialist. He discovered a cancer at the base of my tongue. Talking about lightning bolts, that was a massive strike.

I was blessed also in having wonderful doctors and an excellent ENT specialist. On 2 May 2017, I went through an 11-hour surgery. I insisted on walking from the ward to the operating theatre instead of being wheeled in, because I wanted to be strong and was confident that God was walking with me. I had two surgeons. The surgeon doing the robotic surgery on the cancer in my tongue showed me the screen and the robotics controls and explained that he would see inside my mouth on the screen and carry out the operation by manipulating the controls. Then my main ENT surgeon said, "General, you will lie down here. I will be here. We have not decided who will go in first though." To this day I do not know who did what first.

When I woke up in the high dependency ward, I found 16 tubes and leads all over my body, down to my feet. I had a tracheostomy tube inserted for me to breathe, so that if there was any bleeding I would not suffocate. I could not speak because of this and the only way I could communicate was by writing, using a pen and a pad. How frustrating it was being unable to speak! I was there for one very painful and harrowing month; and Kate was by my bedside all the while. But throughout the ordeal I was not afraid. I had my faith and I believed that God was there with me always. There was a board near my bed where my granddaughter wrote a Bible verse. It was Psalm 121: 1-2 which reads: "I lift up my eyes to the hills. From where does my help come? My help comes from the Lord, who made heaven and earth."

The nurse told her that the board was for the doctors to write instructions, whereupon my granddaughter said under her breath, "This is God's instruction." The Bible verse remained on the board. I was also comforted by the fact that my former colleagues, retired SAF officers, friends and family were praying for my recovery. They were my steadfast prayer warriors.

I went through 30 sessions of radiotherapy, with a plastic mask over my face. Then I knew what "The Man in the Iron Mask" must have felt like. I lost my sense of taste and my mouth was constantly dry because my salivary glands were affected. After the radiotherapy, I went for radioiodine treatment. A follow-up CT scan showed I had three nodules in my lung and the doctors did a deep needle biopsy guided by CT scan, during which they put a needle right into my lung to take samples from the nodules. To my utter dismay, they turned out to be malignant. The cancer had spread from my tongue to my lung. My faith was shaken but my family stood by me. Then I was on chemotherapy for six weeks. Again, I felt that God was faithful to me. I was spared from the debilitating side effects of chemotherapy; I did not suffer from nausea, neither did I lose my hair. My grandson said in jest that he was most relieved that I had not lost my iconic moustache.

I was going to the hospital so frequently, always accompanied by Kate, that the National University Hospital was like my second address. It was not easy to sit in the chemotherapy treatment room while being infused with the drugs. Of the three sessions in a week, two took almost a day, seated in a chair. Halfway through the chemotherapy sessions, a CT scan showed 95 per cent regression of the nodules. At the end of the six weeks, there were no traces of the cancerous nodules. I had gone to a healing service in church and had been inspired by those who shared their testimonies, so I felt moved to share my blessings with others and gave a testimony at the next healing service.

After that, I started on immunotherapy. This had other side effects; I got rashes, but while it was uncomfortable, I could wear long sleeves to prevent injuring myself from scratching. After the operations and procedures, though I could eat a little, food kept getting into my lungs because I was not swallowing well. The worst episode was when I was on holiday in Phuket. I spent six out of the eight days there in hospital. Instead of celebrating at the resort, we rang in the New Year in my hospital room with my family camping on the floor, feasting on food bought from a 7-Eleven. Again, it tested my faith. But I know that God knows best. And I always say, "I surrender myself to you, Lord. Thy will be done." I had to undergo a procedure called PEG (percutaneous endoscopic gastrostomy) to insert a semi-permanent feeding tube. I accepted that I was going to miss enjoying food orally, but if it was God's will that I forego that, I accepted it. I am still accepting it. And in His wisdom, God has compensated me with good health. Because I am on tube feeding, my diet is so well controlled that I no longer have hypertension, diabetes, and potential kidney problems. That I am alive today is through God's grace. I had been in the operating theatre and high dependency wards countless times until, on my last visit, the technician and the nurses looked at me and said, "Aiyah Sir, you again!" Knowing that it is God's decision that I am alive is something that keeps me at peace.

Throughout my journey with cancer, I have been grateful for two things – that my faith remained strong and my God heard my pleas, answered my prayers and walked with me and, most comforting of all, that my wife and my family stood by me all the way through. They prayed and kept faith and encouraged me throughout. I am very proud of and grateful for my children, Karina and Warren whom Kate has blessed me with, my four grandchildren, Dana, Daniel, Ethan and Deanne, and my daughter-in-law, Su-Yin. They have made such a difference in my life, standing by me through thick and thin, in good times and in difficult moments.

My wife was most wonderful as she nursed me throughout. She is still nursing me – she has to dress my rashes, ensure that I get the proper food supplement for my tube feeding, and manage my medication. I really do not know what I would do without her. Frankly, sometimes I do not know what medicine I am supposed to take. Kate has kept me comfortable and kept me in my faith. As I said, in my life, God in His grace has favoured me with many blessings but His greatest gift to me is Kate for my wife.

To God Be The Glory!

HONOURS, AWARDS AND DECORATIONS

NATIONAL

Uniformed Services of Malaysia Medal, 1966
The Defence Medal, 1970
SAF Long Service and Good Conduct Medal (12 years), 1973
SAF Long Service and Good Conduct Medal (22 years), 1982
SAF Long Service and Good Conduct Medal (30 years), 1989
SAF Good Service Medal, 1975
The Public Administration Medal (Gold), 1978
The Public Administration Medal (Gold) (Military), 1981
Long Service Medal, 1985
The Meritorious Service Medal (Military), 1990
The Public Service Medal, 2005
The Public Service Star, 2009
The Distinguished Service Order, 2015

FOREIGN

United States of America
The Legion of Merit (Degree of Commander), 1978
The Legion of Merit (Degree of Commander), 1988

Philippines
The Legion of Honor (Degree of Commander), 1978

Taiwan
The Order of Resplendent Banner with Grand Cordon, 1984
The Order of Precious Tripod with Grand Cordon, 1991

Republic of Korea
The Order of National Security Merit – Tong-il Medal, 1984

Republic of Indonesia
Bintang Yudha Dharma Utama (1st Class), 1986

Brunei

Darjah Paduka Keberanian Laila Terbilang Yang Amat
Gemilang Darjah Pertama, 1987

Malaysia

Darjah Kepalahwanan Angkatan Tentera Malaysia
(Kerhormat) – Panglima Gagah Angkatan Tentera, 1987
Darjah Yang Mulia Setia Mahkota Malaysia, 1989

Thailand

The Most Noble Order of the Crown of Thailand, 1987
The Most Exalted Order of the White Elephant, 1991

France

The Legion of Honour (Degree of Commander), 1991

Chile

Commander of The Order of Bernardo O'Higgins, 2000

RECOGNITIONS

United States Command and Staff College
Allied Officer Hall of Fame, Certificate of Honor, 1975

AUSTCHAM President's Medal, 2005

The Boys' Brigade in Singapore
The Distinguished Service Recognition, 2010

NTUC Friend of Labour Award, 2012

The Singapore Red Cross Society
Humanitarian Award, 2013

GLOSSARY OF ACRONYMS

ABC	Australian Broadcasting Corporation
ABRI	Angkatan Bersenjata Republik Indonesia (Armed Forces of the Republic of Indonesia)
ACS	Anglo-Chinese School
ADC	Aide-de-Camp
AFP	Armed Forces of the Philippines
AMP	Advanced Management Program
ANZUK	Australia, New Zealand, United Kingdom
ASEAN	Association of Southeast Asian Nations
BB	Boys' Brigade
BOQ	Bachelor Officers' Quarters
CCA	Co-curricular Activity
CDF	Chief of Defence Force
CGS	Chief of the General Staff
C&E	Communications and Electronics
CINCPAC	Commander-in-Chief, Pacific Command
CIS	Chartered Industries of Singapore
CO	Commanding Officer
CUO	Cadet Under-Officer
DFAT	Department of Foreign Affairs and Trade
DGS	Director General Staff
EDB	Economic Development Board
FMC	Federation Military College
FPDA	Five Power Defence Arrangements
GAM	Gerakan Aceh Merdeka or Free Aceh Movement
GB	Girls' Brigade
GSO	General Staff Officer
GRE	Graduate Record Examinations
HDB	Housing and Development Board
HSC	Higher School Certificate

ICRC	International Committee of the Red Cross
IDF	Israel Defense Forces
LST	Landing ship, tank
MAF	Malaysian Armed Forces
MFA	Ministry of Foreign Affairs
MID	Ministry of Interior and Defence
Mindef	Ministry of Defence
MO	Medical Officer
MP	Member of Parliament
NCO	Non-Commissioned Officer
NGO	Non-Governmental Organisation
NRA	Non-Resident Ambassador
NS	National Service
NSmen	National Servicemen
OC	Officer Commanding
OCS	Officer Cadet School
PACAF	Pacific Air Forces
PACOM	Pacific Command
PANGAB	Panglima ABRI (Commander, Armed Forces of the Republic of Indonesia)
PAP	People's Action Party
PIM	Pasokan Infantry Malaysia
PNG	Papua New Guinea
PWD	Public Works Department
Pre-U	Pre-University
RSAF	Republic of Singapore Air Force
RSM	Regimental Sergeant-Major
RSN	Republic of Singapore Navy
RSO	Regimental Signals Officer
SAF	Singapore Armed Forces
SAFOS	SAF Overseas Scholarship
SAFTI	Singapore Armed Forces Training Institute
SATO	School of Advanced Training for Officers
SCSC	Singapore Command and Staff College
SEATO	Southeast Asia Treaty Organisation
SIA	Singapore Airlines

SMF	Singapore Military Forces
SMU	Singapore Management University
SRCS	Singapore Red Cross Society
SVC	Singapore Volunteer Corps
2 SIB	2nd Singapore Infantry Brigade
3 SIB	3rd Singapore Infantry Brigade
1 SIR	1st Battalion Singapore Infantry Regiment
2 SIR	2nd Battalion Singapore Infantry Regiment
4 SIR	4th Battalion Singapore Infantry Regiment
5 SIR	5th Battalion Singapore Infantry Regiment
TNI	Tentera Nasional Indonesia (Indonesian National Armed Forces)

ABOUT THE CO-WRITERS

Chua Siew San had a 45-year career in the civil service. She was Deputy Secretary (Policy) in the Ministry of Defence and then Deputy Secretary (Asia-Pacific) in the Ministry of Foreign Affairs. She was Ambassador to Thailand before she retired. She is a co-founder of Clarity The Word Factory.

Judith d'Silva spent 44 years in the civil service, 39 of which were in the Ministry of Defence. She served in various departments before retiring as Director (Plans & Content) in Nexus. She was an active member of the Speak Good English Movement from 2006 to 2018. She is a co-founder of Clarity The Word Factory.